CONSUMER BEHAVIOUR

Of Related Interest

MARKETING RESEARCH
Text, Applications and Case Studies

Ramanuj majumdar

The book shows the sequential steps involved in the conduct of marketing research with numerous illustrations drawn from the Indian market. It will help management students and executives in preparing research brief, formulate suitable design, contract questionnaire, choose appropriate data analysis technique (s) and communicate findings in a given situation.

The book is essentially application oriented. Emphasis had been laid on how skilful handling or secondary sources of data can yield valuable information about business trends.

Extensive discussion on the utility of several multivariate techniques and non-parametric tests in marketing studies stand out as the unique features of the book. It shows proper use of statistical tests by indicating the linkage between the assumptions of various statistical tests and marketing data. Also, to sharpen the perspectives of the reader, the book offers a discussion on some marketing research studies conducted by the author

RESEARCH METHODOLOGY
Methods and Techniques

C.R. Kothari

The book discusses several quantitative methods widely used in social science. The presentations are uniformly economical and cogent. Illustrations given are meaningful and relevant. The book can be used as a well-organised guide by researchers whose methodological background is not extensive.

The book is to serve as a textbook for students of social sciences and management students

CONSUMER BEHAVIOUR

(SECOND EDITION)

Matin Khan
Retd. Head of Business Administration
Lucknow University
Lucknow, UP

NEW AGE MANAGEMENT

An Imprint of

NEW AGE INTERNATIONAL (P) LIMITED, PUBLISHERS

New Delhi • Bangalore • Chennai • Cochin • Guwahati
Hyderabad • Kolkata • Lucknow • Mumbai
Visit us at **www.newagepublishers.com**

Published by New Age International (P) Ltd., Publishers
First Edition: 2001
Second Edition: 2004
Reprint: 2018

GLOBAL OFFICES

- **New Delhi** **NEW AGE INTERNATIONAL (P) LIMITED, PUBLISHERS**
 7/30 A, Daryaganj, New Delhi-110002, (INDIA)
 Tel.: (011) 23253771, 23253472, **Telefax:** 23267437, 43551305
 E-mail: contactus@newagepublishers.com • Visit us at www.newagepublishers.com
- **London** **NEW AGE INTERNATIONAL (UK) LTD.**
 27 Old Gloucester Street, London, WC1N 3AX, UK
 E-mail: info@newacademicscience.co.uk • Visit us at www.newacademicscience.co.uk
- **Nairobi** **NEW AGE GOLDEN (EAST AFRICA) LTD.**
 Ground Floor, Westlands Arcade, Chiromo Road (Next to Naivas Supermarket), Westlands, Nairobi, KENYA
 Tel.: 00-254-713848772, 00-254-725700286
 E-mail: kenya@newagepublishers.com

BRANCHES

- **Bangalore** 37/10, 8th Cross (Near Hanuman Temple), Azad Nagar, Cnamarajpet, Bangalore- 560 018
 Tel.: (080) 26756823, **Telefax:** 26756820, **E-mail: bangalore@newagepublishers.com**
- **Chennai** 26, Damodaran Street, T. Nagar, Chennai-600 017, **Tel.:** (044) 24353401, **Telefax:** 24351463
 E-mail: chennai@newagepublishers.com
- **Cochin** CC-39/1016, Carrier Station Road, Ernakulam South, Cochin-682 016, **Tel.:** (0484) 2377303, **Telefax:** 4051304
 E-mail: cochin@newagepublishers.com
- **Guwahati** Hemsen Complex, Mohd. Shah Road, Paltan Bazar, Near Starline Hotel, Guwahati-781 008,
 Tel.: (0361) 2513881, **Telefax:** 2543669, **E-mail: guwahati@newagepublishers.com**
- **Hyderabad** 105, 1st Floor, Madhiray Kaveri Tower, 3-2-19, Azam Jahi Road, Near Kumar Theater, Nimboliadda Kachiguda, Hyderabad-500 027, **Tel.:** (040) 24652456, **Telefax:** 24652457
 E-mail: hyderabad@newagepublishers.com
- **Kolkata** RDB Chambers (Formerly Lotus Cinema) 106A, 1st Floor, S N Banerjee Road, Kolkata-700 014
 Tel.: (033) 22273773, **Telefax:** 22275247, **E-mail: kolkata@newagepublishers.com**
- **Lucknow** 16-A, Jopling Road, Lucknow-226 001, **Tel.:** (0522) 2209578, 4045297, **Telefax:** 2204098
 E-mail: lucknow@newagepublishers.com
- **Mumbai** 142C, Victor House, Ground Floor, N.M. Joshi Marg, Lower Parel, Mumbai-400 013
 Tel.: (022) 24927869, **Telefax:** 24915415, **E-mail: mumbai@newagepublishers.com**
- **New Delhi** 22, Golden House, Daryaganj, New Delhi-110 002, **Tel.:** (011) 23262368, 23262370, **Telefax:** 43551305
 E-mail: sales@newagepublishers.com

ISBN: 978-81-224-1531-5

C-17-08-10715

Printed in India at Saras Graphics, Rai, Haryana.
Typeset at Laser Crafts, Delhi.

NEW AGE INTERNATIONAL (P) LIMITED, PUBLISHERS
7/30 A, Daryaganj, New Delhi-110002
Visit us at **www.newagepublishers.com**
(CIN: U74899DL1966PTC004618)

Acknowledgements

The department of Business Administration started its MBA course in 1974 and had the good fortune to celebrate the silver jubilee year in Year 2000. I have been associated with the department since its inception. After doing my MBA with the first batch and enjoying the UGC scholarship, I did my Ph. D from this department and have since been associated with the department in some capacity or another.

I thank the students, teachers, office staff and the Dean, Faculty of Commerce, Prof. R.A. Sharma, for extending their full support and cooperation to me whenever needed. I would like to thank the former Head of Department, Dr. O.P. Kaushal who was my guide and who helped me considerably.

I wish to express my gratitude to Dr. Sanjay Medhabi, Dr. R.R. Daugwal for their help and advice. I shall be failing in my duty if I donot express my gratitude to Mr. L.N. Mishra the local representative of Newage publishers, and to Mr. Rajiv Bannerjee and his entire team for taking an interest in editing and publishing this book and giving it the present form that it is in.

Thanks are due to Mr. Amit Khare who has been a constant source of encouragement. My thanks are due to Ms. Sara Khan for editing this book.

MATIN KHAN

Acknowledgements

Preface to the Second Edition

Some changes have been incorporated in the new edition of the book. One extra chapter on the changing consumer behaviour has been added in the end. Some examples and a case study have been added in chapter one. The chapter on cultural variation has been extended by a write on Marketing implications and Marketing strategies. Additions have been made in chapter 7 of group behaviour. In outlet selection and purchase (chapter No. 12) stress has been added on store location. The chapter on Diffusion of Innovation (chapter 18) contains strategies as well.

MATIN KHAN

Preface to the First Edition

This book is designed in such a way that it covers the relevant syllabi of the universities in India. The book presents a comprehensive coverage of the subject with examples from the Indian scenario. The book stresses on consumer decision-making and clearly explains the five stages of problem recognition, information search, evaluation of alternatives, purchase and post-purchase behaviour. It also explains outlet selection and purchase.

The external environment and its influence on decision-making is highlighted. These are demographical, political, cultural and technological factors. Along with these, the internal determinants of beliefs, attitudes, personality, memory and values have also been discussed in this book.

Contemporary developments like e-consumer behaviour and consumer delight in place of consumer satisfaction have also been discussed.

The marketing manager must know about the changing attitudes, beliefs, interests and moods of consumer and must be able to woo the consumer by changing the marketing mix. While marketing, the satisfaction of the consumer is of prime importance and the repeat purchases must be ensured so that the product is on a sound footing. All these factors have been highlighted throughout the text.

It is hoped that this book will serve as a useful text for students and teachers. The author will be happy to receive any feedback which may help in improving the book in its subsequent editions.

MATIN KHAN

Contents

1

Consumer Behaviour

Customer is profit, all else is overload....

This chapter provides an introduction to consumer behaviour. "Consumer is the most important person. The business revolves around the consumer."

After finishing this chapter one should be able to understand:

- What is meant by consumer behaviour
- Consumer decision-making process
- Marketing strategy and consumer behaviour
- Indian consumer and his characteristics

INTRODUCTION

All of us are consumers. We consume things of daily use, we also consume and buy these products according to our needs, preferences and buying power. These can be consumable goods, durable goods, speciality goods or, industrial goods.

What we buy, how we buy, where and when we buy, in how much quantity we buy depends on our perception, self concept, social and cultural background and our age and family cycle, our attitudes, beliefs values, motivation, personality, social class and many other factors that are both internal and external to us. While buying, we also consider whether to buy or not to buy and, from which source or seller to buy. In some societies there is a lot of affluence and, these societies can afford to buy in greater quantities and at shorter intervals. In poor societies, the consumer can barely meet his barest needs.

The marketers therefore tries to understand the needs of different consumers and having understood his different behaviours which require an in-depth study of their internal and external environment, they formulate their plans for marketing.

Management is the youngest of sciences and oldest of arts and consumer behaviour in management is a very young discipline. Various scholars and academicians concentrated on it at a much later stage. It was during the 1950s, that marketing concept developed, and thus the need to study the behaviour of consumers was recognised. Marketing starts with the needs of the customer and ends with his satisfaction. When every thing revolves round the customer, then the study of consumer behaviour becomes a necessity. It starts with the buying of goods. Goods can be bought individually, or in groups. Goods can be bought under stress (to satisfy an immediate need), for comfort and luxury in small quantities or in bulk. For all this, exchange is required. This exchange is usually between the seller and the buyer. It can also be between consumers.

Consumer behaviour can be defined as the decision-making process and physical activity involved in acquiring, evaluating, using and disposing of goods and services.

This definition clearly brings out that it is not just the buying of goods/services that receives attention in consumer behaviour but, the process starts much before the goods have been acquired or bought. A process of buying starts in the minds of the consumer, which leads to the finding of alternatives between products that can be acquired with their relative advantages and disadvantages. This leads to internal and external research. Then follows a process of decision-making for purchase and using the goods, and then the post purchase behaviour which is also very important, because it gives a clue to the marketers whether his product has been a success or not.

To understand the likes and dislikes of the consumer, extensive consumer research studies are being conducted. These researches try to find out:

- What the consumer thinks of the company's products and those of its competitors?
- How can the product be improved in their opinion?
- How the customers use the product?
- What is the customer's attitude towards the product and its advertising?
- What is the role of the customer in his family?

The following key questions should be answered for consumer research. A market comes into existence because it fulfils the needs of the consumer. In this connection, a marketer has to know the 70's framework for consumer research. Taking from an example of soap.

Who constitutes the market?	Parent, Child, Male, Female	Occupants
What does the market buy?	Soap, Regular, Medicated, with Glycerine, Herbal what Brand, what size	Objects
Who participates in buying?	Parent, Child, Male, Female	Organisations
How does the market buy?	Cash, Credit, Mail-order etc.	Operations
When does the market buy?	Monthly, Weekly etc. Prescribed by Doctor (Medicinal)	Occasions

Where does the market buy?	Supermarket, Retail store etc.	Outlet
Why does the market buy?	For Cleansing, Bathing, Fresh feeling etc.	Objectives

(taken from Multi-marketer)

Consumer behaviour is a complex, dynamic, multidimensional process, and all marketing decisions are based on assumptions about consumer behaviour.

Marketing strategy is the game plan which the firms must adhere to, in order to outdo the competitor or the plans to achieve the desired objective. In formulating the marketing strategy, to sell the product effectively, cost-benefit analysis must be undertaken.

There can be many benefits of a product, for example, for owning a motor bike one can be looking for ease of transportation, status, pleasure, comfort and feeling of ownership. The cost is the amount of money paid for the bike, the cost of maintenance, gasoline, parking, risk of injury in case of an accident, pollution and frustration such as traffic jams. The difference between this total benefit and total cost constitutes the *customer value*. The idea is to provide superior customer value and this requires the formulation of a marketing strategy. The entire process consists of market analysis, which leads to target market selection, and then to the formulation of strategy by juggling the product, price, promotion and distribution, so that a *total product* (a set of entire characteristics) is offered. The total product creates an image in the mind of the consumer, who undergoes a decision process

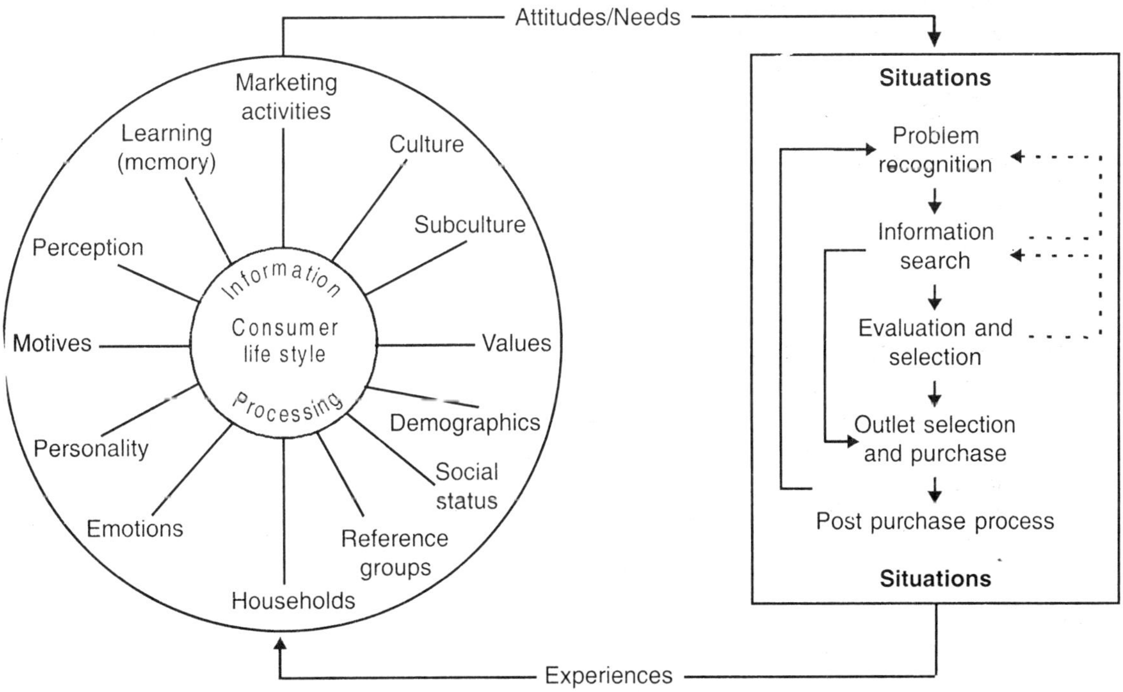

Fig. 1.1 A simplified framework for studying consumer behaviour.

which leads to the outcome in terms of satisfaction or dissatisfaction, which reflects on the sales and image of the product or brand.

Figure 1.1 gives in detail the shaping of consumer behaviour, which leads a consumer to react in certain ways and he makes a decision, keeping the situations in mind. The process of decision-making varies with the value of the product, the involvement of the buyer and the risk that is involved in deciding the product/ service.

The figures shows the consumer life style in the centre of the circle. The consumer and his life style is influenced by a number of factors shown all around the consumer. These are culture, subculture, values, demographic factors, social status, reference groups, household and also the internal make up of the consumer, which are a consumers' emotions, personality motives of buying, perception and learning. Consumer is also influenced by the marketing activities and efforts of the marketer.

All these factors lead to the formation of attitudes and *needs* of the consumer.

Marketing Strategy and Consumer Behaviour

(i) Marketing Analysis

(a) Consumer
(b) Company
(c) Competition
(d) Condition

(ii) Marketing Segmentation

(e) Identify product related needs
(f) Group customers with similar need sets
(g) Describe each group
(h) Select target market

(iii) Marketing Strategy

(i) Product
(j) Price
(k) Distribution
(l) Communication
(m) Service

(iv) Consumer Decision Process

(n) Problem recognition
(o) Information search—internal, external
(p) Alternative evaluation
(q) Purchase
(r) Use
(s) Evaluation

(v) Outcomes

(t) Customer satisfaction
(u) Sales
(v) Product/Brand image

Fig. 1.2 Marketing strategy and consumer behaviour.

Then follows the process of decision-making, as shown in the rectangle which consists of the problem recognition, information search (which is both internal and external) then the evaluation and selection procedure, and finally the purchase. After the purchase and use of the product the customer may be satisfied or dissatisfied with the product. This is known as post-purchase behaviour. The existing situations also play an important role in the decision-making process. The dotted line show the feedback.

◆ MARKET ANALYSIS

Market analysis requires an understanding of the 4-Cs which are consumer, conditions, competitor and the company. A study is undertaken to provide superior customer value, which is the main objective of the company. For providing better customer value we should learn the needs of the consumer, the offering of the company, vis-a-vis its competitors and the environment which is economic, physical, technological, etc.

A consumer is anyone who engages himself in physical activities, of evaluating, acquiring, using or disposing of goods and services.

A customer is one who actually purchases a product or service from a particular organisation or a shop. A customer is always defined in terms of a specific product or company.

However, the term consumer is a broader term which emphasises not only the actual buyer or customer, but also its users, i.e. consumers. Sometimes a product is purchased by the head of the family and used by the whole family, i.e. a refrigerator or a car. There are some consumer *behaviour roles* which are played by different members of the family.

Role	*Description*
Initiator	The person who determines that some need or want is to be met (e.g. a daughter indicating the need for a colour TV).
Influencer	The person or persons who intentionally or unintentionally influence the decision to buy or endorse the view of the initiator.
Buyer	The person who actually makes a purchase.
User	The person or persons who actually use or consume the product.

All the consumer behaviour roles are to be kept in mind but, the emphasis is on the buyer whose role is overt and visible.

(a) The Consumer

To understand the consumer; researches are made. Sometimes motivational research becomes handy to bring out hidden attitudes, uncover emotions and feelings. Many firms send questionnaires to customers to ask about their satisfaction, future needs and ideas for a new product. On the basis of the answers received, changes in the marketing mix is made and advertising is also streamlined.

(b) The External Analysis (Company)

The external analysis may be done by the feedbacks from the industry analyst and by marketing researches. The internal analysis is made by the firm's financial conditions, the quantum of the sales, force and other factors within the company.

The study of these factors leads to a better understanding of the consumer and his needs.

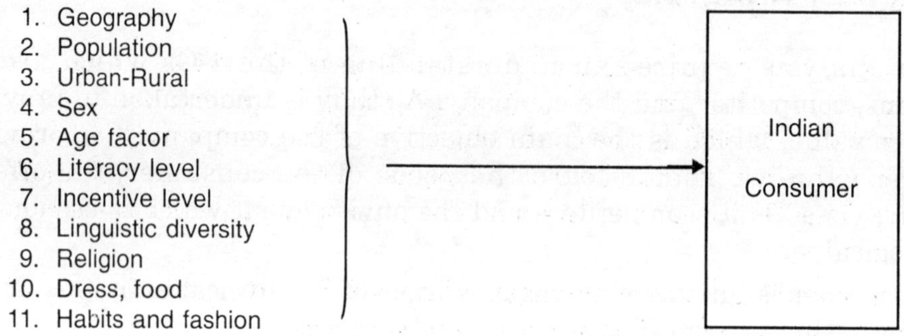

Fig. 1.3 Characteristic features of Indian consumer.

(c) The Competition

In the analysis of the market, a study of the strengths and weaknesses of the competitors, their strategies, their anticipated moves and their reaction to the companies' moves and plans is to be made. The company after getting this information, reacts accordingly and changes its marketing mix and the offering is made in a manner which can out do the competitor. This is a very difficult process and it is easier said than done. To have correct information about the competitors and to anticipate their further moves is the job of the researcher.

(d) The Conditions

The conditions under which the firms are operating has also to be seriously considered. The factors to be studied are the economy, the physical environment, the government regulations, the technological developments, etc. These effect the consumer needs, i.e. the deterioration of the environment and its pollution may lead to the use and innovation of safer products. People are health conscious and are concerned with their safety. Hence, in this case, safer products have a better chance with the consumer. In case of recession, the flow of money is restricted greatly. This leads to the formulation of different marketing strategies.

(e) Market Segmentation

The market is divided into segments which are a portion of a larger market whose needs are similar and, they are homogeneous in themselves. Such segments are identified with similar needs.

(f) Need Set

By need set, it is meant that there are products which satisfy more than one need. An automobile can fill the transportation needs, status need, fun needs or time saving needs. So the company tries to identify the need sets which its product can fulfil. Then we try to identify the groups who have similar needs, i.e. some people need economical cars, others may go for luxury cars.

(g) Demographic and Psychographic Characteristics

These groups are identified and they are described in terms of their demographic and psychographic characteristics. The company finds out how and when the product is purchased and consumed.

(h) Target Segment

After all the above preliminary work is done, the target customer group known as the target segment is chosen, keeping in mind how the company can provide superior customer value at a profit. The segment which can best be served with the company's capabilities at a profit is chosen. It has to be kept in mind that different target segments require different marketing strategies and, with the change in the environmental conditions the market mix has to be adjusted accordingly.

Attractiveness of the segment can be calculated by marking the various criterion on a 1 to 10 scale as given below:

Table 1.1

1 2 3 4 5 6 7 8 9 10

Criterion	*Score on 1 to 10 scale with company being most favourable*
Segment size	—
Segment growth rate	—
Competitor strength	—
Customer satisfaction with existing product	—
Fit with company image	—
Fit with company objectives	—
Fit with company resources	—
Fit with other segments	—
Investment required	—
Stability/Periodicability	—
Zest to serve	—
Sustainable advantage available	—
Leverage to other segments/markets	—
Risk	—
Other factors	—

Marketing Strategy

Strategies are formulated to provide superior customer value. In formulating market strategies, the 4-ps are directed at the target market.

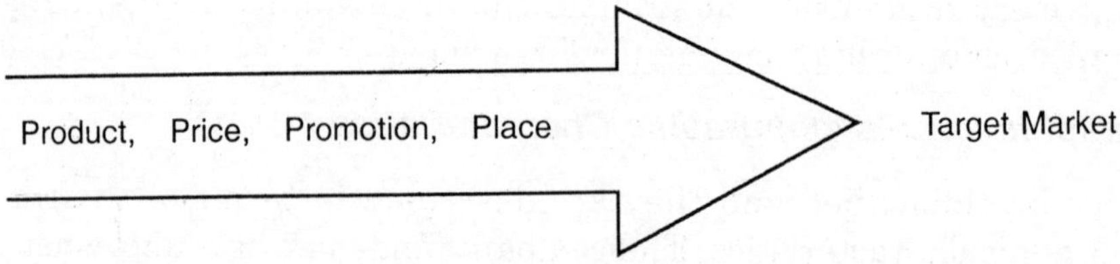

Fig. 1.4 Decision-making process generally followed by consumers.

(i) Product

Product is anything that is offered to the consumer which is tangible and can satisfy a need and has some value.

(j) Price

Price is the amount of money one must pay to obtain the right to use the product.

(k) Distribution (Place)

The goods can be distributed by many channels. These could be retailers, wholesalers, agents or by direct selling. Distribution outlets play an important role in reaching the goods to the consumer. They provide, time, place and possession utilities. Some goods need to be marketed through the channels or the middleman. Others can be marketed directly by the company to the actual consumer.

(l) Promotion

Promotion is the means of changing the attitudes of the consumer, so that it becomes favourable towards the company's products. Various means of promotion are advertising, personal selling, sales promotion and publicity.

(m) Service

Service refers to auxiliary service that enhances the value of the product or the service. For instance, while buying a car. Free services are provided over a certain period of time. Check-ups are free and maintenance is also covered on the charge of an adequate amount along with the product purchased. These auxiliary services are provided at a cost with money. These provide value to the product or the customer. These services give an advantage to the customer and he is free from the botheration of occasional checkups or risk. The risk is considerably reduced and, the customer derives satisfaction with his decision to purchase.

(n) Consumer Decision Process

The decision-making process consists of a series of steps which the consumer undergoes. First of all, the decision is made to solve a problem of any kind. This may be the problem of creating a cool atmosphere in your home.

For this, information search is carried out, to find how the cool atmosphere can be provided, e.g. by an air-conditioner or, by a water-cooler. This leads to the evaluation of alternatives and a cost benefit-analysis is made to decide which product and brand image will be suitable, and can take care of the problem suitably and adequately. Thereafter the purchase is made and the product is used by the consumer. The constant use of the product leads to the satisfaction or dissatisfaction of the consumer, which leads to repeat purchases, or to the rejection of the product.

The marketing strategy is successful if consumers can see a need which a company's product can solve and, offers the best solution to the problem. For a successful strategy, the marketer must lay emphasis on the product/brand image in the consumer's mind. Position the product according to the customers' likes and dislikes. The brand which matches the desired image of a target market sells well. Sales are important and sales are likely to occur if the initial consumer analysis was correct and matches the consumer decision process. Satisfaction of the consumer, after the sales have been effected, is important for repeat purchase. It is more profitable to retain existing customers, rather than looking for new ones. The figure below gives an idea of the above discussion.

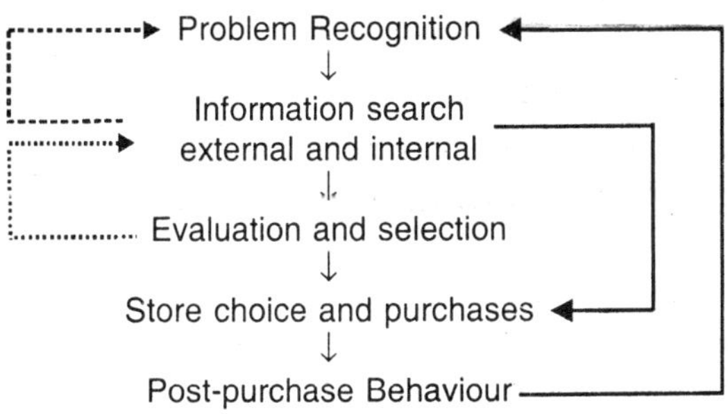

Fig. 1.5 Decision Process.

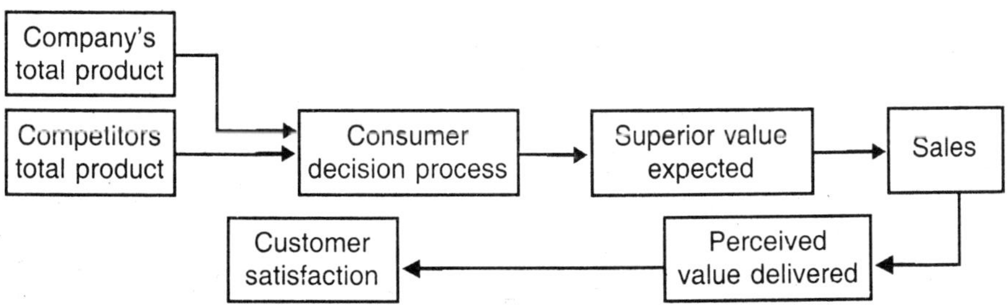

Fig. 1.6 Creating Satisfied Customers.

Source: Adapted from Hawkins, Best, Canly, *Implementations of Marketing Strategy.*

Questions

1. What do you understand by consumer behaviour? What information is sought in consumer researches?
2. How is consumer behaviour related to the formulation of marketing strategy?
3. What are the elements of marketing strategy in consumer behaviour?

Case Study

The marketer has to learn about the needs and changing of the consumer behaviour and practice the Marketing Concept. Levi strauss & Co. were selling jeans to a mass market and did not bother about segmenting the market till their sales went down. The study into consumer behaviour showed their greatest market of the baby boomers had outgrown and their NEEDs had changed. They therefore came out with Khaki or dockers to different segments and comfortable action stocks for the consumers in the 50 age group. Thus by separating the market and targetting various groups and fulfilling their needs, they not only made up for the lost sales but far exceeded the previous sales. They also targeted the women consumers for jeans and both men and women started wearing jeans in greater numbers. The offering given by the company must be enlarged to suit various segments.

For example Maruti Udyog Ltd has come out with many models. Maruti 800, Maruti Van, Zen, Alto, Veagon R, Versa Gypsy, Esteem, Boleno and other models. For successful marketing one should:

1. Find consumer needs of various segments.
2. Position Products (new & existing) to these segments.
3. Develop strategies for these segments. Practice greater selectivity in advertising and personal selling and creating more selective media and distribution outlets.

2

Factors Influencing Consumer Behaviour

Think of the customer first, if you would have the customer think of you.

This chapter deals with the internal and external factors that influence consumer behaviour. Consumer is affected by changes in his personality, attitudes, etc. and also by the external environment. One should be able to explain the following:

- Various factors influencing consumer behaviour
- The joint effects of internal and external determinants
- The elements of the decision-making process

INTRODUCTION

The factors that influence consumer behaviour can be classified into internal factors or (individual determinants) and, external environmental factors. External factors do not affect the decision process directly, but percolate or filter through the individual determinants, to influence the decision process as shown in Fig. 2.1.

The arrow shows how the external influences are filtered towards the individual determinants to affect the decision process.

The individual determinants that effect consumer behaviour are:

- ➢ Motivation and involvement
- ➢ Attitudes
- ➢ Personality and self concept
- ➢ Learning and memory
- ➢ Information processing

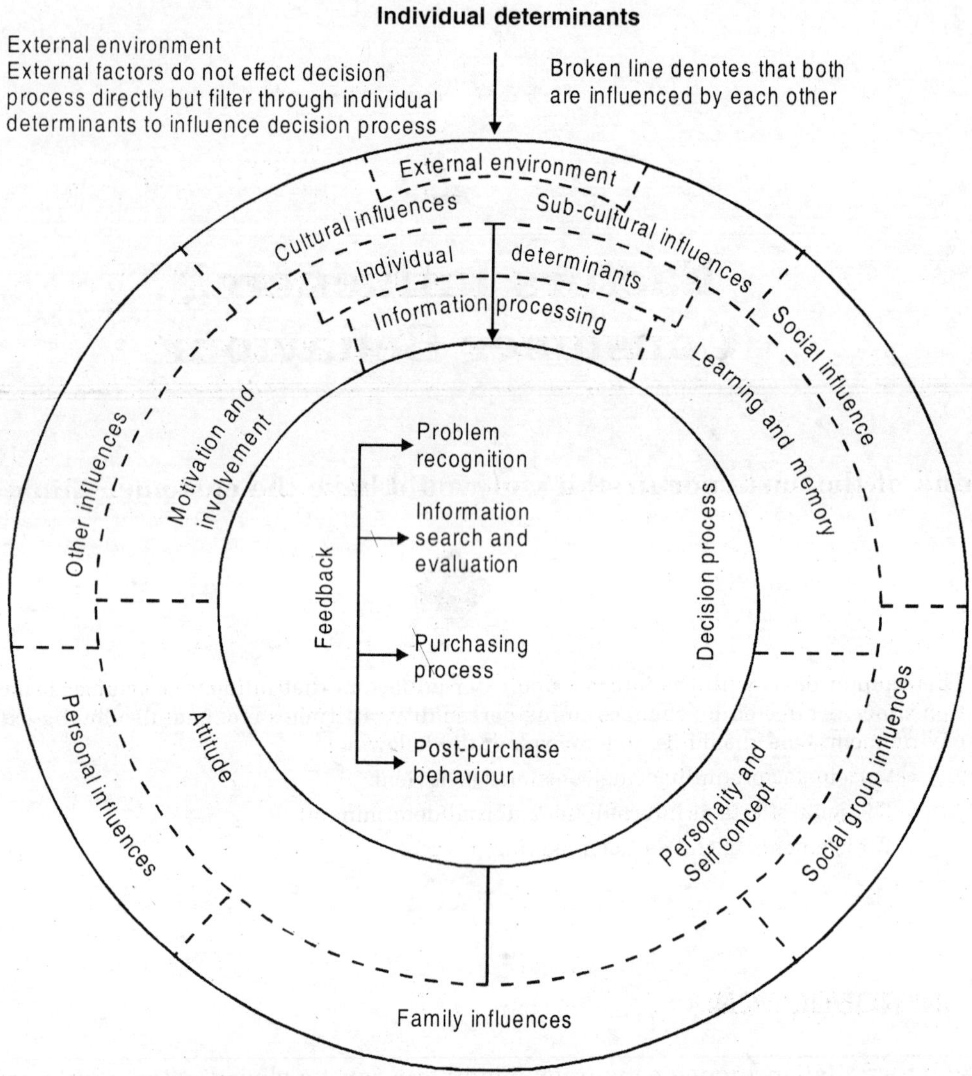

Fig. 2.1 A simplified framework for studying consumer behaviour.

The external influences or factors are:

- ➢ Cultural influences
- ➢ Sub-cultural influences
- ➢ Social class influences
- ➢ Social group influences
- ➢ Family influences
- ➢ Personal influences
- ➢ Other influences

We shall give a brief description of these influences in this chapter and they will be dealt with in greater detail in the subsequent chapters.

◆ INDIVIDUAL DETERMINANTS

Motivation and Involvement

In a society, different consumers exhibit different consumer behaviour because they are unique and have unique sets of needs. Motivation is that internal force that activates some needs and provides direction of behaviour towards fulfilment of these needs.

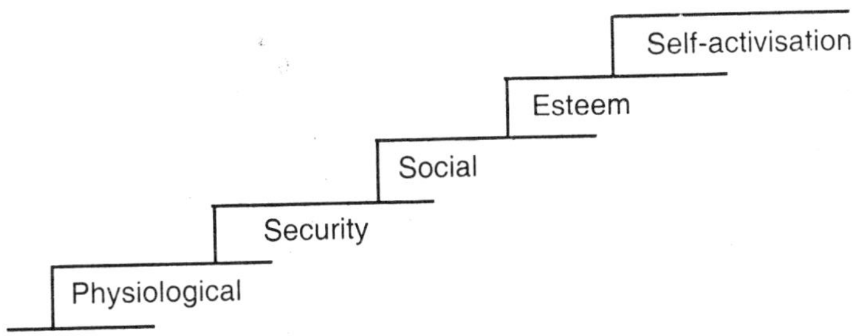

Fig. 2.2 Maslow's hierarchy of needs.

While talking of motivation, we cannot afford to forget the Maslow's Hierarchy of needs which tells us about the primary and secondary needs.

First the biological needs of hunger, thirst, shelter are satisfied then the safety needs and then the psychological desires of being accepted in society, seeking status, esteem, etc. are satisfied. People adopt different methods to fulfil their needs. The need of transport can be met by car, rail, bus or aeroplane. People choose different modes of transport because of their level of involvement in different activities.

Involvement refers to the personal relevance or importance of a product or a service, that a consumer perceives in a given situation. Depending on the value and personal interest, a consumer can have a high or low involvement. For a professional tennis player, the choice of a tennis racket is made with great care. He sees the weight, size, grip and tension of the strings, etc. The racket is his most important professional tool. Similarly, a professional photographer has to buy a camera with the right specifications and attributes. For another person, a tennis racket may only be a means of entertainment or in the case of a camera, the recording of family and other events by a camera which is convenient and handy.

Attitudes

These are our learned predispositions towards people, objects and events. Attitudes are responsible for our responses and are not inborn but are learnt from people around us.

Our attitudes influence our purchase decisions and consumer behaviour. A person having a carefree attitude will buy an object without much involvement. People who want to play safe and avoid risk taking, will go for a safe investment. People who want convenience and are short of domestic help, will have a positive attitudes towards canned and frozen foods.

Personality and Self Concept

It is the sum total of our mental, physical and moral qualities and characteristics that are present in us and that make us what we are. Consumers try to buy the products that match their personality. People wanting to look manly will buy products with a macho appeal, which would enhance their image and personality. People who give emphasis on comfort and care, will purchase comfort products and so on. If one wants to emulate a film star his choice will be different from others.

Learning and Memory

Every day we are exposed to a wide range of information, but retain only a small portion of it. We tend to remember the information that we are interested in or, that is important to us. In a family different members of the family are interested in different types of information which they individually retain. Mothers retain information regarding household items. Father retains information regarding his interest in cars, motor cycles and other objects. Children are interested in objects of their interest like amusement parks, joy rides, Barbie dolls, etc.

Our motives, attitudes, personality filters the information. Keeping only relevant information in our minds and, keeping the others out. This is known as selective retention. We retain in our memory only selective information that is of interest to us.

Information Processing

All consumers analyse and process the information they receive. These are activities that a consumer engages in, while gathering, assimilating and evaluating information. Consumers assimilate and evaluate selective information and this reflects on their motives, attitudes and personality and self concept. Same information can be evaluated in a different manner by different individuals. The most common example is a glass half filled with a liquid. It can be interpreted as "half empty" or half full. The first is a pessimistic view and the other is an optimistic view of processing the information.

◆ EXTERNAL ENVIRONMENTAL FACTORS AFFECTING CONSUMER BEHAVIOUR

Cultural Influences

It is defined as a complex sum total of knowledge, belief, traditions, customs, art, moral law or any other habit acquired by people as members of a society. Our consumer behaviour, that is the things we buy are influenced by our background or culture. Different emphasis is given by different cultures for the buying, use, and disposing of products. People in South India have a certain style of consumption of food, clothing, savings, etc. This differs from the people in the North of India. Different cultures and habits are predominant in different parts of the world. Japanese have a different culture from that of USA, England or Arabian countries. Therefore, in consumer behaviour culture plays a very important part.

Sub-Cultural Influences

Within a culture, there are many groups or segments of people with distinct customs, traditions and behaviour. In the Indian culture itself, we have many sub-cultures, the culture of the South, the North, east and the West. Hindu culture, Muslim culture, Hindus of the South differ in culture from the Hindus of the North and so on. Products are designed to suit a target group of customers which have similar cultural backgrounds and are homogeneous in many respects.

Social Class

By social class we refer to the group of people who share equal positions in a society. Social class is defined by parameters like income, education, occupation, etc. Within a social class, people share the same values and beliefs and tend to purchase similar kinds of products. Their choice of residence, type of holiday, entertainment, leisure all seem to be alike. The knowledge of social class and their consumer behaviour is of great value to a marketer.

Social Group Influences

A group is a collection of individuals who share some consumer relationship, attitudes and have the same interest. Such groups are prevalent in societies. These groups could be primary where interaction takes place frequently and, consists of family groups. These groups have a lot of interaction amongst themselves and are well knit. Secondary groups are a collection of individuals where relationship is more formal and less personal in nature. These could be political groups, work group and study groups, service organisations like the Lions, Rotary, etc. The behaviour of a group is influenced by other member of the group. An individual can be a member of various groups and can have varied influences by different members of groups in his consumption behaviour. An individual can be an executive in a company, can be a member of a political party. He may be a member of a service organisation and of entertainment clubs and study circles. These exert different influences on his consumption.

Family Influence

As has already been said, the family is the most important of the primary group and is the strongest source of influence on consumer behaviour. The family tradition and customs are learnt by children, and they imbibe many behavioural patterns from their family members, both consciously and unconsciously. These behaviour patterns become a part of children's lives. In a joint family, many decision are jointly made which also leave an impression on the members of the family.

These days the structure of the family is changing and people are going in more for nucleus families which consists of parent, and dependent children. The other type of family is the joint family where mother, father, grandparents and relatives are also living together.

Personal Influences

Each individual processes the information received in different ways and evaluates the products in his own personal way. This is irrespective of the influence of the family, social class, cultural heritage, etc. His own personality ultimately influences his decision. He can have his personal reasons for likes, dislikes, price, convenience or status. Some individuals may lay greater emphasis on price, others on quality, still others on status, symbol, convenience of the product, etc. Personal influences go a long way in the purchase of a product.

Other Influences

Consumers are also influenced by national or regional events which could be like the Asiad, the Olympics, cricket test matches, World Cup, the war or a calamity. These leave permanent or temporary impressions on the mind of the consumer and affect his behaviour. In these events, products are advertised and sometimes the use of product like drugs, etc. is discouraged. People are urged to adopt family planning methods. Situation variables such as product display, price reduction, free gifts and attractive offers also influence consumer behaviour.

In Fig. 2.1 the broken lines indicate that these factors influence and in turn are influenced by each other. The various factors percolate from the external to the individual determinant, to finally influence the decision process.

External factors cannot affect the decision process directly but, these are also instrumental and exert an influence on consumer behaviour.

Factors affecting consumers can also be studied by dividing the factors into four groups as shown below. This can be done under four broad headings which can have sub headings as shown in Fig. 2.3 on next page.

Classification in four broad categories

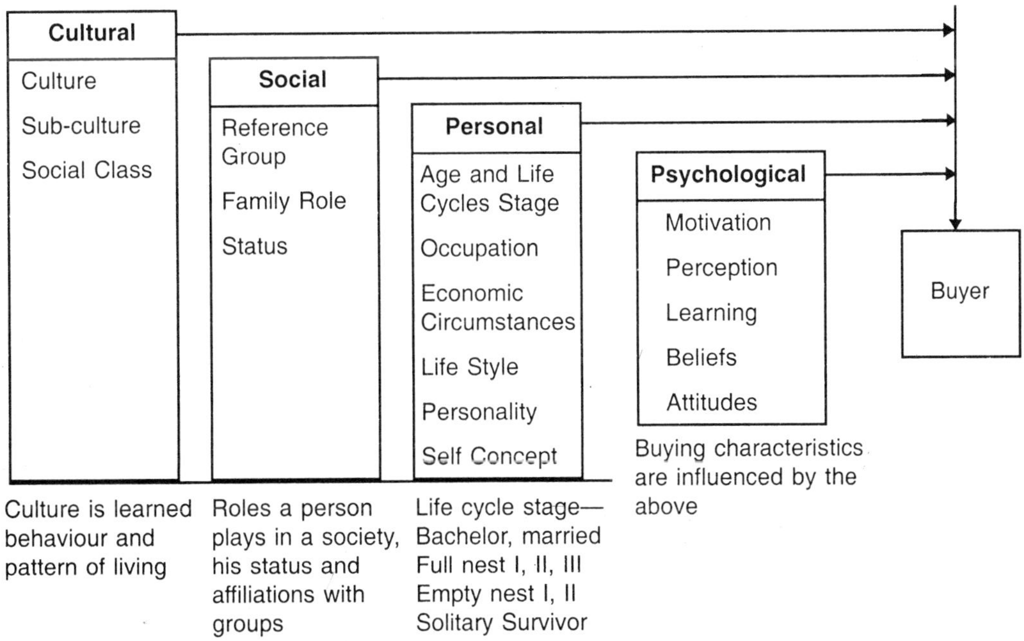

Fig. 2.3 Factors influencing consumer behaviour classification in four broad categories.

Questions

1. List and explain the individual determinants of consumer behaviour.
2. How does the external environment help and influence the individual determinants in consumer behaviour?
3. Illustrate and explain with a diagram the decision-making process and how are they influenced by various factors.

3

Models of Consumer Behaviour

**The only goose that lays golden eggs everyday...
forever... is your customer.**

In this chapter, various models of consumer behaviour are explained. These models explain how a consumer searches and gets the information and goes on to make a decision for himself, for his family or for the organisation. The student must understand the:

- Input, process and output model
- Individual decision-making
- Family decision-making

INTRODUCTION

We have already seen that there are many factors which influence the decision-making of consumers. There are various consumer models which help in the understanding of consumer behaviour. These are listed below. We shall discuss these briefly.

1. Economic Model
2. Psychological Model
3. Pavlovian Model
4. Input, Process Output Model—Gandhi: Philip Kotler
5. Sociological Model
6. Howarth Sheth Model
7. Engel-Blackwell-Kollat Model
8. Model of family decision-making
9. Nicosia Model
10. A Model of Industrial buying behaviour.

1. Economic Model

In this model, consumers follow the principle of maximum utility based on the law of diminishing marginal utility. The consumer wants to spend the minimum amount for maximising his gains.

Economic man model is based on:

Price effect: Lesser the price of the product, more will be the quantity purchased.

Substitution effect: Lesser the price of the substitute product, lesser will be the utility of the original product bought.

Income effect: When more income is earned, or more money is available, more will be the quantity purchased.

This model, according to behavioural scientists, is not complete as it assumes the homogeneity of the market, similarity of buyer behaviour and concentrates only on the product or price. It ignores all the other aspects such as perception, motivation, learning, attitudes, personality and socio-cultural factors. It is important to have a multi-disciplinary approach, as human beings are complex entities and are influenced by external and internal factors discussed in Chapter 2. Thus, price is not the only factor influencing decision-making and the economic model according to scientists have shortcomings.

2. Psychological Model

Psychologists have been investigating the causes which lead to purchases and decision-making. This has been answered by A.H. Maslow in his hierarchy of needs. The behaviour of an individual at a particular time is determined by his strongest need at that time. This also shows that needs have a priority. First they satisfy the basic needs and then go on for secondary needs.

The purchasing process and behaviour is governed by motivational forces. Motivation stimulates people into action. Motivation starts with the need. It is a

Fig. 3.1 Maslow's hierarchy of needs.

driving force and also a mental phenomenon. Need arises when one is deprived of something. A tension is created in the mind of the individual which leads him to a goal directed behaviour which satisfies the need. Once a need is satisfied, a new need arises and the process is continuous.

3. Pavlovian Learning Model

This model is named after the Russian Physiologist Ivan Pavlov. He experimented on a dog and observed how it responded on the call of a bell and presenting it with a piece of meat. The responses were measured by the amount of saliva secreted by the dog. Learning is defined as the changes in behaviour which occur by practice and, based on previous experience. This is important to marketers as well.

The learning process consists of the following factors:

Drive

This is a strong internal stimuli which impels action. Because of the drive, a person is stimulated to action to fulfil his desires.

Drives

Can be innate (inborn) which stem from physiological needs, such as hunger, thirst, pain, cold, sex, etc. Learned drive, such as striving for status or social approval.

Cause are weak stimuli that determine when the buyer will respond. We have:

(a) ***Triggering Cues:*** These activate the decision process for any purchase.

(b) ***Non-triggering Cues:*** These influence the decision process but do not activate it. These are of two kinds:

1. *Product cues* are external stimuli received from the product directly, e.g. colour of package, weight, style, price, etc.
2. *Informational cues* are external stimuli which provide information about the product, like advertisement, sales promotion, talking to other people, suggestions of sales personnel, etc.

Response is what the buyer does, i.e. buys or does not buy.

Reinforcement

Thus when a person has a need to buy, say clothing, and passes by a showroom and is attracted by the display of clothing, their colour and style, which acts as a stimulus, and he makes a purchase. He uses it, and if he likes it, an enforcement takes place and he is happy and satisfied with the purchase. He recommends it to his friends as well, and visits the same shop again. Learning part, thus is an important part of buyer behaviour and the marketer tries to create a good image of the product in the mind of the consumer for repeat purchases through learning.

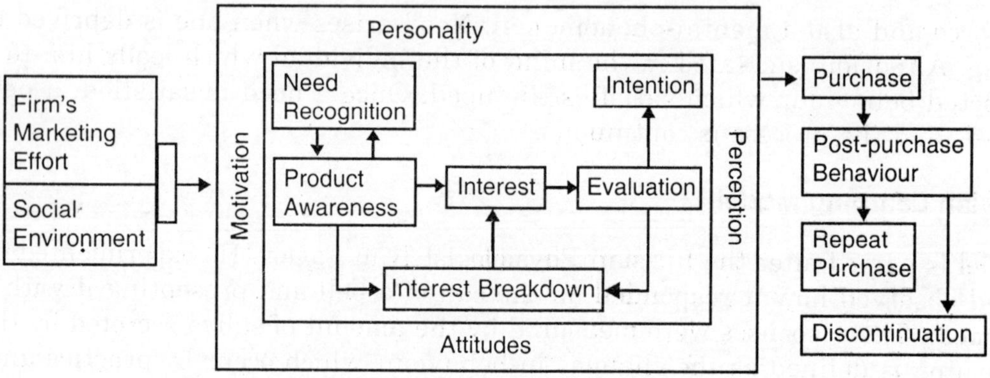

Fig. 3.2 Input, Process and Output Model.

4. Input, Process and Output Model

This is a simple model of consumer behaviour, in which the input for the customer is the firm's marketing effort (the product, price, promotion and place) and the social environment. The social environment consists of the family, reference groups, culture, social class, etc. which influences the decision-making process. Both these factors together constitute the input in the mind of the consumer.

Need Recognition

When one is aware of a want, tension is created and one chooses a product to satisfy his needs. There is also a possibility that a person may be aware of a product before its need is recognised. This is indicated by the arrows going both ways from the need to the product and vice-versa.

Product Awareness

Product awareness can be had from advertisement or exposure to different types of media or by the social circle. The awareness and the need leads to the building of interest. In some cases, the interest may also breakdown and, the decision process also stops or may be postponed for the time being.

Evaluation

Evaluation may consist of getting more information about the product and comparing and contrasting it with other products. This can be done theoretically or by taking a trial. Once the evaluation is completed, the consumer's interest may either build up and he has intentions to buy, or he may lose interest and the decision process may again stop or be postponed.

Intention

Once there is intention to purchase the product, the consumer goes ahead and acts or purchases the product. Once the product is purchased, it is used to fulfil the need and, the more the product is used, the more the consumer becomes aware of the positive and negative points of the product.

Post-purchase Behaviour

If, after the purchase and use of the product the customer is satisfied, he is happy and goes in for repeat purchases or recommends the same to his friends and acquaintances. If, however, the customer is dissatisfied, he discontinues further purchase of the product and builds a negative attitude towards it, which may be harmful to the company.

The post purchase behaviour is very important for the marketer and the company because it leads to proper feedback for improvement and maintaining the quality and features desired by the product. If the customer is very happy with the purchase, he forms a good impression about the product and the company.

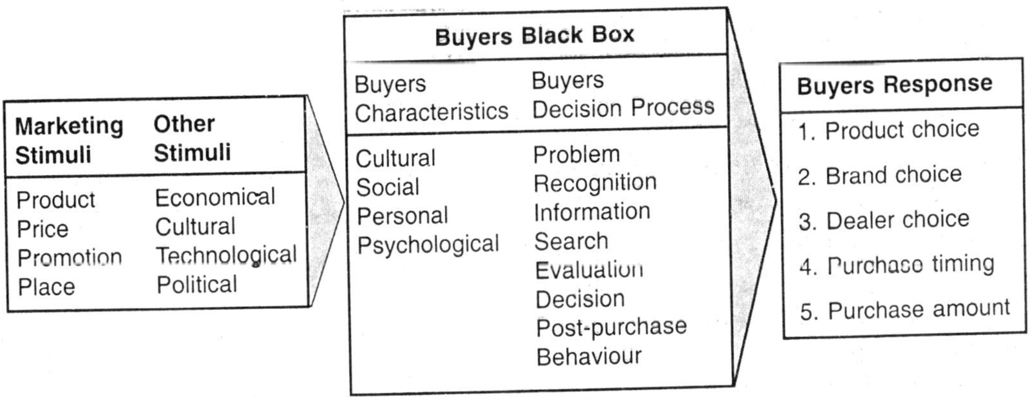

Fig. 3.3 Buyer's Black Box Model.

The above figure shows three stages in terms of stimuli buyer's black box and buyer's response.

The consumer gets the input from the marketing effort of the firm (4 ps) and the other stimuli. This input is processed in the mind (Black Box), which constitutes the characteristics of the buyer and the process of decision-making. Once the buyer has decided to buy then, he responds in terms of his choice of product, brand, dealer, timing and amount.

The post purchase behaviour of being satisfied or dissatisfied is also important, and is shown in the decision-making process.

5. Sociological Model

This is concerned with the society. A consumer is a part of the society and he may be a member of many groups in a society. His buying behaviour is influenced by these groups. Primary groups of family friends and close associates exert a lot of influence on his buying. A consumer may be a member of a political party where his dress norms are different. As a member of an elite organisation, his dress requirements may be different, thus he has to buy things that conform to his lifestyles in different groups.

6. Howarth Sheth Model

This model is slightly complicated and shows that consumer behaviour is a complex process and concepts of learning, perception and attitudes influence consumer behaviour. This model of decision-making is applicable to individuals. It has four sets of variables which are:

(i) Input
(ii) Perceptual and Learning constructs
(iii) Outputs
(iv) Exogenous or external variables.

Input

Some inputs are necessary for the customer for making decisions.

These inputs are provided by three types of stimuli as shown in Fig. 3.4.

(a) *Significative stimuli:* These are physical tangible characteristics of the product. These are price, quality, distinctiveness, services rendered and availability of the product. These are essential for making decisions.

(b) *Symbolic stimuli:* These are the same as significative characteristics, but they include the perception of the individual, i.e. price is high or low. Quality is upto the mark or below average. How is it different from the other products, what services can the product render and, what is the position of after sales service and how quickly or easily is the product available and, from where.

(c) *Social stimuli:* This is the stimuli provided by family, friends, social groups, and social class. This is important, as one lives in society and for the approval and appreciation of the society, buying habits have to be governed.

Perceptual and Learning Constructs

These constructs are psychological variables, e.g. motives, attitudes, perception which influence the consumer decision process.

The consumer receives the stimuli and interprets it. Two factors that influence his interpretation are stimulus-ambiguity and perpetual bias.

Stimulus ambiguity occurs when the consumer cannot interpret or fully understand the meaning of the stimuli he has received, and does not know how to respond. Perceptual bias occurs when an individual distorts the information according to his needs and experiences.

These two factors influence the individual for the comprehension and rating of

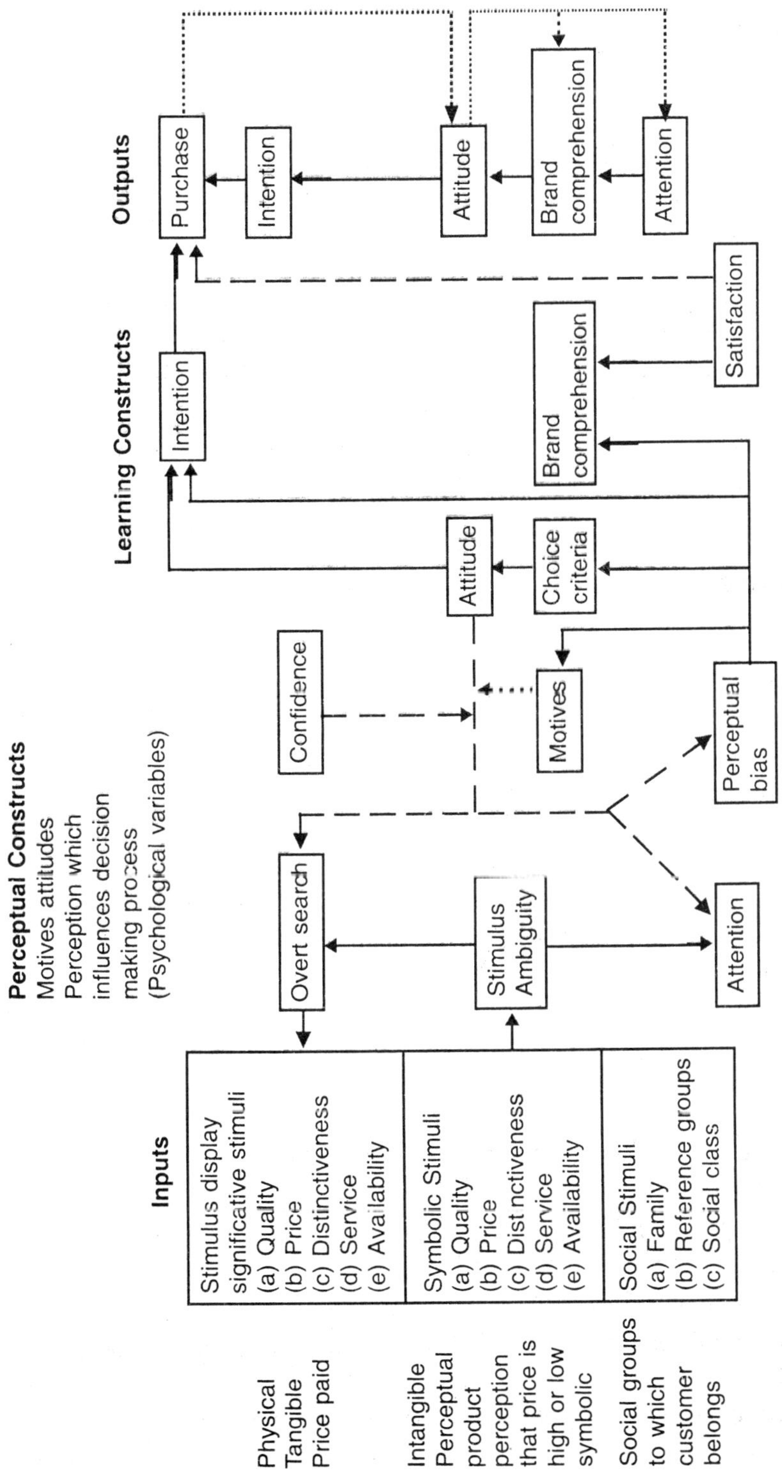

Fig. 3.4 Simplified version of the Howarth-Sheth Model of Buyer Behaviour.

the brand. If the brand is rated high, he develops confidence in it and finally purchases it.

Output

By output we mean the purchase decision. After purchase there is satisfaction or dissatisfaction. Satisfaction leads to positive attitude and increases brand comprehension. With dissatisfaction, a negative attitude is developed. The feedback shown by the dotted line and the solid lines shows the flow of information.

Exogenous or External Variables

These are not shown in the model, and do not directly influence the decision process. They influence the consumer indirectly and vary from one consumer to another. These are the individual's own personality traits, social class, importance of purchase and financial status.

All the four factors discussed above are dependent on each other and influence the decision-making process. The model though complicated, deals with the purchase behaviour in an exhaustive manner.

7. Engel-Blackwell-Kollat Model

It consists of four components:

(i) Information processing
(ii) Central control unit
(iii) Decision process
(iv) Environmental influences.

Information Processing

As shown in the diagram, the information processing consists of exposure, attention, comprehension and retention of the marketing and non-marketing stimuli. For successful sales the consumer must be properly and repeatedly exposed to the message. His attention should be drawn, such that he understands what is to be conveyed and retains it in his mind.

Central Control Unit

The stimuli processes and interprets the information received by an individual. This is done by the help of four psychological factors.

(a) Stores information and past experience about the product, which serves as a standard for comparing other products and brands.
(b) Evaluative creteria which could be different for different individuals.
(c) Attitudes or the state of mind which changes from time to time, and helps in choosing the product.
(d) The personality of the consumer which guides him to make a choice suiting his personality.

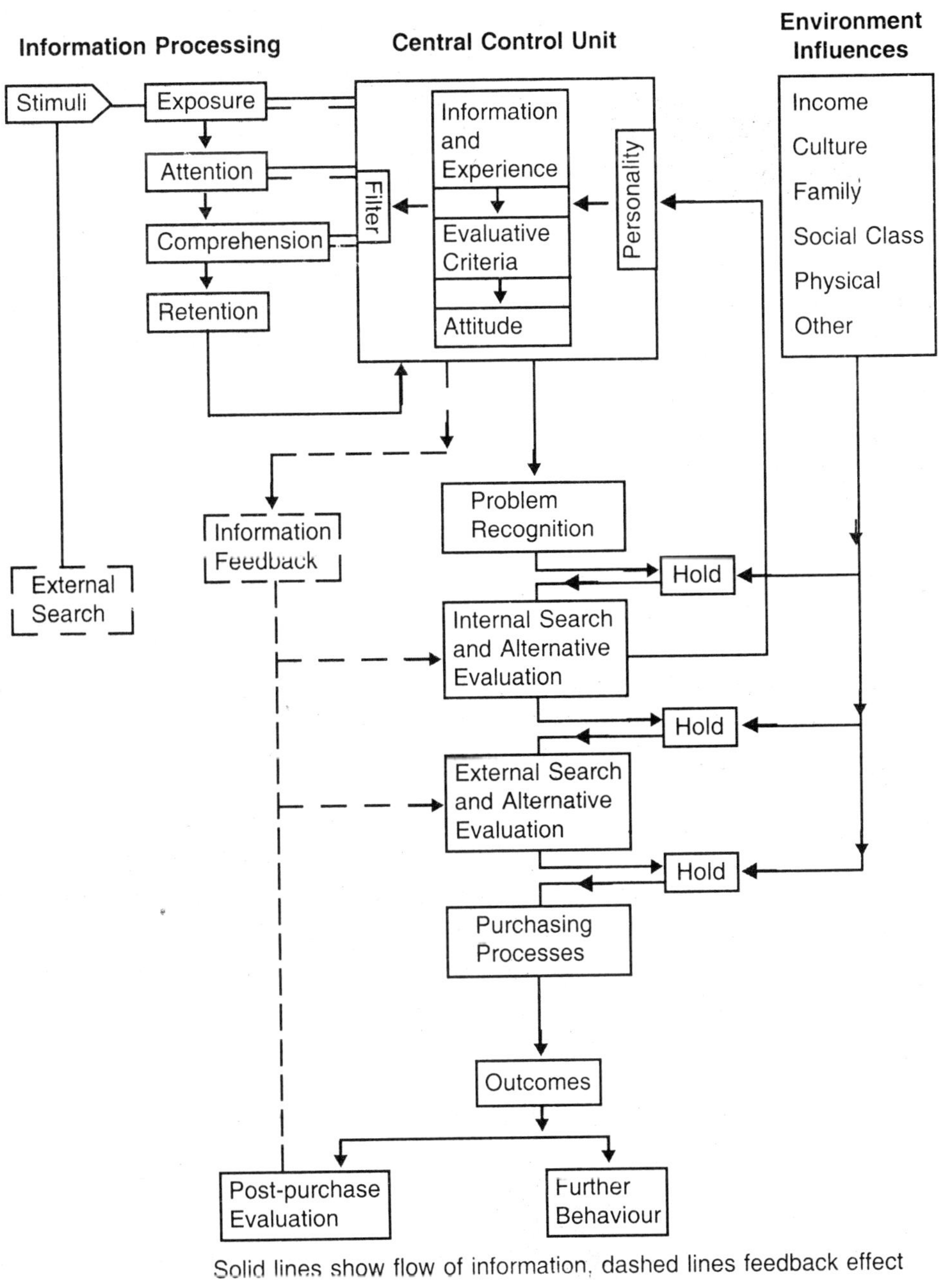

Fig. 3.5 Engel-Blackwell-Kollat Model of Buyer Behaviour.

Decision Process

This chapter is dealt with later in the text, and consists basically of probelm recognition, internal and external search, evaluation and the purchase. The decision outcome or the satisfaction and dissatisfaction is also an important factor which influences further decisions.

The decision process may involve extensive problem solving, limited problem solving or routinised response behaviour. This depends on the type and value of the product to be purchased.

Environmental Influences

The environmental influences are also shown in a separate box and consist of income, social class, family influences, social class and physical influences and other considerations. All these factors may favour or disfavour the purchase decisions.

8. Model of Family Decision-making

In a family decision-making model, it is important to understand how the family members interact with each other in the context of their consumer decision-making. There are different consumption roles played by various members of the family. These roles are as follows:

(i) Influencers

The members who influence the purchase of the product by providing information to the family members. the son in a family may inform the members of a new fast food joint. He can influence the family members to visit the joint for food and entertainment.

(ii) Gate keepers

These members control the flow of information for a product or brand that they favour and influence the family to buy the product of their choice. They provide the information favourable to themselves and, withhold information about other product which they do not favour.

(iii) Deciders

These are the people who have the power or, money and authority to buy. They play a major role in deciding which product to buy.

(iv) Buyers

Buyers are the people who actually buy. A mother buying ration for the house, etc. Father buying crayons for his children.

Preparers

Those who prepare the product in the form it is actually consumed. Mother preparing food by adding ingredients to the raw vegetable. Frying an egg for consumption, sewing clothes for the family, etc.

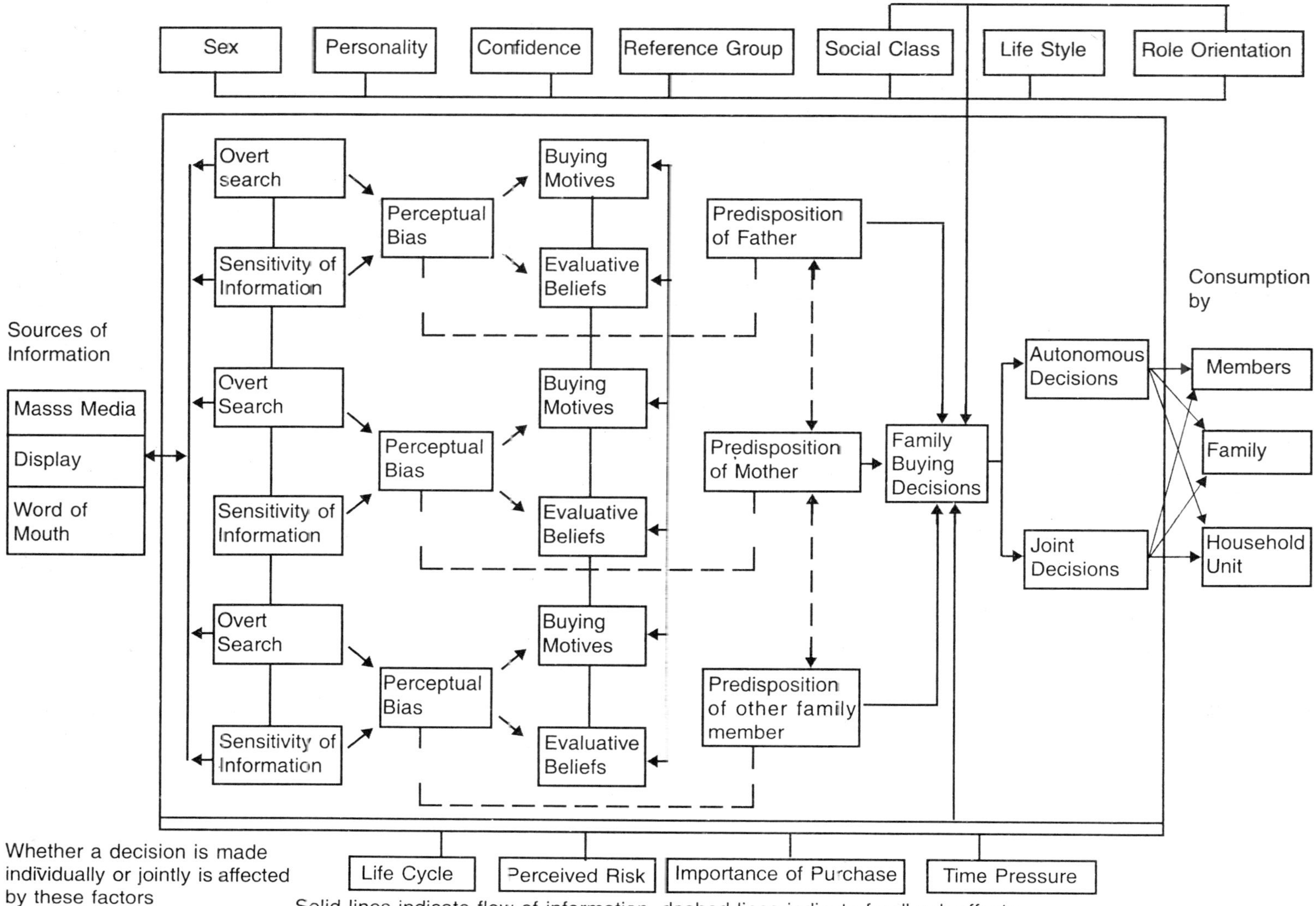

Solid lines indicate flow of information, dashed lines indicate feedback effects

Fig. 3.6 A Model of Family Decision-making

User

The person who actually uses or consumes the product. The product can be consumed individually or jointly by all members of the family. Use of car by the family, use of refrigerator, TV, etc.

The roles that the family members play are different from product to product. Some products do not involve the influence of family members—vegetables bought by the housewife. She can play many roles of a decider, preparer as well as the user. In limited problem solving or extensive problem solving there is usually a joint decision by family members.

The diagram shows the predisposition of various family members, which when influenced by other factors leads to joint or individual decisions. These factors are shown in the diagram and consist of social class, lifestyle, role orientation, family lifecycle stage, perceived risk, product importance and time pressure.

9. Nicosia Model

This model explains the consumer behaviour on the basis of four fields shown in the diagram. The output of field one becomes the input of field two, and so on.

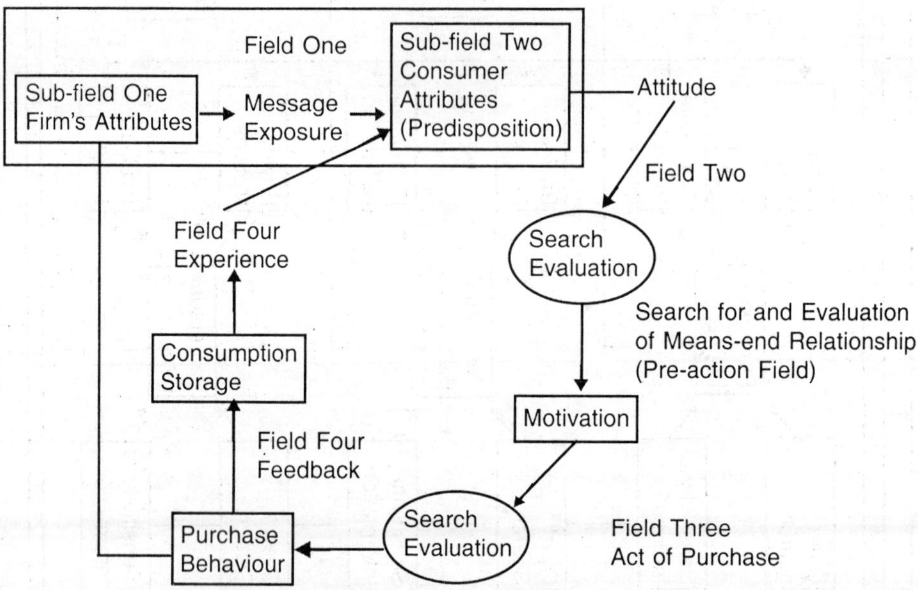

Fig. 3.7 Nicosia Model.

Field one consists of subfields one and two. Subfield one is the firm's attributes and the attributes of the product. The subfield two is the predisposition of the consumer and his own characteristics and attributes, which are affected by his exposure to various information and message, and is responsible for the building of attitude of the consumer.

Field two is the preaction field, where the consumer goes on for research and evaluation and gets motivated to buy the product. It highlights the means and end relationship. Field three is the act of purchase or the decision-making to buy the product. The customer buys the product and uses it. Field four highlights the post purchase behaviour and the use of the product, its storage and consumption. The feedback from field four is fed into the firms attributes or field one, and the feedback from the experience is responsible for changing the pre-disposition of the consumer and later his attitude towards the product.

Nicosia Model is a comprehensive model of dealing with all aspects of building attitudes, purchase and use of product including the post purchase behaviour of the consumer.

10. A MODEL OF INDUSTRIAL BUYER BEHAVIOUR

The purchases made in an Industrial organisation involve many more people of different backgrounds and it is more complex.

There are three main features in this model:

1. There are different individuals involved who have a different psychological make up.
2. Conditions leading to joint decision-making by these individuals.
3. Differences of opinion on purchases or conflicts that have to be resolved to reach a decision.

These are shown in Fig. 3.8 as (1), (2) and (3).

The persons involved in the decision-making are from quality control, manufacturing, finance, research and development and other possible areas. These may be named as purchase agents, engineers, and users, as referred to in the model.

These constitute a purchasing committee. They have:

(1a) Different backgrounds

(1b) Different information sources

(1c) Undertake active search

(1d) They have perceptual distortion

(1e) Satisfaction with past purchase.

With these characteristics, they develop certain expectations from the product to be bought. The obvious ones are product quality, delivery time, quantity of supply, after sales service and price. These are known as explicit objectives. There are other objectives as well, which are the reputation of the supplier, credit terms, location of the supplier, relationship with the supplier, technical competence and even the personality, skill and lifestyle of the salesman. These are known as implicit objectives.

Different individuals in the purchasing committee give emphasis on different aspects of the product. Engineers look for quality and standardisation of the product.

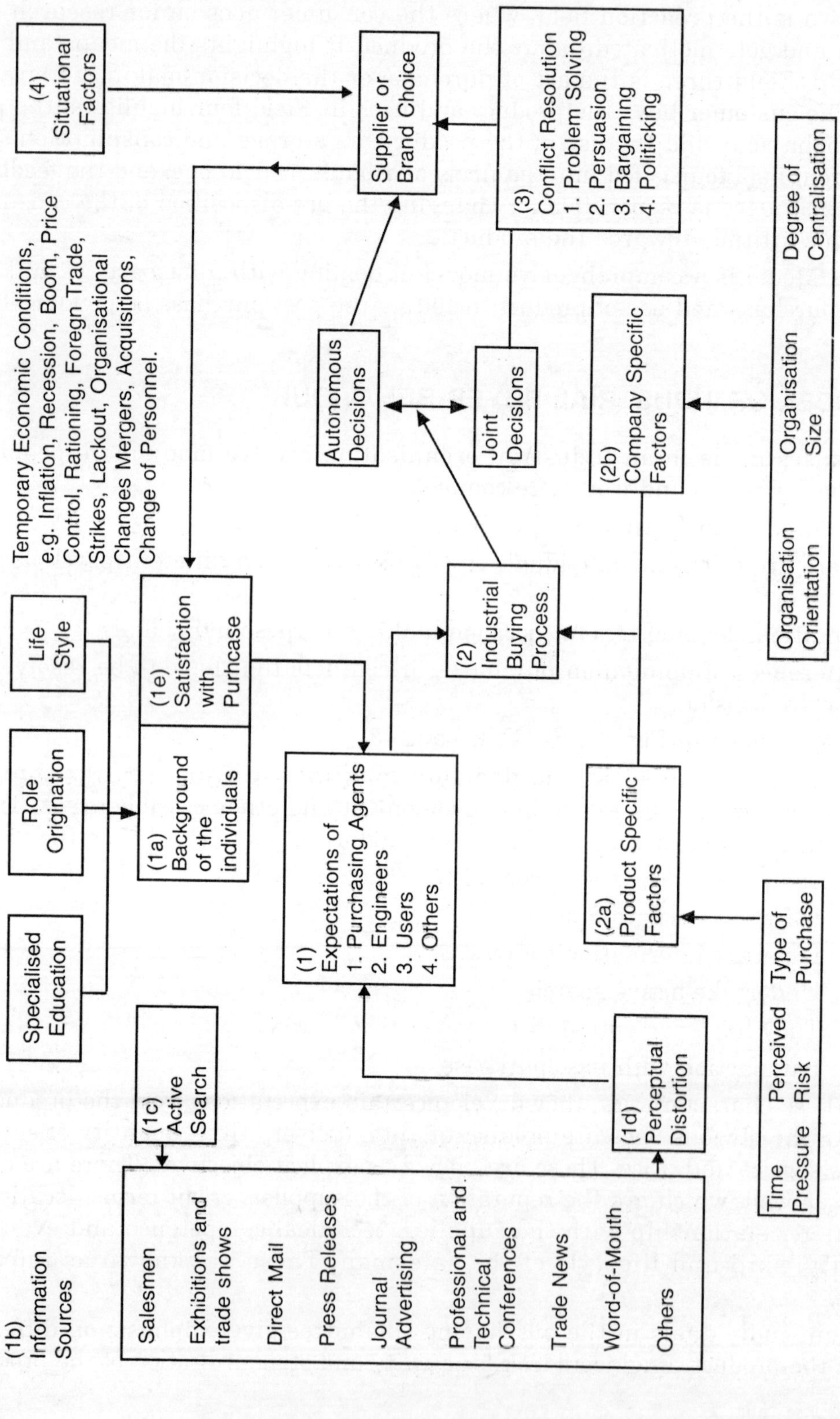

Fig. 3.8 An integrative model of industrial buyer behaviour.

Users think of timely delivery, proper installation and after sales service. Finance people look for maximum price advantage. Thus, there are conflicting interests and views that have to be resolved. If autonomous decisions are made, these issue do not surface. There are conditions leading to autonomous or joint decisions.

(2a) Product Specific Factors

Perceived risk: With higher risks joint decisions are favoured.

Type of purchase: Items involving heavy investments are made jointly, routine and less costly decisions can be made independently.

Time pressure: If goods are urgently required, individual decisions are favoured.

(2b) Company Specific Factors

Size of the organisation: Larger the size of the organisation, the more the emphasis laid on joint decision.

Organisation Orientation: In a manufacturing organisation, the purchases are dominated by production personnel and in a technology oriented organisation, the decisions are based on engineers.

(3) The conflict that arises for buying decision has to be resolved. The resolution can be done by:

(a) Problem solving

(b) Persuasion

(c) Bargaining

(d) Politicking.

The fourth aspect is the influence of situational factors which must be considered. These are economic conditions such as inflation, recession or boom, price contracts, rationing foreign trade, strikes or lock outs. Organisational change such as a merger, acquisition change of key personnel, etc. Sometimes these factors outweigh the realistic criteria of decision-making.

This model explains how purchase decision are made in an industrial organisation.

All the models discussed in this chapter give us an idea of the buying behaviour in diverse situations. An understanding of these models gives the marketer clues to formulate his strategies according to the target audiences, e.g. an individual, a family or an industry, etc.

Questions

1. What is the significance of the Pavlovian Model? Discuss in brief.
2. Discuss and illustrate the Input, Output Process Model by means of a diagram.

3. Discuss the Howarth Sheth Model, the Engel-Blackwell-Kollat Model as applicable to individuals.
4. Discuss the model of family decision-making and its importance.
5. Discuss the various fields of the Nicosia Model.
6. How is industrial buying different from individual buying? Illustrate by means of an industrial buyer model.

4

Concept of Culture

Ask the advice of a thousand men
Ignore the advice of a thousand more
Then go back to your original decision.

This chapter deals with the concept of culture, which is a very broad concept and includes knowledge, belief, customs and pattern of living acquired from predecessors. The student should be able to understand:

- Concepts of culture and its characteristics
- Function of culture
- Variation in cultural values

◆ INTRODUCTION

"CULTURE is the distinct way of life of a group of people and their complete design for living."

Culture is that complex whole which includes knowledge, belief, art, law, morals, customs and any other capabilities and habits acquired by humans as members of society. Culture influences the pattern of living, of consumption, of decision-making by individuals. It has certain characteristics and is transmitted from one generation to another.

It is a comprehensive concept and includes all those things that influence an individual in his thinking and behaviour, e.g. people in the western world have a different culture than those in the east. Their behaviour, living style and decision-making is different from those in the eastern countries.

Characteristics of Culture

- Culture is invented by 3 interdependent systems
  - (i) Ideological system—mental system consisting of ideas, beliefs, values and ways of reasoning (good or bad).
  - (ii) Technological system consists of skills, techniques to produce.
  - (iii) Organisational system (family and social class) coordinates behaviour.
- Culture is learned: It begins early in life and is learned through generations.
- Culture is socially shared, by human beings living in societies.
- Culture as similar yet different. Athletics, sports language music rituals are observed by all but are different.
- Culture is gratifying and persistent: You get satisfaction yet change is difficult.
- Culture is integrated and organised.
- Culture forms no runs and is prescriptive.
- Culture is acquired. It can be acquired from the family, from the region or from all that has been around us while we were growing up and learning the ways of the world.
- Culture forms a boundary within which an individual thinks and acts. When one thinks and acts beyond these boundaries, he is adopting a cross-cultural behaviour and there are cross-cultural influences as well.

The nature of cultural influence is such that we are seldom aware of them. One feels, behaves, and thinks like the other members of the same culture. It is all pervasive and is present everywhere.

Culture is a very broad concept and pervades like the air in the atmosphere.

Culture can be divided into two distinct components.

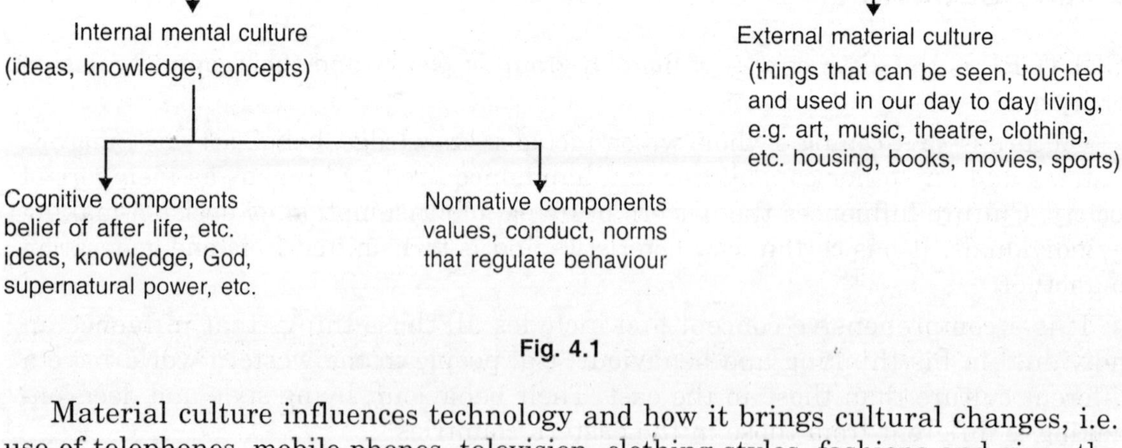

Fig. 4.1

Material culture influences technology and how it brings cultural changes, i.e. use of telephones, mobile phones, television, clothing styles, fashions and gives the marketers a chance to improve the product, packing, etc. to meet the needs of the consumer, etc.

The Functions of Culture

We have already seen that culture influences the behaviour of individuals. It provides a framework within which individuals and households build their pattern of living or exhibit their lifestyles.

Norms are the boundaries that culture sets on the behaviour. There are rules that encourage or prohibit certain behaviour in specific situations. Norms are derived from cultural values, which are widely told beliefs that specify what is desirable and what is not. When these rules are violated, it results in sanctions or penalties which are either disapproved of by the society, and in extreme cases the individual violating the norms are banished or ostracised from the society. Most individuals obey norms because it is natural to obey them. Culture outlines many business norms, family norms, behaviour norms, etc. How we greet people? How close one should stand to others while conducting business? The dress we wear and any other patterns of behaviour.

Culture keeps changing slowly over time; and is not static. Changes takes place due to rapid technologies. In case of emergency, war, or natural calamities, marketers and managers must understand the existing culture as well as the changing culture and culture of the country where the goods are to be marketed. Major companies have adapted themselves to international culture and are accepted globally.

Coca Cola is sold all over the world. Procter Gamble and other companies give cross-cultural training to their employees. By making cross-culture mistakes, many companies have difficulty in pushing their products for example, (i) Coca Cola had to withdraw its 2 litre bottle from Spain, because it did not fit in the local refrigerator; (ii) Many countries are very traditional and do not like women displayed on the products. This acts as a detriment to business in those countries.

Variation in Cultural Values

There are three broad forms of cultural values as shown in Fig 4.3.

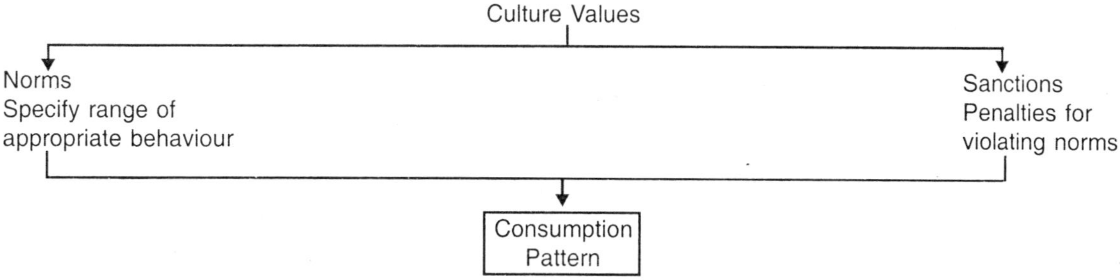

Fig. 4.2 Values, norms sanctions and consumption pattern.

Source: Adapted from *Consumer Behaviour*—Hawkins, Best, Coney.

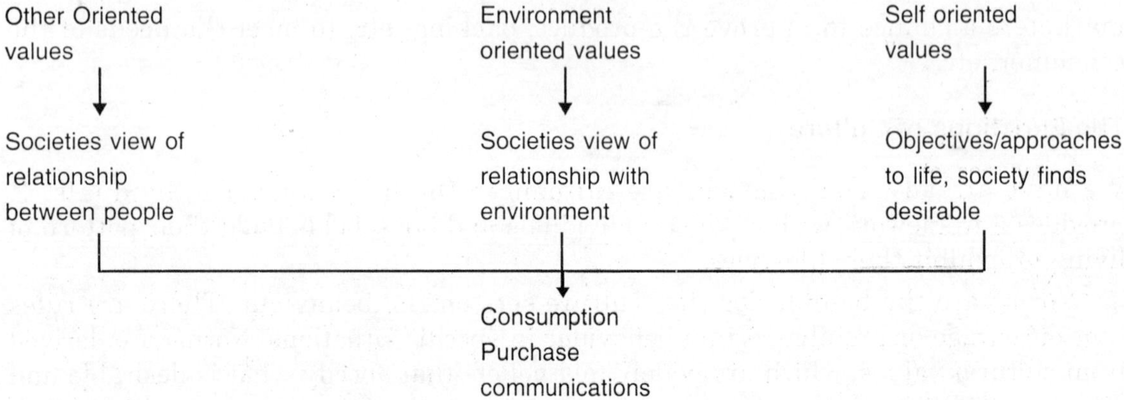

Fig. 4.3 Values orientation influence behaviours.

Source: Hawkins, Best, Coney.

Other Oriented Values

This shows the relationship between individuals and the society. The relationship influences marketing practices. If the society values collective activity—decisions will be taken in a group. It gives rise to following questions which affect consumer behaviour.

Individual / collective: Whether individual initiation has more value than collective activity?

Romantic orientation: This depicts whether the communication is more effective which emphasises courtship or otherwise. In many countries a romantic theme is more successful.

Adult / child theme: Is family life concentrated round children or adults? What role do children play in decision-making?

Masculine / Feminine: Whether the society is made dominant or women dominant or balanced.

Competitive / Cooperation: Whether competition leads to success. This is achieved by forming alliances with others.

Youth / age: Are prestige roles assigned to younger or older members of the society. American society is youth oriented and Korean is age oriented. Decisions are taken by mature people in Korea.

Environment Oriented Values

Cleanliness: If a culture lays too much stress on cleanliness. There is scope for the sale of beauty creams, soaps, deodorants, insecticides, washing powder, vacuum cleaner, etc. In western countries, a lot of emphasis is placed on this aspect and perfumes and deodorants are widely used.

Performance status: A status oriented society cares for higher standards of living, and chooses quality goods and established brand names and high prices items. This is true for the United States, Japan, Singapore, Malaysia, Indonesia, Thailand and most Arabic countries.

In performance oriented societies, where rewards and prestige is based on an individual's performance, less importance is given to brand names. Products which function equally well and may not be big brand names are used. Germans do not give the same amount of emphasis to brand names. The marketers adopt strategies accordingly.

Tradition/change: Traditional oriented societies stick to the old product and resist innovation or new techniques. In traditional societies, there is less scope for new products, and old traditional products are in greater demand. In some societies which are upwardly mobile, consumers are looking for modern methods, new products, new models and new techniques.

Risk taking/security: An individual who is in secure position and takes a risk can be either considered venturesome or foolhardy. This depends on the culture of the society. For developing new entrepreneurs risk taking is a must. It leads to new product development, new advertising themes and new channels of distribution. Security oriented societies have little chances of development and innovation.

Problem solving/fatalist: A society can be optimistic and have a problem solving attitude or, be inactive and depend on fate. This has marketing implications on the registering of complaints when consumers are dissatisfied with the purchase of the products. Advertising plays an important part and gives guidance to the consumer, and removes these doubts to a great extent.

Nature: There are differences in attitude over nature and its preservation. Consumers stress on packing materials that are recyclable and environment friendly. Some countries give great importance to stop environmental pollution and to recycling of products.

Companies like—P&G, Colgate-Palmolive captured a great extent of the market by offering products which are less harmful to the environment. They also use ingredients in the products which are not harmful in any way.

Self-Oriented Values

Active/passive: Whether a physically active approach to life is valued more highly than a less active orientation. An active approach leads to taking action all the time and not doing nothing. In many countries, women are also taking an active part in all activities. This makes the society a highly active one, where everybody is involved in work.

Material/non-material: In many societies money is given more importance, and a lot of emphasis is on being material minded. While in many societies things like comfort, leisure and relationships get precedence over being materialistic.

Materialism can be of two types. Instrumental materialism, which is the acquisition of things to enable one to do something or achieve something. Cars are used for transportation. People like to possess things of material value which would help them to bring efficiency; other material objects can be computers, washing machines, microwave ovens, etc.

Terminal materialism: It is the requisition of materialism for the sake of owing it rather than for use—Art is acquired for owing it. Cultural differences play an important role in this type of materialism. Instrumental materialism is common in the United States of America, where Japanese advertisements are mostly dominating terminal materialism. Antique collections is another example of terminal materialism.

Hard work / leisure: This has marketing implications on labour saving products and instant foods. Some societies value hard work and consider it as a fuller life. Others adopt labour saving devices and instant foods to have more leisure time at their disposal.

Postponed gratification / immediate gratification: Should one save for the rainy day or live for the day? Sacrifice the present for the future, or live only for the day? Some countries like The Netherlands and Germany consider buying against credit cards as living beyond one's means, whereas credit cards are very popular in America and other countries having a different cultural orientation, some prefer cash to debt. Some societies save for the morrow, others enjoy the present and spend lavishly.

Sexual gratification / abstinence: Some traditional societies curb their desires, food, drinks or sex, beyond a certain requirement. Muslim cultures are very conservative, and do not want their women to be seen in public or be exposed, so the Polaroid camera which gives instant photographs can be purchased and pictures can be taken by the family members without their women being exposed to the developers in a photo lab.

In other cultures, attractive female pictures are used for the advertisement of products. This may be considered very normal in these societies whereas, other societies may consider it strange.

Humour / serious: Should we take life lightly and laugh it off on certain issues or, take everything seriously? This is another aspect of culture. Advertising personnel selling techniques and promotion may revolve around these themes and the way the appeal for a product is to be made in various cultures.

Question

1. Explain culture and its characteristics.
2. Explain the function of culture and its components.
3. What are the variations in cultural values. Explain with examples.

5

Cultural Variations in Non-verbal Communications

Communication with the customer is the core of good customer service Coming together is the beginning, keeping together is progress, working together is success.

People from different cultures behave differently and have different ways of conducting themselves and interacting with people. This chapter should be able to explain:

- Variables in non-verbal communication
- Behaviours of people governed by culture
- Cultural values
- Marketing implication of culture

◆ INTRODUCTION

In a culture we have many variations in non-verbal communications. Each culture assigns a meaning to non-verbal signs utilised by it. There are some variables in non-verbal communication. These are:

(a) Use of time
(b) Use of space
(c) Friendship
(d) Agreements
(e) Things
(f) Symbols
(g) Etiquette

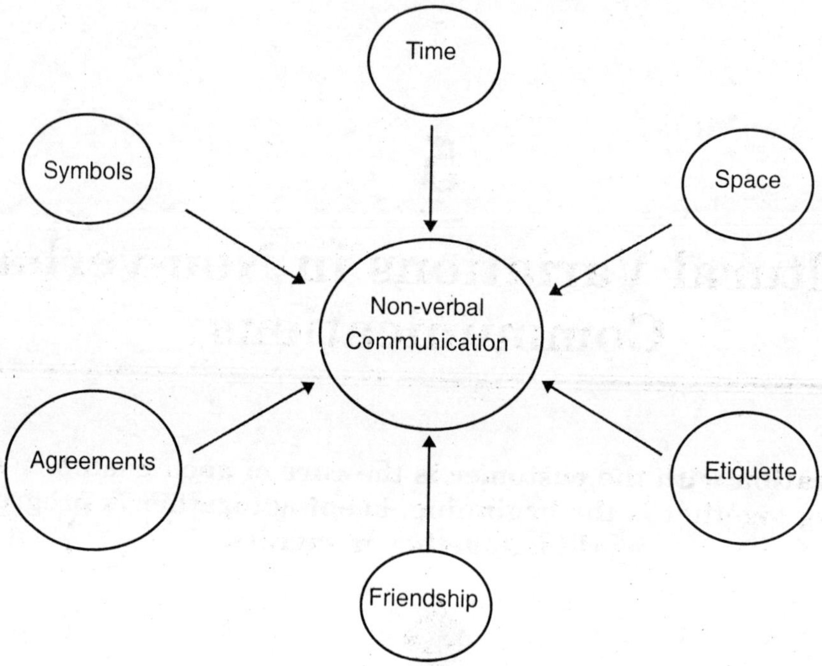

Fig. 5.1

Source: Adopted from Hawkins, Best, Coney.

Time

Time is a resource which is distributed equally amongst everybody. Every person has the same amount of time at his disposal. What view individuals and societies take of time makes them different. Some can be classified under monochronic culture and others in polychronic culture.

Some of the important differences between monochronic and polychronic culture are given in the table below.

Table 5.1

Monochronic culture	Polychronic culture
Do one thing at a time.	Do many things at once.
Concentrate on the job.	Highly distractible and subject to Interruption.
Take deadlines and schedules seriously.	Consider deadlines and schedules secondary.
Committed to job.	Committed to people and relationships.
Adhere religiously to plans.	Change plan often and easily.
Emphasise promptness.	Base promptness on relationship.
Accustomed to short term relationships.	Prefer long term relationships.

Source: Adapted from Hawkins, Best and Coney.

The meaning of time may be different in different cultures. Some people take time in making decisions according to the importance of decisions. Some insist on coming to the point directly in business transactions and are well prepared.

Some keep appointments by the minute, others make people wait for a long time.

Space

Space may be related to prestige rather than the need. The higher the office, the bigger the office space and so on. Americans have the offices of executives on the top floor and tend to separate the office of subordinates whereas, the French like to put the executives in the midst of subordinates. Japanese have their discount stores on the upper floor. Some cultures and individuals maintain a fair distance while transacting, others co-mingle easily. Americans maintain a fair distance while interacting with associates. Arabs stand very close to each other. This is known as the personal distance maintained by the people.

Friendship

Friendship plays an important role in business transactions. Good personal relationship and feelings matter most in a long term agreement. Social contacts developed by parties gain priority over technical specifications. Americans make friends easily, and drop them easily as well, because of both social and geographical mobility. Some cultures like Indian or Latin Americans have lasting relationships that endure for a long time and so does the business. Personal ties, personal trust leads to cooperation and a lot of transaction can take place between parties. Some want to transact business only with those whom they get along and, making money is secondary.

Some try to develop mutual confidence and trust, so that a lasting business results.

Agreements

All business when transacted is done under some agreements. These agreements may be written or just on an understanding between the two parties. Most people enter into an agreement, but friendship and kinship are also given a lot of importance. Verbal commitments are also binding in some cultures, where signing a contract is just a mere formality.

Things

Different cultures attach different meaning to things. Things include products as well as gifts given in certain business and social situations. An appropriate product in the form of a gift is to be carefully chosen. The gifts can be big or small. They can be given openly or presented privately. This depends on the practices followed in that particular country. Some want to make a show of the gift, by giving it in front of others. Others are secretive about it.

Symbols and Colours

Different countries attach different meanings to symbols, numbers and colours. Symbols can be flowers, triangles, pictures and animals, etc. Some numbers are considered lucky, and others not so lucky, or even unlucky, like 13, 4, etc. Colours have different interpretations. Pink is associated with a female, and blue with the male in the US, whereas it is just the opposite in Holland.

A list of colours and their interpretations is given below:

White: Symbol of mourning or death in the Far East, happiness, purity and peace in the United States.

Purple: Associated with death in many Latin American countries.

Blue: Symbolises feminity in Holland and masculinity in the United States, Sweden, India, etc.

Red: Colour for brides and children in India. Sign of masculinity in the UK and France, negative in Nigeria, Germany and positive in Denmark, Rumania and Argentina.

Yellow: Sign of death in Mexico, infidelity in France, celebrations in many other countries including India.

White lilies: Suggestion of death in England.

Symbol of Numbers

7: Lucky in India, USA, Morocco, Nicaragua and Czechoslovakia.

13: Unlucky in many countries including India.

4: Symbol of death in Japan. Packing in 4s is avoided.

Triangle: Negative in Hong Kong and Taiwan positive in Columbia.

Owl: Wisdom in the United States, bad luck in India.

Deer: Speed, grace in the United States; Homosexuality in Brazil.

Etiquette

These are accepted norms of behaviour. Some behaviour may be rude or abusive in one culture and quite acceptable in other cultures, e.g. sitting with legs crossed or sitting in a manner that shows the sole of a shoe. In Japan it is considered impolite to say no directly to a business offer. They put it differently, by saying it is very difficult, which means no. The exchange of business cards in Japan is essential, and indicates the level of your status in your business.

Similarly, there are many different habits and ways of doing things socially that effect the making of advertisement. Eating with the fork in the right hand and the left hand kept under the table is quite common in America. Whereas, in European culture, the fork should be in the left hand and the right hand holding the knife or spoon.

These non-verbal communications in different countries or different languages have a direct bearing on the marketing activity and must be taken care of. As people recognise verbal languages, they act accordingly. In a similar manner, non-verbal communication must also be recognised and understood so that there is less misinterpretation. The advertisement of the communication we want to give should be appropriate and match with the culture of the country.

Cross-cultural Marketing strategies specially advertising can be standardised to save cost. One campaign can be used in several countries e.g. An Asian Model for Asian countries in a low cut short dress. The appeals to youth beauty and sophistication etc. This standardisation has to appealed against cost and its impact. This is however a controversial issue.

There are seven consideration for approaching a Foreign Market

(i) Is the **Geographical area having a** homogeneous or a hetrogeneous culture? Marketing efforts are usually directed on geographical area mostly an economic and Political entities. Some times one area is considered as a single cultured unit but this may not be true. The culture of Kashmir is different to the culture in South India. Similarly Canada may have English Canadian and French Canadian who have different buying habits and different attitudes towards products. Therefore the marketing compaign should be directed on cultural groups rather than countries in geographical areas.

(ii) What need the product can fulfil in a culture? -for example the bicycle and motor cycle may satisfy recreational needs in many countries whereas these products fill the transportation needs in India and other developing countries.

(iii) **Affordability of the product:** Whether the groups or individuals can afford the product. It becomes difficult due to economic constraints or recession. Marketers therefore resort to credit strategy or exchange of old goods with new products.

(iv) Values for owning or purchasing the product: The value system must be investigated for influencing the purchase of the product.

(v) Consideration of Distribution, Political & Legal structures: Some products are distributed through general stores in one country while the same products may be distributed through medicine stores. eg. Vanilla is considered a chemical & is distributed through chemical stores in many countries. Similarly political & legal constraints have to be considered for formulating market strategies.

(vi) Communication about the product: Communication should be based on the (i) Media Inavailable (ii) Need that the product fulfils (iii) Values associated with the product (iv) Verbal & non-verbal commutation systems in culture. Commutation can be made effective through promotion mix. Consideration of the culture is important and the marketing mix has to be juggled to cater to different cultural needs while developing & marketing programmes ethical issue should be kept mind. These issues relate to credibility of the benefits provided by the product. Proper cost charged from the customer & giving due importance to legal constraint meeting the expectation of the customer an fixing due importance to legal constraints imposed by the government.

Marketing implications

Cultural values are not fixed or static but keep changing and are dynamic. They come slowly but surely. One of the factors that leads to the cultural change is the increased craving for fun excitement and enjoyment which open more opportunities for travel, thrills, fun oriented, entertainment and liesure oriented products. Other factors could be the paucity of time that people have. Most people are so busy and want to save time on travel, on cooking, on marketing and on repairs of items etc. The urge of saving time leads to the fast moving and safer moving vehicle etc. Fast food centres, convenience foods, cooking aids microwave ovens, disposable diapers, telemarketing, E business etc. The services are now being delivered at home by just a phone-call in servicing of cars, the cars are taken from your place and an alternative car provided for use till your car is delivered.

The urge for spending more time at home also known as cocooning has also brought a new dimension in purchasing of products like exercise machines. Swimming pools, Sauna bath in the house, owning of computers and video casette and recorders. People also want to make use of the money they get as a golden Handshake or as retirement benefits and want to live a healthier life. Comprehensive health care and direct housing. Many consumers want to live an inner-directed life and spend on improving themselves—improving their looks, vigour, vitality and well being and live life to the fullest. Another change that is taking place is that consumers want to live a more natural and healthier life by using natural products i.e. rejection of the artificial and acceptance of the natural material. This can be in many areas of pharmaceuticals: use of natural hurbs.

Cosmetics—natural hurbs and not chemicals household items and plants.

Clothes—Pure cotton, Pure silk.

Furnishing—Change synthetic to natural fibres.

These cultural changes leads the marketer to rethink his strategies of products Mix, Promotion pricing and distribution for the targeted consumer. They try to offer more than what the customer expects, offering products that truly perform giving more guarantees building stranger relationships. The market is to be segmented in terms of cultural values. Environmental oriented values, self oriented values are other values and accordingly the products are to be tailored to their needs and products be positioned to appeal to this target segment. Distribution methods may include in home catalogue shopping, toll free telephone shopping. Latest are the drive in churches & funeral parlours for short of time consumers.

The promotion can have a new approach and stress more on realistic aspects and acknowledging the women's role in our society. Advertising focussed on the desired segment and more and accurate information delivered to the consumer.

Questions

1. Explain the term culture.
2. How are behaviours of groups and individuals governed by culture?
3. What are the characteristics of culture? Explain the function of culture.
4. What are the 3 forms of cultural values?
5. What are the factors influencing non-verbal communications? Explain with reference to time and symbols.
6. What are marketing implications of culture? What is the role of a marketer in this connection?

6

Social Stratification

There are two classes of people—those who create weatlth and those who consume it.

After reading this chapter the student should understand:

- Social class
- Behaviour—unique, shared and excluded
- Social class system
- Buying patterns of various social classes
- Market strategy applied to social classes

◆ WHAT IS A SOCIAL CLASS

A social class refers to a social position that an individual occupies in a society. People belonging to a social class have many characteristics, such as education, occupation, ownership of property and source of income. We, in India have many social classes and these divide the society into a hierarchy of classes, varying from the high class to low. The members within each group have almost the same status, income, buying characteristics. Social class influences the decision-making of groups and individuals.

We are aware of our social class to a certain extent, which gives us an idea of our status. Social class is a reality of life. It reflects on the marketing behaviour of consumers. The products we buy, the style we prefer the stores we visit and want to buy from.

Definition

1. A social class is a hierarchical division of a society into relatively distinct and homogeneous groups with respect to attitudes, values, lifestyles, etc.

2. It is a relatively permanent and homogeneous division or strata in a society, which differs in their wealth, education, possession, values, beliefs, attitudes, friendship and manner of speaking.

Status difference also reflects on prestige, power and privilege.

The concept of social class involves families rather than individuals. Members of the same family enjoy the same status, as they belong to the same social class and share the same house, share a common income and have similar values. These characteristics effect their relationship with others. Social class results from large groups in a population sharing approximately the same life styles, who are stratified according to their social status and prestige.

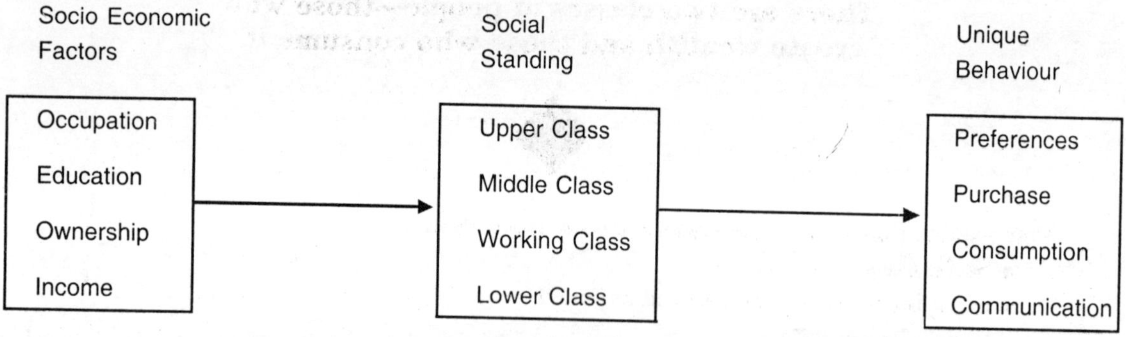

Fig 6.1 Social Standing: How it is derived and influences behaviour.

All countries and societies have variations in social standing—many countries, including China, tried to have a classless society but not with great success. Social stratification is thus a reality of life. As shown in Fig. 6.2 the behaviour of all social classes are unique within themselves.

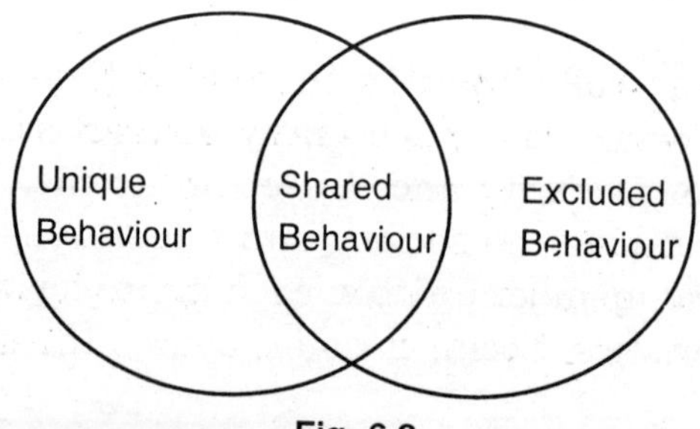

Fig. 6.2

Source: Adapted from *Consumer Behaviour*, Hawkins, Coney and Best.

By unique behaviour we mean that each social class has its own pattern of purchase, education, occupation, recreation, etc. This is important to marketers, in order to understand the needs of the consumer, and accordingly to frame a marketing strategy. There are many behaviours ,that are common between social classes, and all social classes behave in a similar manner without much difference. This is shared behaviour. Excluded behaviour is one which the social classes do not indulge in. They try to avoid that behaviour, as it is against their standards and norms. These could be eating behaviour, i.e. the choice of the eating place. Buying behaviour: the places one avoids going to, like discount stores, etc. for the upper class. Social classes usually meet the following five criterion.

Bounded

The social classes are bound by certain tacit restrictions which include or exclude certain individuals, places or objects. These are tacit rules they follow by themselves. They restrict behaviour as they share similar educational background occupation lifestyle etc.

Ordered

All social classes have a hierarchy or stratification in terms of income, prestige and status that distinguishes them from the others.

Mutually Exclusive

The individual only belongs to one class and behaves and acts accordingly. However, the movement from one class to another is possible and goes on with time. We have a new rich class which has moved upward with the time. They are upwardly mobile and belong to the open system. Those in closed system have inherited and scribed status. They cannot leave their social class.

Exhaustive

That every member of a social class must fit into some class and be identified with it.

Influential

There must be behavioural variations between classes or they may be expected to behave differently.

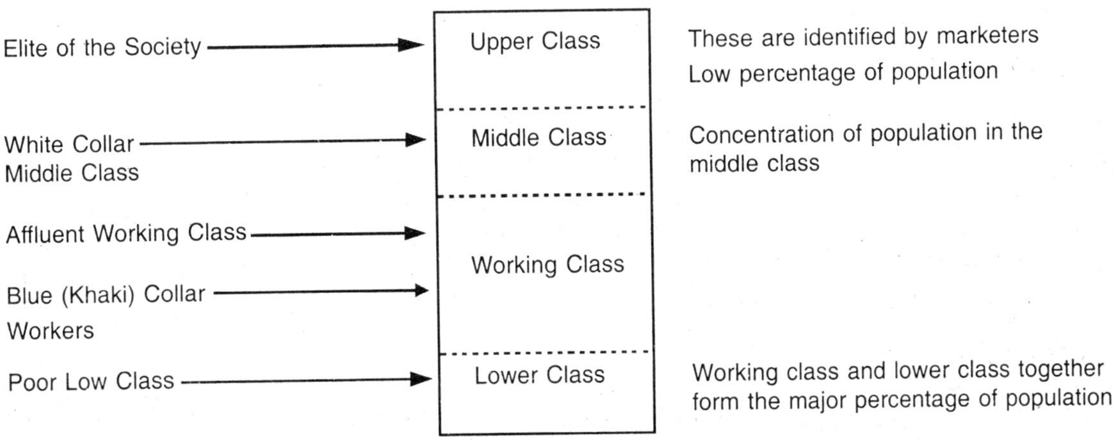

Fig. 6.3 Social Class System.

Based on the above criteria, it is clear that a strict and tightly defined social class system does not exist. Social classes are basically divided into three major categories—upper, middle and lower. For the great spread, we have further classified them into four classes by bringing the working class in between the middle and lower.

The classes have also been classified into six categories by Warner.

1 Upper Upper	3 Upper Middle	5 Upper Lower
2 Lower Upper	4 Lower Middle	6 Lower Lower

Fig. 6.4 Social Class System.

Warner's index uses 4 variables as an index of social class. These are occupation, income, house and dwelling area. Warner has categorised the social class into 6 categories. This helps the marketers in deciding their target group and the marketing strategy for each. For instance, the concept of mass marketing can be more successfully applied to middle or the lower classes, rather than the upper class. The upper class is a target for speciality goods and rare commodities which depict their social status.

Social Classes and their Buying Patterns

The buying behaviour of individuals and groups are strongly influenced by the social class to which they belong, or aspire to belong. Social class is also linked to demographic and geographic data. These classes are found living in clusters and have relatively homogeneous geo-demographic segments in terms of housing, urbanisation and other, viz. class difference in status is symbolic for food, housing, clothing, purchases, lifestyle.

In a social class, people try to make the same kind of purchases as are expected by their peers. Marketers try to target their products on class based market segments.

Upper Upper Class

This is the most wealthy, aristocratic class having a lot of property. This is a small sized segment and has to be targeted for novelty, expensive and luxury goods by the marketers. This class has access to property, prestige and power. They have a lot of discretionary income and can buy the right product and services and socialise with the right people. They are an attractive market segment for leisure goods designer clothes, foreign travel and special services.

Lower Upper Class

They are lower in status than the upper upper class and try to imitate their lifestyle. They are known by their conspicuous consumption and are also a smaller target

Table 6.1 Lifestyle orientation and purchasing pattern of a social class

Social Class	*Lifestyle Orientation*	*Purchasing Tendencies*
Upper Class	Good taste Greaceful living Good things in life Individual expression Interest in art and culture	Quality merchandise; Expensive hobby and recreation equipment, art, books, travel
Middle Class	Respectability, conformity, propriety, social esteem	Items in fashion and related to self presentation; Good clothing, neighbourhood and house items for children
Working Class	Fun oriented parochial (restricted in scope) Unsophisticated taste. Foucus on possession and not ideas	Newest appliances, sporting events newest and biggest items
Lower Class	Close family relationships No interest in world affairs Neighbourhood oriented Want immediate gratification	Status symbol products enhancing self esteem; Pseudo symbols of prosperity, such as used scooters; readily available products

Source: Adapted from Hawkins, Best, and Coney—*Consumer Behaviour*, p. 173.

market for luxury goods. They try to acquire the habits and lifestyle of the upper upper class. The products used by the upper class trickle down to this class and is known as the trickle down effect. The upper upper class becomes a reference groups and the members of the lower upper class strive to achieve a higher status in the society. The marketers knowing this, formulate a strategy for this group or class of people.

Upper Middle Class

This class has achieved success in life and consists of managers, professionals, lawyers, professors. They are also owners of medium sized business. They therefore take membership of clubs and have a broad range of cultural interests. They are hard working and want to reach higher in society. Their aspirational group is the upper class.

Lower Middle Class

The common man represents this group. Some are highly paid workers and small business owners and may not have a very high education.

This class aspires for respectability. They wish to have well maintained houses in good neighbourhoods. Marketers sell products, to this group, which have respectability and social acceptance in the society.

Upper Lower Class

They live for the present. They and the lower lower class constitute the major percentage of population. Their buying habits are influenced by their cultures and sub-cultures. Their social activities influence the purchase of product.

Lower Lower Class

They live in utter poverty. Their main concerns to fulfil their basic physiological needs. They need shelter, clothing, food and go for economical purchases. Their first priority is the price and they cannot afford any unnecessary expenditures.

Marketing Strategy and the Social Classes

Marketers are interested in supplying the right products to the right customer (target segment) at the right price at the right time and with the right promotion. For this, first the target segment is selected and this can be done on the basis of a social class, which is a better prediction of a consumer's lifestyle than income. Reasons for shopping and purchases also differ among the social classes. The upper classes shop for pleasure, and tend to visit stores which are exclusive and sophisticated. The situation of stores are also important. They visit boutiques and are particular where they go shopping. The upper and middle classes indulge in greater information search and get information through the TV, magazines, newspapers, and from groups and individuals of their social status.

The lower classes are involved in buying less costly products and have much less information. They are more concerned with social relationship and respond too products and promotion of a different nature.

Marketers thus find that a combination of social class and income are superior for product classes that are visible. These products require moderate expenditure and are symbols of social status like TV sets, cars, clothing, etc.

In designing a market strategy using social stratification, a process is follwed in which

(a) The marketer relates the status of the group to the product.

(b) Data is collected as the targeted social strata.

(c) Positions the product according to social status.

(d) Develops a proper marketing mix.

While relating a product to the status of the group or individual, one has to understand that the product or brand consumed varies according to income, which may restrict the purchase of expensive items like cars. Education influences the consumption of fine arts, of imported goods and varies with social class. Credit cards, etc. are also used by different social classes for different purposes. This provides a motivation for purchase. Some use it for convenience and safety, or both, others use it to pay the monthly bills. Some products are used for symbols of prosperity, and to

Table 6.2 Developing Marketing Strategy for Social Class

Relate status to product	*Gather data on social class*	*Position the products*	*Marketing Mix*
Product Brand Usage Purchase Motivation Symbolic meaning Use situation	Actual life-style Desired life-style Media usage Shopping habits	Select desired image and correlate with desired life-style	Develop Marketing mix to achieve desired position Product price Promotion Distribution Service

project their social class. Products are offered for different use situations, i.e. parties, marriages gifts, daily use, etc.

The next step is to gather data on the lifestyles of people and how they want to become upwardly mobile by aspiring to have a desired lifestyle. To promote the product to their lifestyle, proper media must be chosen and used effectively. The shopping habits of buyers and their patterns of buying are also to be studied carefully.

In the third step the product is positioned. It is positioned according to different income groups and social classes, e.g. Maruti-800 is an economy car; Zen is a world car; Esteem is more spacious and expensive.

Consumable products can also be positioned as a health drink—Bournvita, economical drink (Rasna), fizz drinks, etc. The products can be positioned according to the needs of the social classes.

The last step is to find out and offer, a proper marketing mix to the social class. This consists of product, price, promotion and distribution, which have many alternatives and have to be juggled to suit the target market. The after sales service is also very important and must be given due emphasis to satisfy the customer, and ensure repeat sales.

Questions

1. Explain the concept of social class.
2. Describe the social stratification and their buying patterns.
3. How would you develop a marketing strategy for social class?

7

Group Influences on Consumer Behaviour

If there is any secret of succes, it lies in the ability to get the other person's point of view, and seeing things from his angle—Henry Ford.

This chapter explains:

- Groups of various types
- How groups influence behaviour
- Influence of reference groups on individuals
- Opinion leaders and their role

INTRODUCTION

All of us belong to some group or the other and, we also associate ourselves with different groups in our daily life. Of course, the most primary group with whom we are mostly in touch with, is our family. The groups that we associate with or, the groups that we meet and interact with influence our behaviour to a certain extent.

Definition

A group consists of two or more individuals who share a set of norms, values or beliefs and have certain implicitly or explicitly defined relationship with one another, such that their behaviour is interdependent. Groups give an opportunity to individuals to learn and socialise. Marketers use the knowledge of group influences when designing market strategy.

Reference group is a group of people who your refer to, while making buying decisions. They help you in buying items like clothing, etc. Reference groups influence consumer behaviour by building aspirations for the individual and, helping him to choose the product for a particular lifestyle. They are small groups and consist of family, close friends, work groups, neighbours or any other group of people you associate with.

These groups regulate the lives and set standards for norms and conduct. In a family, influence is exerted by the members of the family in the purchase-consumption process.

Reference groups affect consumers by imparting information and by influencing value expressive needs of the consumers. If one wants to be a member of the group, one has to conform to the standards of the group. Their values and attitudes have to be appreciated and adopted, and one tends to buy and use the products which the group uses and appreciates. More homogeneous groups, or group members having similar characteristics are more susceptible to attitude changes than the groups whose members are less homogeneous. Some individuals have a strong sense of identification with a group because they derive strong material or psychological benefit by being associated with that group. Sometimes, there are pressures of buying, known as conformity pressures, and one adheres to the norms of the group. Conformity pressures can be noticed with norms set by schools and colleges, other membership organisation and military or police organisation and the like. These can be exerted directly or indirectly on the members of the group.

There are three levels of group involvement. These are:

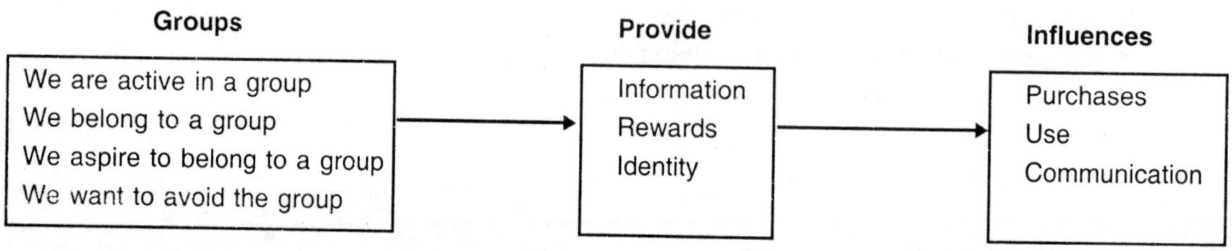

Fig. 7.1 Group Influence Consumption.

Compliance

The members of the group have to comply only by overt or open behaviour with the norms and standards, i.e. comply by paying certain fixed fees. Being present on time. Wearing the same clothes, etc. It makes no demand on the change of attitudes, beliefs of the person concerned. You can only be a passive member of a service organisation, pay fees, eat food, meet people and go away without being service minded, e.g. Lions Clubs and Rotary Clubs.

Identification

This is a deeper relationship where the individual not only complies to the standards, but also maintains a social relationship and changes his perception to a great extent, i.e. you can join a service organisation only for being a member or, you can change your perception and become service minded and actually start believing in service doing and, appreciating to achieve the service objectives of the organisation. You can become involved deeply and take pride in identifying yourself as a Lion or a Rotarian.

Internalising

Here you become more committed and, not only believe in service, but also try to enforce the objects and views on others, to get more deeply involved in it. You make or force others to follow the norms and rules of the organisation.

An example of the process can be that your are born in religious surroundings and perform rituals enforced on you. The next stage is that you start being religious yourself and the third stage is that you start preaching the same to others.

There are four types of reference groups. These are:

Membership and Non-membership Groups

This is a simple and self explanatory classification. A membership group is one to which one belongs. Non-membership group are groups of which you are not a member but may aspire to belong to.

Formal or Informal Group

A formal group has a structure and some objectives and the roles of the members are defined. Certain rules and regulations are followed. An informal group has no structure. People come and go at random, e.g. a group meeting in the market place having tea and snacks together, meeting without much purpose.

Primary or Secondary Group

This depends on the frequency of contact. Primary groups consist of family, close friends, peers and business associates with whom one has regular contact. Secondary groups meet infrequently and are not so closely knit. Club membership groups and shopping groups are secondary groups.

Aspirational Groups

Aspirational groups are the groups you aspire to belong to and want to join at some future time. These are known as anticipatory aspirational groups. We also have symbolic aspirational groups to which a person is attached but not likely to belong to. These are professional sports groups, or some other elite group.

Marketers use a symbolic group by using celebrities to advertise the products.

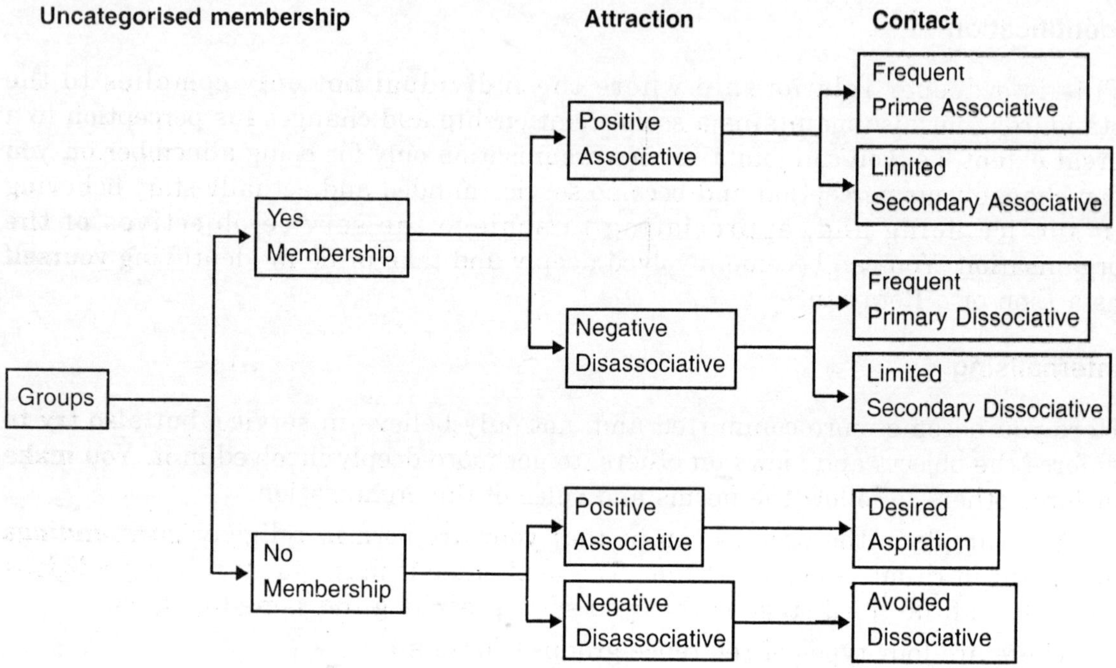

Fig 7.2

Source: Adapted from Hawkins, Best and Coney, p. 147.

The above figure shows the classification of groups. It is important for marketers to make a study of the behaviour of groups and accordingly formulate strategies. Consumers use these groups as a point of reference at different times. Primary groups exert greater and more direct influence on purchasing behaviour, and the advertisers use family settings and family events as a means of advertising them to influence consumers.

Reference Groups and the Influence Exerted by Them

Reference groups can be further classified into 4 categories given below, depending on the functions they perform and, the kind and degree of influence exerted by them. These groups lay down certain norms, roles and status that are followed by members.

Norms are unwritten codes, or standards of conduct that are assigned to individuals within a group.

Roles are the part that the members play as initiator, influencer, gate keeper, decision maker, the purchaser and final user.

Status is the position of authority that is designated within a group. High status relates to more power, e.g. father and mother in a family have greater status than the other family members. Also the chief executive has greater authority and power than the subordinates in an organisation. Products are also bought and consumed, which relate to the status of the individual or group.

Thus, there are four categories of reference groups namely normative, comparative, status and dissociative groups. We shall discuss these one by one.

Normative Groups

These are groups that uphold the norms of the groups. There are values that must be adhered to, while exhibiting consumer behaviour. There is also the judgement or the perspective one uses in defining personal situations.

These norms also influence the choice of clothing or how much a person should eat or drink at a party—normative influence may lead to normative behaviour. The influences are exerted on purchase of clothing, furniture, appliances, food, etc. These are visible items. Other items like mouth-wash, perfumes, etc. may not be visible, but are used for the approval of group members. Normative influence is also known as utilitarian influence, which occurs when an individual fulfills group expectations to receive a direct reward or to avoid a sanction. You may purchase a given brand of coffee to win approval from a spouse or a neighbourhood group, or you may refrain from wearing the latest fashion for fear of being teased by friends.

Comparative Reference Groups

These are groups with whom the individual compares himself and his attitudes. He compares himself to other members of the group to find out whether they support his views and attitudes.

The new resident in the neighbourhood are attracted to neighbours who are similar to themselves, because they reinforce existing attitudes and behaviours. Advertisers also use spokesmen who are perceived by consumers as similar to themselves, because they reinforce existing attitudes and behaviour. Comparative reference groups provide the basis for validating beliefs, values and attidudes. Consumers need not be in direct social contact with a reference group to be influenced by it.

In the case of comparative reference groups, if values are expressed, they can be practised and one can come closer to the group and be accepted by it. This is known as value expressive influence, e.g. where drinking is prohibited and expressed. One practices the same to be accepted by the group. In groups where chappals and sandals are not allowed and is expressed, then one has to conform with the values of the group to come closer to it.

Dissociative Group

Some individuals do not want to be likened to, or identified by a group of individuals. They try to dissociate themselves from that group. These groups are known as dissociative groups. You may try to dissociate yourself from a group in your office who may be dishonest and you want to uphold your image of honesty. This is also done to move upwards into a higher social class. You may not buy products used by the dissociative group. You may want to move away from this dissociative group of people.

Status Reference Group

When one refers to the status or a position of the people in a group, he is referring to status reference group. An individual who may not belong to this group may aspire to achieve that status and, want to be a member of that group (aspiration group).

Reference Group, Social Influence and Social Power

The influence of reference groups as consumer behaviour is felt through the influence of social power. There are five basis of social power. These are:

Reward Power

It is the ability to give rewards in the form of money, gifts, psychological rewards such as recognition practice. In some cases, products like clothes, durables goods, etc. are also offered.

Coercive Power

It is the ability to give threats or withhold rewards. It is the threatening or coercive power to influence consumer behaviour, e.g. The purchase of accepted clothing, deodorants, mouthwash and LIC Policies, are sold by using coercive power.

Legitimate Power

It is linked to cultural or group values. The groups influences the consumption pattern to which they belong. It is the power one has, because of his legitimate position in an organisation, i.e. a manager.

Referent Power

It is used to buy a status oriented product which identifies the feeling of oneness with the group. The group member is urged to obtain a similar status by purchasing the recommended items.

Expert Power

Buying behaviour is influenced by the expertise of the people in the group. People who are experienced and technically qualified in an area.

A person may be attracted to and conform to group norms, either in order to gain praise or recognition, or in response to coercive power.

Factors Affecting the Influence of Reference Groups

A reference group provides benefits to individuals and that is why people associate with reference groups. It exerts an influence on the individual's behaviour and the degree of influence is determined by:

Firstly, how informed and experienced the individual is? If the individual is less informed, he relies heavily on the reference group or, if he has little or no experience even then he looks up to the groups for information and guidance.

Secondly, if the group has high credibility, greater influence can be exerted by it on the individual's behaviour. It can thus change the attitudes and beliefs of the consumers. Consumers will look upon it and refer to it more for information on product quality.

The Nature of Reference Group Influences on Products and Services

When people meet in a social setting they discuss their experiences with the products that they have used and, express their likes and dislikes and preference and, attributes of the product. The individuals also buy products or use services which they see others using or buying.

Reference group influences the product and brands when the product is conspicuous. The conspicuousness can be measured by:

Exclusivity and Visibility Dimensions

Exclusivity refers to few people possessing or using the product, and if many are using the product it is less exclusive. Necessity goods are less conspicuous than luxury goods. Products which are necessities will be used by many consumers whereas, luxury products will be used by few chosen customers only.

Exclusivity / Visibility	*Necessity* Weak reference group influence (–) on product.	*Luxury* Strong reference group influence on product (+)
Public Strong reference group influence on brand (+)	*Public Necessities* Influence—weak product and strong brand wrist watch, automobile, men's suit.	*Public Luxuries* Influence—strong product and brand, e.g. golf club
Private Weak reference group influence on brand (–)	*Private Necessities* Influences—weak product and brand, e.g. mattress, floor lamp and refrigerator.	*Private Luxuries* Influence—Strong and weak brand, e.g. home video-game, ice maker.

Fig. 7.3 Reference group influence on product and brand purchase decision.

Source: Peter J.P. Olson, J.C. *Consumer Beli Marketing Strategy Perspective,* p. 443.

Visibility Dimension

If the product can be seen and identified by many, it is more visible. Products consumed in public are more conspicuous than products consumed in private.

The figure shows four categories which are public necessities and public luxuries and private necessities and private luxuries. The examples of products used in each category is shown in Fig. 7.3 on page 63.

Reference Group Application in Marketing

A wide application of reference groups is used in advertising by marketers. They use pleasant situations and attractive and prominent people to promote their products. The products are used by these people who are sought after and, have made a mark in life. They try to identify lifestyle characteristics of a certain group and then design effective advertising strategies. The designing of advertising is done by:

Using Celebrities

Celebrities who endorse the product to the consumer, e.g. film stars for beauty products including soaps (Lux), etc. sports people for the use of health products, e.g. Kapil Dev for Boost; Shahrukh Khan for Smoodles; Pierce Brosnan for Reid and Taylor; Cindy Crawford for Revlon.

Use of Experts and Professionals

Experts in various fields are used to promote the products. The prospective customers evaluate the products advertised by experts and are affected by these experts and professionals.

Doctors are used to promote tooth-pastes, e.g. Forhans, Sachin Tendulkar promoting Visa Cards, etc.

Use of Spokesman

For product endorsements, spokesmen for a particular product refer to the appeal for the common man. It is propagated that somebody from the common man uses the product and is satisfied. Lalitaji of the Surf advertisement.

Opinion Leaders

These are key persons in a group who influence their group and are innovators or early buyers. The marketer focuses his strategies on key persons in the group, some are opinion leaders, and others are opinion seekers. Thus, key persons are knowledgeable with a lot of experience. They are also known as influencers and others are receivers. They consist of friends, associates, neighbours, etc. In this group persuasive communication is more fruitful, as opinion leaders can affect and influence the behaviour of others in a group.

There are opinion leaders who mediate the transmission of information from Mass Media to the general public:

(a) Firstly, the Mass Media transmits information to the general public.

Mass Media → Transmission
of Information → General Public

(b) Secondly, Mass Media may send through opinion leaders to general public

Mass Media → Opinion Leaders → General Public
(Target Customers)

(c) Thirdly, there is interaction between people and information goes forward and backwards, interaction and positive and negative discussions are made, attitudes are made, and thus information goes to the general public

Mass Media → Opinion Leader → General Public
(Target Customers)

The Opinion leaders transmit the products relative information, which consists of:

(a) use of specific product, e.g. washing machine, vacuum cleaner, electric shaver, etc.

(b) which of several brands is the best—Whirlpool, Kelvinator, BPL, etc.

(c) which is the best place to shop from, which dealer, locality, etc.

Opinion leaders for one specific product may not be the opinion leaders for other products, as well. An opinion leader for infants foods may not be the opinion leader for kitchen ware, etc. Opinion leaders in one area may not necessarily influence other areas.

Characteristics of Opinion Leaders

Opinion leaders are more knowledgeable, and have a keen level of interest.

- More involved in the product category.
- Have local friendship and social interaction.
- Can disseminate information.
- Have high credibility.
- Have more self-confidence, are more sociable and cosmopolitan, can take risks.

Opinion leaders are activated greatly to reduce distance process for the products they have bought; may want to influence neighbours and friends. They involve themselves, to confirm their own judgement.

They are younger, have more education, have a higher income, and higher occupational status.

They are exposed to media. See more movies and television. Also read information magazines and technical publication devoted to the product category. Having greater knowledge about the product, they can disseminate more and true information about the products and their usage. Opinion leaders are therefore a case of study to marketers and their strategies are evaluated and formed, keeping the opinion leaders and their roles in mind.

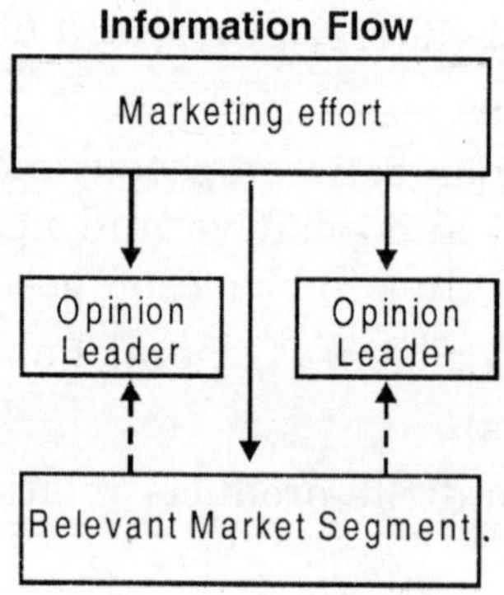

Fig. 7.4 Information flow

The figure shows that the opinion leaders seek relevant information from the mass media and other sources, and transmit the same to members of the group. The dashed line show the feedback from the group to the opinion leaders.

Gate-keepers: They may be distinct from opinion leaders. They introduced ideas and information, but are not able to influence the group.

Market Maven: Maven is an expert having knowledge and information over many kinds of products. Shopping places and other facts of the markets. Their expertise is of a general market rather than of a product specific market. They enjoy brousing and shopping and participate in marketing activities. They are well read, they read classified newspapers Mail advertising etc. Communication can be source initiated or recipient initiated and may have one or two way influence.

Source Initiated: The marketer or the user transmits information to the user. e.g. Mohan told me how good is the performance of his washing machine so I bought one.

Receiver Initiated: (One way influence) The receiver makes an effort to get the information—

I asked the salesman which mixie does he recommend.

Source Initiated: (2 way influence) I showed my expensive set of crockery to Mohan and he now plans to buy one for himself. He felt that it was a good set. This made me feel better and offset my anxiety of having bought an expensive one.

Receiver Initiated: (2 way influence) Mohan asked me to show my collection of arms to him. We had an interesting discussion on the subject and both learnt from the commenis of each other.

Word of Mouth Communication to be Effective: For communication to be effective the following points must be considered—

1. The product is visible and purchase behaviour is apparent.
2. The product is distinctive and can be matched with life style, taste and personal likes.
3. The product is newly introduced and the consumers have not formed any opinion about it.
4. The product is important to the reference group's norms and belief systems. Suger free coca cola for diabetic patients or low cholestrol foods for older people prone to disease.
5. When consumers have doubt about the product and considered it risky and initiate a lot of discussion and product related discussions (Maruti Van) risky from the accident point of view.

Marketing Strategy and Opinion Leadership

There are different opinion leaders for different products. The marketer must determine through research, experience or logic, the role an opinion leader plays in the existing situation for a product or service.

Consumers talk to each other about their experiences and performance of the product. If their experiences do not meet expectations then there is cause for concern, and the marketer must take relevant steps to redress their complaints. When the product falls short of the customer's expectations, dissonance occurs, which has to be reduced or removed by the marketer.

This can be reduced by utilising the knowledge of opinion leaders, which are rather difficult to identify. Opinion leaders are gregarious and tend to belong to clubs and associations. Some product categories have professional opinion leaders who are also very influential.

Hairstylists serve as opinion leaders for hair-care products. For healthcare products-pharmacists are important opinion leaders. Computer professionals can give an opinion about the purchase of personal computers. The idea is to identify the opinion leaders, and then undertake a marketing research on them and formulate a marketing strategy.

The marketing research conducted on opinion leaders gives ideas of the likes and dislikes of the product users and their categories. Various tests should include the product use test, the pre-testing of the advertising copy, the media preferred for customers to respond favourably to the firm's marketing mix. The sampling should be done from amongst the opinion leaders. In retailing and personnel selling various techniques can be adopted to attract customers like, one meal extra for every three meals or, pay for two and take three or, a "fashion advisory board" can be constituted in clothing stores. An automobile dealer can provide a free wash or a free servicing or oil change to the customers and opinion leaders who send customers to their workshop. Estate agents may offer a free stay in attractive locales for people who promote or bring in customers for real estates.

In advertising, people of prominence and, owners can be used and their experiences and satisfaction received can be projected through conversation and, by giving their impression to the general public and non-owners of the product. Opinion leaders can be used effectively in commercials to promote the product to the masses.

Questions

1. What is a group? Give some examples of groups and their level of involvement.
2. How can groups be classified?
3. What are factors affecting the influence of reference groups? What are the basis of social power?
4. What are opinion leaders? What role do they play in transmitting information?
5. What are the characteristics of opinion leaders?
6. What factors influence reference groups to make decisions on products and brands?

8

Individual Determinants

There was a wise man whose constant prayer was that he may see today with the eyes of tomorrow.

This chapter deals with individual determinates, and the goals of this chapter are to understand:

- How information is processed
- How decisions are made
- Memory and product positioning
- Factors influencing learning

PERCEPTION

Perception is the most important psychological factor that affects human behaviour. It is a process consisting of several sub-processes. These are stimulus, registration, interpretation, feedback and reaction. The first step is the presence of stimulus, or the situation which an individual faces. This is followed by registration which affects the psychological organs. Thus, the individual interprets (attaches meaning to the stimulus) and learns. Factors like learning help in the perceptual process. Feedback is the fourth element and, the final aspect is the resultant behaviour of the individual.

Our perception of the stimuli and the situation plays an important role on our behaviour. Perception is the critical activity that links the individual consumer to a group, situation and marketer influences.

When a person is exposed to a stimuli, he may show interest in the exposure. His attention is drawn towards the object and the nerves transmit the sensation to the brain for processing. Interpretation is the assignment of meaning to the received sensations. This is retained by the memory (only a part of the registered information may be retained by the memory). This leads to consumption behaviour, which may have positive or negative feedback for the individual.

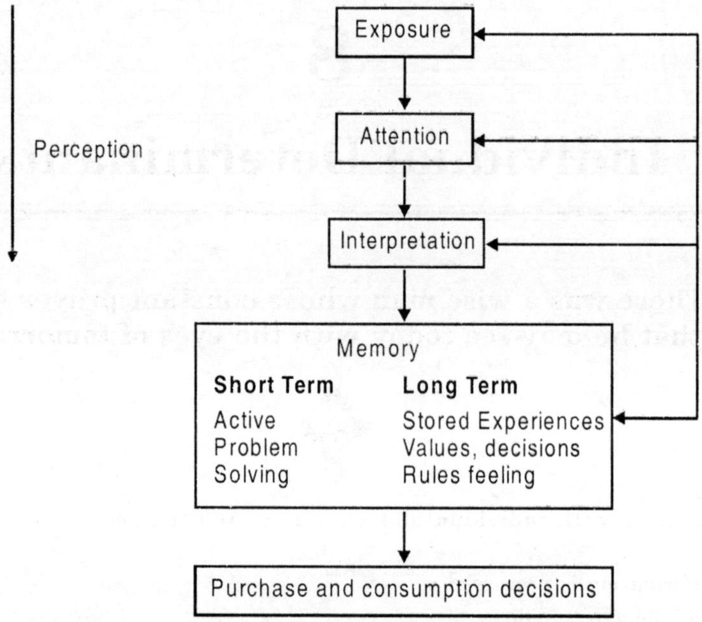

Fig. 8.1 Information processing for consumer decision-making.

Figure 8.1 shows that the individual is exposed to the stimuli. His attention is attracted. He interprets the stimuli and the situation which goes to his memory and, the reaction is shown by means of purchases.

Much of the information may not be available to the memory when an individual decides to purchase something. So, when communicating to the consumers, the marketer has an uphill task, because an individual is exposed to a lot of information but, retains very little in the memory.

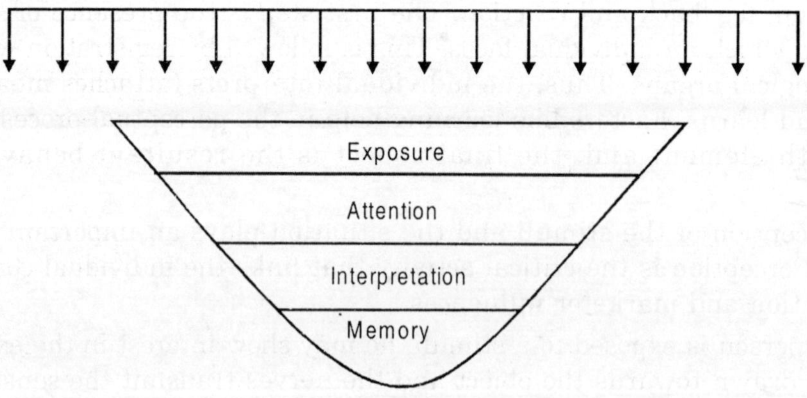

Fig. 8.2

The figure shows that there are very many exposures by the marketers. The individual or the consumer is exposed to only a part of the exposures, some of which is interpreted and little is retained in the memory.

Exposure

When a stimuli comes under the range of sensory perceptor, nerve exposure occurs. Most of the stimuli to which an individual is exposed to, is self selected, e.g. switching channels on TV, skipping pages of magazines, avoiding information that one is not interested in. We deliberately seek and avoid information of our interest. It is done to achieve the goals we aspire for. It is challenge for the marketer to hold the interest of the consumer on his commercials and exposures.

Attention

This occurs when the sensory receptor nerves are activated by the stimuli and, the brain registers sensations for processing. The market offers a variety of goods. It may take us long to go through all of them. Therefore, we selectively choose and attend to products and messages. One may not attend to warnings on cigarette packets or, may see the model more than the clothes. The same individual may devote different levels of attention to the same stimulus in different situations. Attention is determined by three factors—*stimulus,* the *individual* and the *situation*. These together or individually play an important role in attracting the individual.

Stimulus Factor

There are certain features in a product that can attract greater attention. This would be the size, the intensity, the colour and movement, position, format of the message, information quality, information overload.

By size we mean that if an advertisement is on a full page or in a column. The intensity is the number of times a message is repeated in a newspaper or a magazine, TV or any other media. Further, both colour and movement attract attention. An advertisement may be black or white or in multi-colours. It can be shown stationary or in a moving state, which is more noticeable. Position refers to the placement of the object, whether it is placed in the centre or in a corner. Similarly, the right hand page advertisement may be more noticeable than the advertisement on the left hand side.

Isolation is separating an object from other objects. In isolation, an object may stimulate and draw more attention. Similarly the format of the message. How it is presented, what words and structure is used. A simple format can draw greater attention than a complicated message. The messages targeted at a specific audience can also be very effective. Compressed messages which say more in fewer words can make a good impact. Information quality should be balanced or optimum. All consumers have limited capacity to process information. If a lot of information is given, it may confuse the individual and, he is not able to make a choice. This is known as information overload. With too much information consumers get confused and become frustrated. They may also experience pre-purchase dissonance. Marketers give relevant information on packages and labels. Information can also be given in brochures, pamphlets, etc.

Individual Factors

Individuals factors affect the decision-making process. The individual is governed by the interest or the need. Interest also reflects the lifestyle of an individual and, the long term goals (achieving a specific position in life like becoming a senior manager or something). The short term goals are influenced by situations. Individual also differ in their ability to gather and assimilate information. The information sought reflects their needs. An academician is in the pursuit of knowledge and books and, a sportsman will be attentive to advertisement regarding energy foods and health builders. A patient of diabetes gets interested in the medical information regarding the subject.

Situational Factors

Decision-making is also influenced by situational factors like time pressure or cleanliness or crowded places. Noise, atmosphere ambience can stimulate the individual, favourably or adversely in situations. People pressed for time are not able to pay attention to stimuli as well as those who have leisure.

Programme Involvement

In a TV programme, a number of advertisements appear which some individuals watch or some skip them (fast forward) or, take a break. The nature of the programme will influence the nature of response received. The attention can be focussed that is deliberate exposure to stimuli. It can also be without deliberate or conscious focussing of attention.

Interpretation

The same message can be interpreted in different ways. It is how we assign meaning to sensations. Interpretation involves a competitive or factual component and, an effective or emotional response by cognitive or factual component. The stimuli is placed in different categories of meaning. If a firm floats a new brand at a lower price, it can be interpreted that the product is of low quality. This, however may not be true, as the firm may have more efficient means of production and marketing facilities and may be wanting to add another variety or, to extend the brand. The interpretation can also be affected by the semantic and psychological meanings attached to a stimuli. Semantic meaning is the conventional meaning. Whereas, the psychological meaning is the meaning attached by individuals or groups by their experience on the basis of a situation. The word sale may mean that the goods are on reduced price. It can be psychologically interpreted that these goods are going to be out of style soon.

Effective interpretation is an emotional response to an advertisement. The same advertisement or a picture may attract or repel different individuals. Some may feel happy to see a snowfall. Others may dread the cold—some may be happy to see wrestling advertisements, others want to avoid any kind of physical fight.

Misinterpretation of Marketing Messages

The marketers wishing to communicate about their products, must be very careful and present their messages so that they are not misinterpreted, but interpreted accurately. A large number of audiences do not understand the real meaning behind the messages. This may also be due to demographic variables or, their casual approach towards the advertisement.

Memory is the storage factor which could be long term or short term. Memory can be activated. The marketers do it by repetition of messages. When buying items, one tries to recall the past experiences with that item. How pleasant it had been. This affects the decision-making process.

Perception and Marketing Strategies

Marketing strategy consists of directing the four 'ps' on the target market.

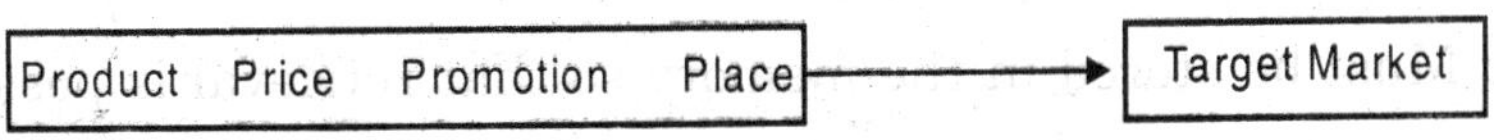

Fig. 8.3

When we talk of perception and marketing strategy, we direct the four 'ps' for proper exposure, attention, interpretation and action.

Thus the ***product***, its brand name, style, packaging and other features should all be such that a proper image or meaning is perceived by the individual.

Price decides the value of goods. A high or a low price may be perceived in different ways. Some may think of a high price as a good quality product from a big company or a prestigious product and brand. Others may think of a high price as a gimmick, whereas, the other lower priced products compare well with the brand in question. Similarly, a low price may interpreted as a low quality product or, as an opportunity given by the company to make its product popular.

Promotion

The selection of the media is important and it should be correlated with the audience one is trying to reach. We can have different media for rural and urban areas. We may also have different media for younger people, as compared to elder people.

Media for men, women, high income, or low income groups may also be different. The advertisements must capture attention and convey meaning. The consumers take an interest in the ads when they are in need of the product, not otherwise. Various strategies of capturing the attention of the consumers can be used, i.e. by giving big ads or the ads of celebrities who can capture the attention. Sometimes garment sellers put an attractive woman, different shades of colours can make the product popular and the sale may increase. A lot of advertisements give importance to sex appeal, e.g. showing an attractive woman with the product in the hand or in use. Branded jewellery advertised with the help of beautiful film actresses or models captures the attention of the audience.

Distribution

Retail shops are well decorated. Interior designing and arrangements of product displays. Point of purchase displays. Visible shelves, lighted with proper background attracts the customer. The ambience and the atmosphere of the shop with proper music, air-conditioning and shining floors and walls, all attract the customers and can increase the traffic in the store, and consequently, register greater sales.

A successful advertisement must accomplish 4 basic tasks:

Exposure: It must be exposed to reach the consumer.

Attention: Should be able to attract the customer and make him interested in the product.

Interpretation: The meaning attached should be consistent with the projected meaning.

Memory: Must be stored in the memory so that retrieval is possible.

◆ LEARNING MEMORY AND PRODUCT POSITIONING

It is strange how much you have got to know
before you know how little you know.

All organisations are interested in highlighting the features of their products and services. They make the consumer aware to know about these features, so that their behaviour can be influenced. It is through learning that the attitudes, beliefs, values, feelings are influenced. We learn a lot from our culture social class, family influences and all these also reflect on our lifestyle. Learning can be described as any change in the content or organisation of long term memory. It is a result of information processing. Learning is the key to consumer behaviour. We learn through and from our culture, sub culture, social class, family friends, and utilise our personal experience, advertising and mass media as shown. These in turn influence our purchase decision as shown in Fig. 8.4 (on next page) learning is defined as a change in behaviour occurring as a result of past experience.

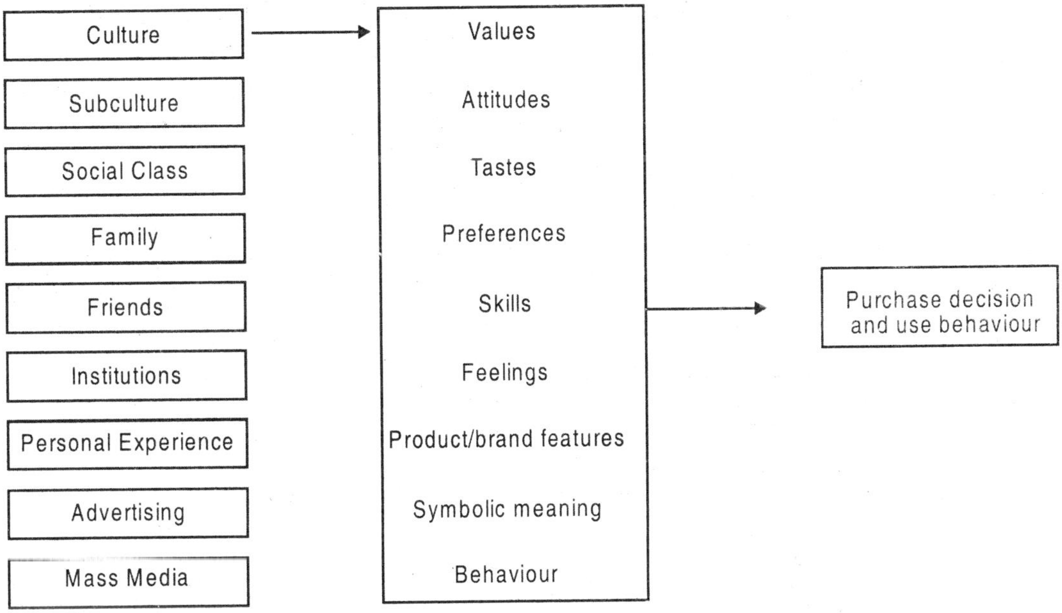

Fig. 8.4

Learning

Learning can be done under a high involvement or low involvement situations. In high involvement learning situation, the consumer is motivated to learn. If a person wants to buy a gadget, he tries to learn about it and is motivated. If a person wants to buy a camera, he learns about cameras. In a low learning situation there is no motivation to learn about the product. Learning situations are of degrees and, depend on situations as well. In low involvement learning, consumers do not have any focussed attention on the advertisements like cigarettes ads. one only glances at the advertisements. The strength of learning can be intensively influenced by four factors which are, importance, reinforcement, repetition and imagery.

Importance

By this we mean how important is the learning for the consumer about the product. If it is important for you to learn about cameras before you buy one, it reflects a high involvement situation.

Reinforcement

Reinforcement is something that increases the likelihood of a response to be repeated in future. Reinforcement can be positive or negative. By positive reinforcement we mean a desired consequence. One feels happy after buying the product. One uses a product, feels happy, and repeats the procedure. An imaginary response removes the unpleasant consequence. If a tablet relieves you from a headache you will continue using it because the negative enforcement. Punishment is the opposite or reinforcement. It is a consequence that decreases the likelihood of the response being repeated in the future, e.g. if one deposits money with a company and does not get good returns this will not be repeated in future.

Repetition

Repetition increases the speed of learning. If a TV commercial is flashed a number of times, it will register more in the minds of the consumers. The exposure must carry important and interesting information.

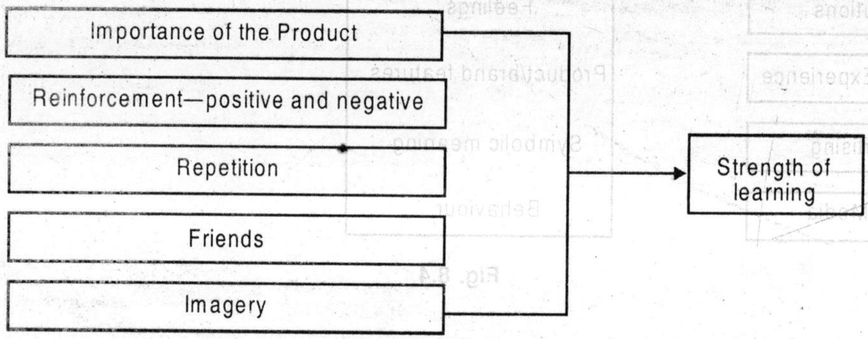

Fig. 8.5 Factors Influencing Learning.

Imagery

By this we mean whether the advertisement is substantiated or accompanied by images. We have brand symbols, names, etc. We have messages substantiated by pictures. The pictures along with the images have a greater impact and can be registered more intensely. The script in which the name is written also gets registered in the mind. The M of McDonald's, the script of Bata, the symbol of Tata, Omega, symbol of Nike, Reebok, etc. are some of the examples which get deeply registered in the consumer's mind.

◆ MEMORY

Your mind is like a camera with a memory, it can take several pictures, which you can file for subsequent use.

Consumers have prior learning experiences, which are accumulated in their minds. The total accumulation of past experiences are known as memory. Memory can be divided into *short term memory* or *long term memory*.

Short term memory: It is the memory which can be recalled immediately and, is activated and in use. It can also be referred to as the working memory, which one can work with and refer to, whenever required. Short term memory can give continued repetition of a piece of information that can be used for problem solving. When elaborate activities are considered, they ride five involvements in the memory. Elaborate activities make use of previously stored experiences, values, attitudes, beliefs and feelings, to interpret and evaluate information and add new elements to memory.

Long term memory: It is a permanent storage in the minds of the consumer. It is active and can store a variety of information consisting of concepts, decisions, rules, processes, affective states, etc. This is important to the marketer because an image of a brand and the concepts that a consumer had heard about a brand, are made up of various elements and the consumer can have a lot of meanings attached to the brand, when the particular brand is mentioned.

Figures 8.6 and 8.7 explain how one can associate various meanings regarding a brand. The various factors that come to a consumer's mind when he thinks of Coca Cola or Bata Shoes are shown in the figure. Similarly, meanings can be associated to various brands and products when one thinks of them. These can be recalled both by short term or long term memory.

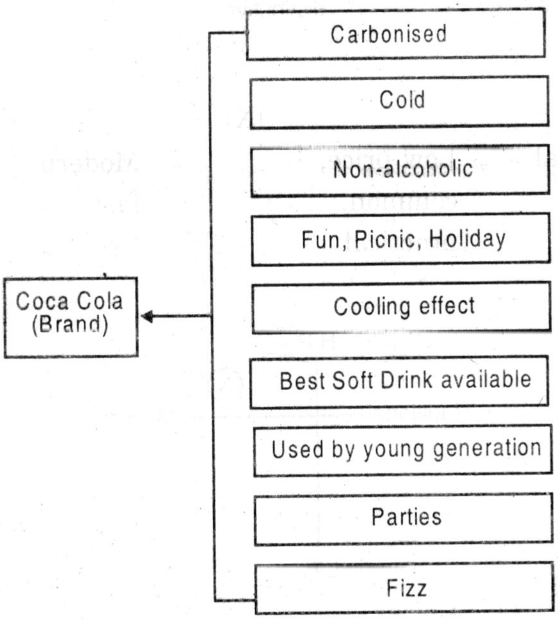

Fig. 8.6

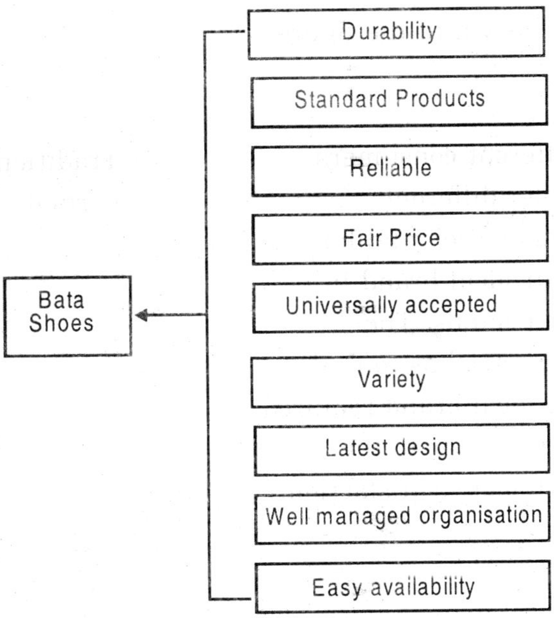

Fig. 8.7

Positioning

Marketers try to position their brands in the minds of the consumer. It relates to the memory of a brand in relation to competing products. By this, the marketer tries to enhance the image of his brand which suits the consumer. Promotes the image of the products and the stores as well. Product position evolves over time, as the marketer gets to know more about the preference of the consumers. Consumers usually have an "ideal brand" concept and, they want to be as close to the ideal brand as possible. The marketer also tries to offer a product by positioning and repositioning the product which comes as close as possible to the consumer's ideal brand. This can be done by finding out the critical dimensions which are preferred. In case of a soft drink, the dimension could be:

If the ideal brand as perceived by the consumer is (X) that is (5, 2) on the graph. The marketer tries to make a product as close to the ideal brand as possible.

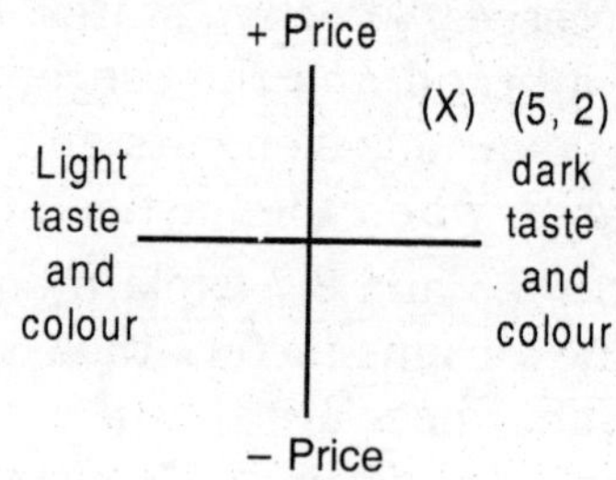

Similarly if a car has to have the dimensions as shown in the figure.

High Price, Prestigious, distinctive

(X)

Traditional normal

Low price, common, practical

Modern fast

Different consumers prefer different combination and have their ideal brand in their minds. The marketer has to find the ideal brand required and to cater to the customer's satisfaction.

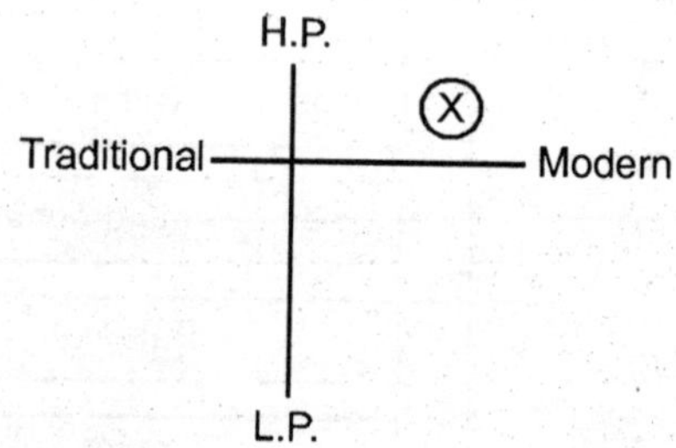

Questions

1. What is perception? How does it help in decision-making?
2. Attention is determined by three factors, comment.
3. What is long term and short term memory?
4. What is positioning? Explain with examples.

9

Motivation and Personality

The best way to get things done is to allow your subordinates to formulate their own methods of operation.

Efficiency can be achieved in work if the people are motivated to achieve the goals. After reading this chapter one must understand:

- The theories of motivation
- Need hierarchy
- Motives and consumption behaviour
- Personality
- Emotions
- Opinion leaders and transmission of information
- Self-concept

INTRODUCTION

In consumer behaviour, motivation plays an important part in making a decision. What is the motive of buying? A motive is why an individual does a thing. Motivation is an inner feeling that stimulates the action that is to be taken by an individual. It provides a specific direction or, results in a response. A person can be motivated to buy a product for convenience, for style, for prestige, for self pride, or for being at par with others.

Maslow's Theory of Motivation

It is a macro theory designed to account for most human behaviour in general. It is based on Maslow's hierarchy of needs, which states that a human being has a variety of needs and, these can be classified as primary and secondary needs or, lower order and higher order needs. Once a need is fulfilled, human beings, try to fulfil other needs. This is usually done in a hierarchy, which can be classified as under:

Physiological

Food, water, sleep, clothing, shelter and sex.

Products in this category include, foods, health foods, medicines, drinks, house garments, etc.

Safety needs

Seeking physical safety and security. Safety of person, safety of belongings, security of job, etc.

Products are locks, guns, insurance policies, burglar alarms, retirement investments, etc.

Social needs

The need to be approved in a society—To love and be loved, friendship, love appreciation and group acceptance.

Products are general grooming, entertainment, clothing cosmetics, jewellery, fashion garments.

Esteem needs

Desire for status, for superiority, self respect and prestige.

Products are furniture, clothing, liquor, hobbies, fancy cars.

Self actualisation needs

The desire for self fulfilment, the desire to become all that one is capable of becoming.

Products are education, art, sports, vacations, garments, foods.

Maslow's hierarchy is a good guide to general behaviour. The same consumption behaviour can fulfil more than one need.

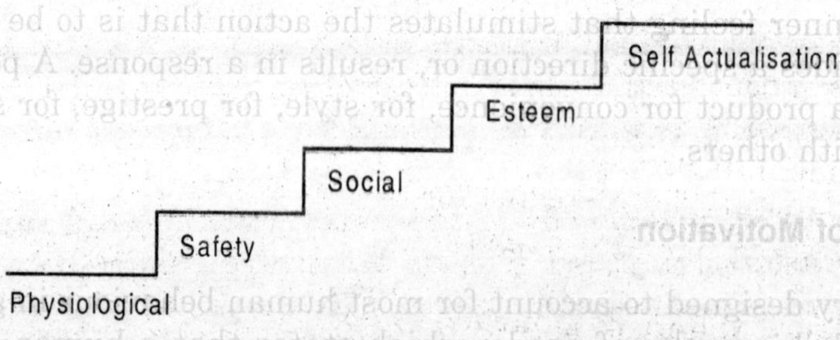

Fig. 9.1 Maslow's hierarchy of needs.

McGuire's Psychological Motives

The classification of motives by McGuire is more specific and used more in marketing.

Need for consistency

People try to buy things which are consistent with their liking and taste. A sophisticated person will be consistent in his choice of colours of clothing, paintings on the wall, colour of rooms. He would prefer sophisticated instead of flashy objects.

Need to attribute causation

We often attribute the cause of a favourable or unfavourable outcome to ourselves or, to some outside element. You can buy shoes by you choice and may not like them. It can be attributed to you. If you buy a dress by the advise of your friends and companions, and do not like it, the causes are attributed to other factors.

Need to categorise

The objects are categorised in a number of ways. The most popular is the price. Cars can be classified around Rs. 2 lakhs or above Rs. 5.5 lakhs. Many products are categorised at 499.00 to keep them under Rs. 500. This is practised in shoes mainly by Bata and others.

Need for cues

These are hints or symbols that affect our feelings, attitudes, impressions, etc. For instance, clothing can be a cue to adopt a desired lifestyle. The use of products can be enhanced by providing proper cues to the purchasers.

Need for independence

Consumers like to own products which give them a feeling of independence, symbols like a white bird flying may predict one to be free and independent.

Need for novelty

We sometimes want to be different in certain respects and want to be conspicuous. This is evident in impulse purchasing or unplanned purchasing. We go in for novelty products, novelty experiences. A different kind of travel with many novelties offered by a travelling agency.

Need for self expression

We want to identify ourselves and go in for products that let others know about us. We may buy a suit not only for warmth but also for expressing our identity to others.

Need for ego defence

When our identity is threatened or when we need to project a proper image, we use products in our defence, Deodorants are used for ego defence. Mouthwash for fresh breath or, false teeth to protect our image. We use hair dye to look younger better, etc. We rely on well known brands to give a correct social image of ourselves.

Need for assertion

These needs are fulfilled by engaging in those kind of activities that bring self esteem and esteem in the eyes of others. We can buy an expensive car which may be for esteem but, if it does not perform well, we tend to complain bitterly. Individuals with a strong need for self esteem tend to complain more with the dissatisfaction of the product.

Need for reinforcement

When we buy a product which is appreciated by others, it reinforces our views, our behaviour, our choice and we go in for repeat purchases. More products can be sold if their reinforcement is greater by their purchases.

Need for affiliation

We like to use product which are used by those whom we get affiliated to. If one's friend appreciates and wears a certain brand then one also tries to use the same brands or objects for affiliation. It is the need to develop mutually helpful and satisfying relationships with others. Marketers use the affiliation themes in advertisements which arouse emotions and sentiments in the minds of the consumers for their children and families.

Need for modeling

We try to copy our heroes and our parents and those we admire. We base our behaviour on the behaviour of others. Marketer's use these themes for selling their product, i.e. "Lux is used by heroines". "Sportsman rely on boost for their energy" and such captions are used regularly and repeatedly.

Utilitarian and Heponic Needs

Utilitarian needs are to achieve some practical benefit such as durability economy, warmth that define product performance. Hedonic needs achieve pleasure from the product they are associated with Emotions & fantasies is derived from consuming a product.

A Hedonic Need is more experiential—The desire to be more masculine or feminine etc. Hedonic advertising appeals are more symbolic & emotional. For utilitarian shoppers the acquiring of goods is a task whereas for Hedonic shoppers it is a pleasurable activity. Shopping Malls may be considered as gathering places and consumers/buyers derive pleasure from these activities besides the selection of goods.

MARKETING STRATEGIES BASED ON MOTIVATION

Consumers do not buy products. They buy motive satisfaction or problem solutions. A person does not buy a sofa set but he buys comfort. A person does not buy cosmetics but he buys hope for looking good. Marketers therefore try to find the motives for buying, and build their products and marketing mixes around these motives. A person may buy a product for a number of motives. One of them could be reward for oneself or to self indulge in them or for a gift. Multiple motives are involved in consumption. Therefore a marketer tries to find out:

(a) the motive for buying,

(b) how to formulate a strategy to fulfil these motives, and

(c) how to reduce conflict between motives.

How to discover motives

This is found out by asking questions from the respondent. Some motives are disclosed by the respondent, others are not divulged or are hidden. For instance, you ask a lady why she wears designer jeans. She can say that (a) they are in style (b) they fit well (c) they are worn by her friends. These motives are disclosed. Latent motives may not be disclosed. These may be (d) they show that I have money (e) they make one look sexy and desirable (f) they show I am young (g) they project my slimness, etc.

Manifest and latent motives

Another important method to find out the motives may be by "Motivational Research" where indirect questions are asked to elicit the information from the respondents. This is done by unstructured disguised interviews or questionnaires.

Once the motives have been known, the marketing strategy is designed around the appropriate set of motives. While designing the strategy, the target market has to be decided and the communication has to be chosen for the said target market. Since there is more than one motive, more than one benefit should be communicated by advertising and other methods of promotion.

In case of a Maurti car as shown in the figure 9.2, the benefit of economy, maneuverability, modern ideology must all be communicated. Usually, direct appeals are used for manifest motives and, indirect appeals for latent motives. Sometimes dual appeals are used and the target market has to be kept in mind.

Motivational conflicts

A consumer wants to fulfil a variety of needs by using a product, therefore, there are conflicts in his mind as to which motive must be given more importance. It is a conflict which has to be resolved. There are three types of motivational conflicts.

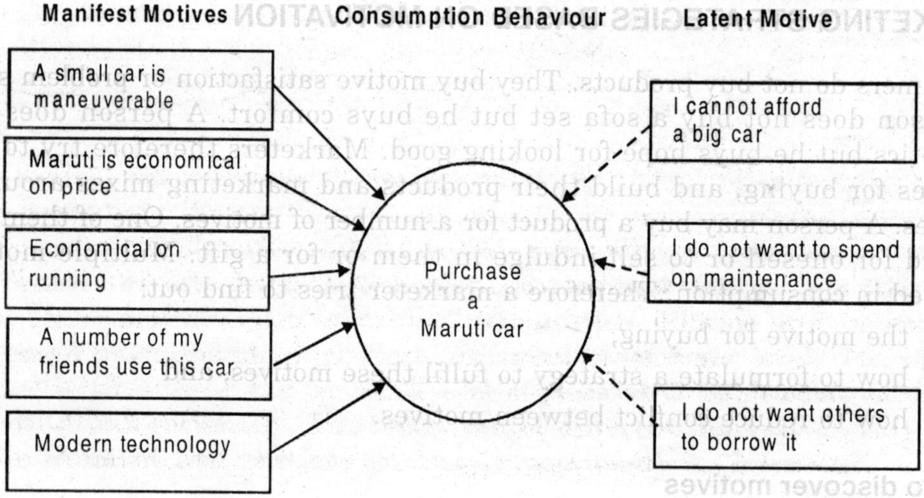

Fig 9.2 Hidden motives are shown by the dotted line.

Approach–approach motivational conflict

There may be two acts of equally attractive choices to make. This can be reduced by the timely release of an advertisement, so that both alternatives can be given importance. A consumer may want a spacious car which is not large—Uno. A consumer may want a medium size fridge with a lot of space inside or, a fridge with a deepfreeze—double door fridge. These two choices create a conflict in the minds of the consumers.

Approach avoidance motivational conflict

In this the consumer is faced both by positive and negative consequences in the purchase of a particular products. If one likes chocolates and is diabetic. This conflict can be resolved by taking sugar free chocolate, or in the case of Coca Cola-Diet free Coke may resolve the conflict.

Avoidance–avoidance conflict

It faces the consumer with two undesirable consequences. Taking an injection once or, taking a bitter medicine a number of times. This can be avoided by choosing a lesser painful alternative according to the convenience of the consumer.

Personality

Personality is another internal determinant which influences our consumption pattern. We tend to use products that go with our personality.

Personality may be defined as those inner psychological characteristics that determine and reflect how a person responds to his or her environment. Inner characteristics are those specific qualities and attributes traits, factors, mannerisms that distinguish one person from another. Personality influences the individual's product choices and brand choices. It also responds to a firm's promotional efforts and, when and how they consume particular products or, services. By associating personality characteristics with consumer behaviour, a marketer can formulate marketing strategies in an effective manner.

Personality reflects individual differences. Therefore we can categorise them into groups on the basis of few traits, e.g. low sociability/high sociability, dull/bright. Practical vs imaginative etc. Personality is consistent and enduring and is only one of the factors that affect consumer behaviour. Personality can change due to major life events. These could be birth, death, marriage. It can also change by a gradual process.

Trait theory

A trait is defined as a predisposition to respond in a particular way. Traits are used to define behaviour of consumers.

There are a number of traits given by Cattell and they are sixteen in numbers.

1. Reserved vs Outgoing
2. Dull vs Bright
3. Docile vs Aggressive
4. Serious vs Happy go lucky
5. Unstable vs Stable
6. Expedient vs Conservative
7. Shy vs Uninhibited
8. Tough minded vs Tender minded
9. Trusting vs Suspicious
10. Practical vs Imaginative
11. Unpretentious vs Polished
12. Self assured vs Self respective
13. Conservative vs Experimenting
14. Group dependent vs Self sufficient
15. Undisciplined vs Controlled
16. Relaxed vs Tense.

Cattell believes that traits are acquired at an early age, or through learning, or are inherited. This theory is representative of multi personality theories (more than one trait influences behaviour).

Trait theory is based on certain assumptions, which are:

1. Traits are relatively stable characteristics,
2. A limited number of traits are common to most people,

3. The degree of traits possessed by an individual can be measured by using a rating questionnaire in a continuum, on a 1 to 10 scale.

Emotions

Emotions control our behaviour. They are relatively uncontrolled feelings which affect our behaviour. We are emotionally charged by environmental factors and events. If somebody misbehaves with us we feel angry. On our achievements we feel happy. Whenever we are emotionally charged, physiological changes also take place within us. These may be faster breathing, perspiration, dilation or moistening of eyes. Increased heart and blood pressure, enhanced blood sugar levels, etc. Mental activation also takes place, and we recall a lot of pleasant or unpleasant incidences and can also think rationally. The behaviour of different individuals vary from situation to situation, and emotions are mostly associated with behaviour.

Types of behaviour

Emotions have been categorised differently be different thikers and philosophers. Plutchick categorises emotions into eight types. These are as under:

Fear
Anger
Joy
Sadness
Acceptance
Disgust
Expectancy
Surprise

According to Plutchick, other emotions are secondary and come out of these basic emotions or, are a continuation of the above emotions, e.g. delight can be a combination of surprise and joy. Similarly, contempt can be a combination of anger and disgust. Others have suggested 3 basic emotions. These are:

P Pleasure
A Arousal
D Dominance

} These basic emotions gives rise to a number of other emotions as shown in the table given below.

Dimension	*Emotion*	*Indicator / Feeling*
Pleasure	Duty	Moral, virtuous, dutiful
	Faith	Reverent, worshipful, spiritual
	Pride	Proud, superior, worthy
	Affection	Loving, affectionate, friendly

(Contd.)

Dimension	*Emotion*	*Indicator/Feeling*
	Innocence	Innocent, pure, blameless
	Gratitude	Grateful, thankful, appreciative
	Serenity	Restful, serene, comfortable, soothed
	Desire	Desirous, wishful, craving, hopeful
	Joy	Joyful, happy, delighted, pleased
	Competence	Confident, in control, competent
Arousal	Interest	Attentive, curious
	Hypoactivation	Bored, drowsy, sluggish
	Activation	Aroused, active, excited
	Surprise	Surprised, annoyed, astonished
	Déjà vu	Unimpressed, uninformed, unexcited
	Involvement	Involved, informed, enlightened, benefited
	Distraction	Distracted, preoccupied, inattentive
	Surgency	Playful, entertained, lighthearted
	Contempt	Scornful, contemptuous, disdainful
Dominance	Conflict	Tense, frustrated, conflictful
	Guilt	Guilty, remorseful, regretful
	Helplessness	Powerless, helpless, dominated
	Sadness	Sad, distressed, sorrowful, dejected
	Fear	Fearful, afraid, anxious
	Shame	Ashamed, embarrassed, humiliated
	Anger	Angry, initiated, enraged, mad
	Hyperactivation	Panicked, confused, overstimulated
	Disgust	Disgusted, revolted, annoyed, full of loathing
	Skepticism	Skeptical, suspicious, distrustful

Source: Adapted from M.B. Holbrook and R. Batra. "Assessing the Role of emotions as Mediators of Consumer Responses to Advertising". Journal of Consumer Research December 1987, pp. 40:20.

A Classification of 12 categories is also made by R. Batra and M.B. Holbrook in their book "Developing a Typology of Effective Responses to advertising".

See Exhibit:

Emotion	Indicator
Activation	Arousal, active, excited
Skepticism	Skeptical, suspicious
Anger	Angry, enraged, mad
Restful	Restful, serene
Bored	Bored, uninvolved, unimpressed, unexcited
Fear	Fearful, afraid
Desire	Desirous, wishful, full of craving

Social affection	Loving, affectionate, pure
Gratitude	Grateful, thankful, benefited
Sadness	Sad, remorseful, sorrowful
Irritation	Disgusted, irritated, annoyed
Surgency	Playful, entertained, lighthearted

Administered as "I felt not at all (adjective/very adjective)" (Seven Point Scale).

Source: Adapted from R. Batra and M.B. Holbrook. "Developing a Typology of Affective Responses to Advertising". Psychology and Marketing, Spring 1990, pp. 22. These authors use the terms affect, emotion is used in this table to be consistent with the text.

Emotions and Marketing Strategy

Marketers have also used emotions to arouse the interest of the consumer. They have used emotion as a product benefit and emotion arousal in context of advertising. When we are emotionally aroused, we try to evaluate the product in a positive or negative manner. "The bunjee jumping was a near death experience. Yet I loved it."

We try to seek positive emotions most of the time but, there are many exceptions as shown. Consumers seek products which arouse emotions. These could be for primary or secondary benefits. Movies, books and music are examples of primary benefit. Khajuraho, Taj Majal, Goa, Essel World positioned as emotion arousing destinations. E-mail or Voice mail are also positioned as emotion arousing products. Excitement and fun can be generated by soft drinks and consumption of alcohol. Luxury cars give a feeling of delight and excitement.

Marketers also take advantage of negative and unpleasant emotions and, when one feels sad, powerless, humiliated or disgusted, they promote the products to prevent or reduce negative emotions. These could be medicines and such products. Flowers are promoted as an antidote to sadness, slimming gimmicks, personal grooming products (toiletries, etc.) are also used to do away with negative emotions. Anxiety and stress reduction products are also designed for the purpose.

Advertising also plays an important part in reducing negative emotions. Advertisements which have an emotional context such as joy, warmth, disgust, do attract attention more than the neutral advertisements. Physiological arousal takes place and more attention is paid to such advertisements. Family relationships are projected in many advertisements, which bring warmth and joy. Repeated exposure to positive emotions, reinforces product and brand preference. Advertisements having positive emotional appeals are gaining popularity. Emotionally charged advertisements, arouse in an individual a feeling of pride, security, happiness and confidence. Most advertisers use emotional appeals to attract customers. This is done by repeated exposures.

Dimensions of self-concept	Actual self-concept	Ideal self-concept
Private self	How I actually see myself	How I would like to see myself
Social self	How others actually see me	How I would like others to see me

Fig 9.3

Self concept

Self concept can be described simply as how one perceives himself and his behaviour in the market place. It is the attitude one holds towards himself. What one thinks of himself. The self concept is not very realistic because an unconcious component is always present. It can be divided into six types, as given below:

(i) *Actual self:* How a person actually perceives himself.

(ii) *Ideal self:* How a person would like to perceive himself.

(iii) *Social self:* How a person thinks others perceive him.

(iv) *Ideal social self:* How a person would like others to perceive him.

(v) *Expected self:* An image of self somewhere in between the actual and ideal self.

(vi) *Situational self:* A person's self image in a specific situation.

Actual self-concept		Products media Services	Desired self-concept	
Private	Social		Private	Social

Self concept is a social phenomenon. It is an attitude to the self. Consequently, the way we dress, the products we use, the services we require, depend on how we want to perceive ourselves. There is a relationship between the self image of a person and the product one wants to buy. Products act as symbols for consumers.

People like to use the products which match their personality. These include clothing, leisure products, personal care products. Marketers want an idea of the self concept and the image of the brand. This can be done on a differential scale of 1 to 7 of several items as shown on next page.

First the consumers are asked to rate their self concept on the differential scale. Then they are asked to rate product brands on the same scales. The responses that match with the brands are expected to be preferred by consumers.

Table 9.1

	1	2	3	4	5	6	7	
1. Rugged	–	–	–	–	–	–	–	Declicate
2. Exciting	–	–	–	–	–	–	–	Calm
3. Uncomfortable	–	–	–	–	–	–	–	Comfortable
4. Dominating	–	–	–	–	–	–	–	Submissive
5. Thrifty	–	–	–	–	–	–	–	Indulgent
6. Pleasant	–	–	–	–	–	–	–	Unpleasant
7. Contemporary	–	–	–	–	–	–	–	Uncontemporary
8. Organised	–	–	–	–	–	–	–	Unorganised
9. Rational	–	–	–	–	–	–	–	Emotional
10. Youthful	–	–	–	–	–	–	–	Mature
11. Formal	–	–	–	–	–	–	–	Informal
12. Orthodox	–	–	–	–	–	–	–	Liberal
13. Complex	–	–	–	–	–	–	–	Simple
14. Colourless	–	–	–	–	–	–	–	Colourful
15. Modest	–	–	–	–	–	–	–	Vain

After matching the self concept with the brand image, the individual tries to find products for his satisfaction. If he is satisfied, his self concept gets reinforced as shown in the figure. The interaction between the product and self concept can be situation specific. In some situations, the self concept can be enhanced or reinforced to a lesser or a higher degree. Marketers use these tools as a guide to product and brand choices.

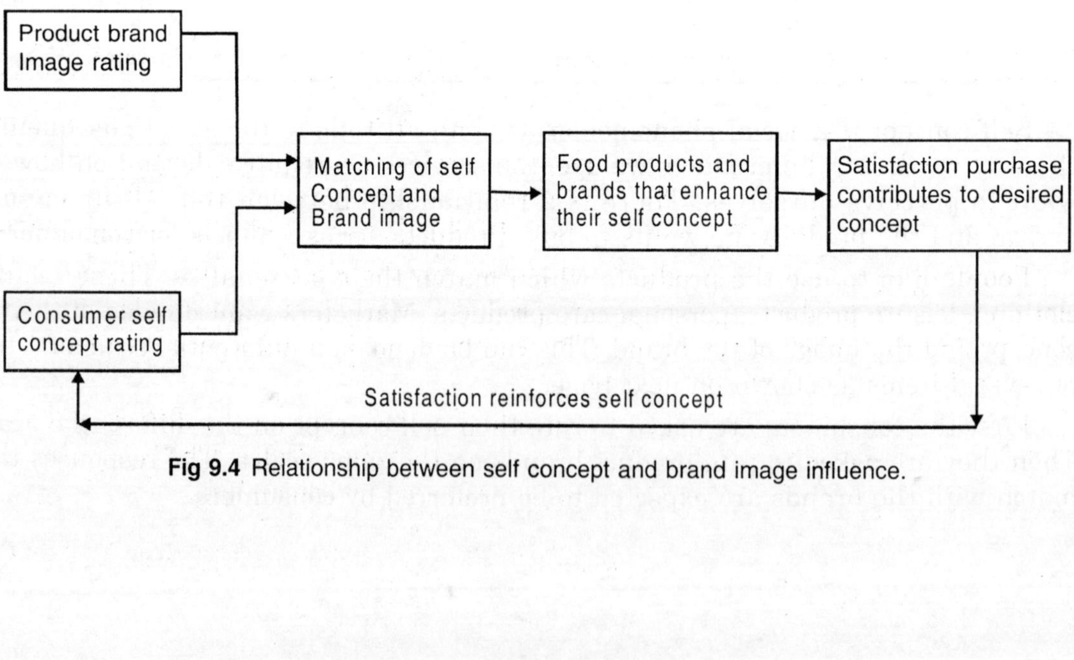

Fig 9.4 Relationship between self concept and brand image influence.

Questions

1. What is the importance of motivation in consumer behaviour?
2. How does Maslow's hierarchy of needs guide a marketer to design and sell his products?
3. What are the categories of needs emphasised by McGuire?
4. Explain manifest and latent motives in consumer behaviour.
5. What is the traits theory and, how does it help marketers?
6. How do emotions help formulate marketing strategy?
7. Explain self concept with reference to marketing.

10

Problem Recognition

Business exists for creating customers, more customers, and many more customers.

Problem recognition is the first stage in the decision-making process. It explains:

- Three types of decision-making
- Gap between the existing and desired consumer position
- Market strategy and problem recognition.

INTRODUCTION

There are five stages in consumer decision-making:

1. *Problem recognition:* A consumer recognises a need to buy a product.
2. *Information search:* Attempt is made to gain knowledge about the product.
3. *Evaluation and alternatives:* The products which can fulfil the needs are evaluated in terms of plus and minus points.
4. *Purchase action:* The actual purchase is made from a store after consideration of a number of factors.
5. *Post-purchase behaviour* (followed sequentially): This is how a consumer feels after using the product, i.e. satisfaction or dissatisfaction.

Importance of Problem Recognition (Need Recognition) or Identification of Needs

It is the first stage in decision-making.

Problem recognition explains:

1. Why a buyer buys.

2. Gives definite direction to subsequent purchase behaviour.
3. Helps the marketer exert his influence, so that the need be recognised.

A virtual circle exists between them (problem recognition and marketers stimuli). The figure shows three types of decision-making:

Fig 10.1

(i) *Habitual decision-making or routinised response behaviour:* Here the information search is low, the risk is low and the involvement is also low. These are products which are bought with greater frequency like a toothpaste, shaving cream, blades, cosmetics, etc. There is hardly any dissonance and very limited evaluation.

(ii) *Limited decision-making:* This is for products which have a higher time, risk and money involvement. In this, information search takes place and the buyer wants to find out a number of features, attributes and aspects of the product before finally making a decision to purchase. The purchase is for items like a TV, computer, a machine, motor cycle, etc. In this there can be limited dissonance if the product does not perform upto expectations.

(iii) *Extended problem solving:* In this category the risk involved is high, the money involvement is much more. The goods are not purchased frequently. These involve a lot of information search and greater physical activity for finding out about the attributes of the products. These items include a house, a motor car, jewellery or something which is valued most. A professional photographer who is keen on taking pictures of very high quality, with a lot of gadgets may also go into his purchases after being highly involved in the same. He may have to undertake a high degree of information search, which is both internal and external. Extended problem sowing is carried out in case of—

- High Priced Products
- Medical Products associated with risk
- Automobiles associated with functions
- Complex Products (computers)
- Products associated with one's ego or emotions (clothings, cosmetics etc.)
- When the product is of great interest to the consumer. It is identified with the norms of the group (all steps shown in fig 10.2).

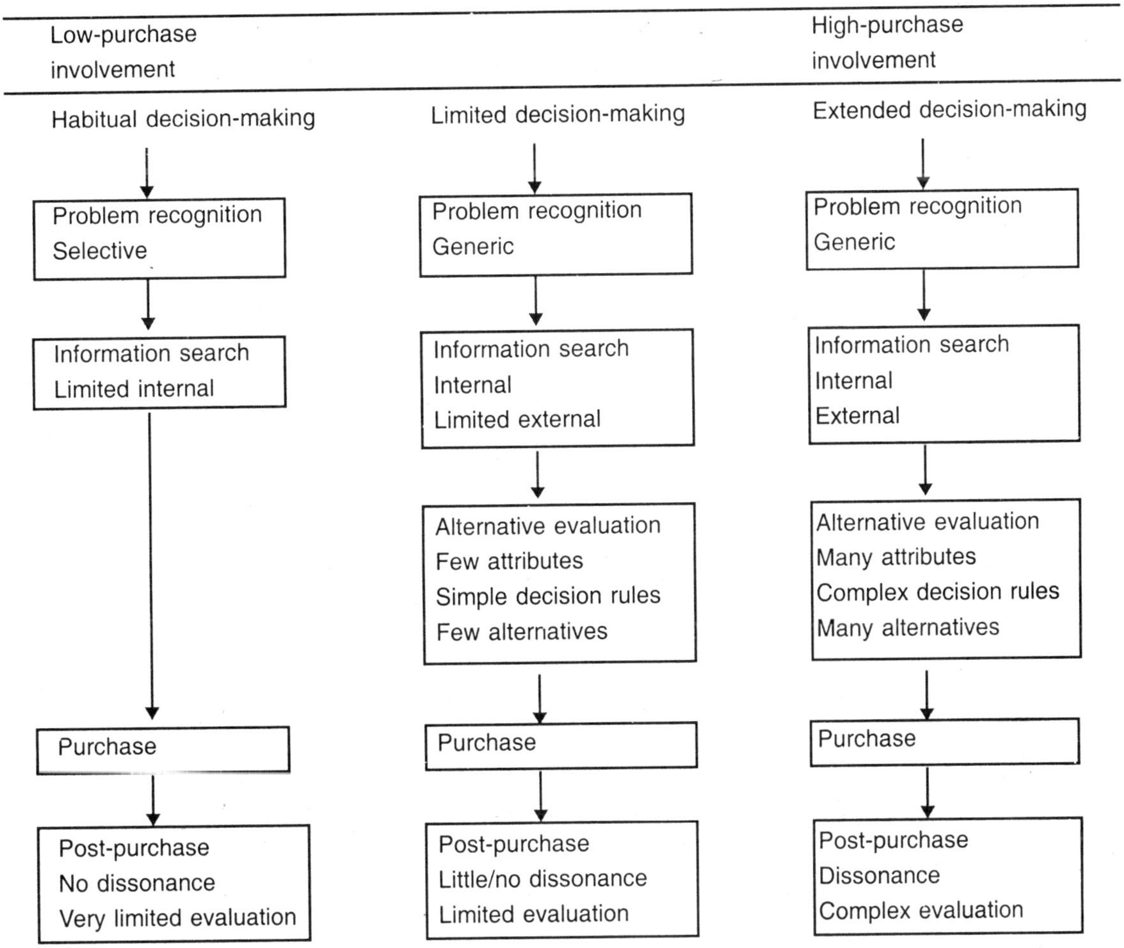

Fig 10.2 A consumer-marketer nexus.

Dissonance

In this type of decision making one can feel pre & post purchase dissonance. Pre purchase dissonance is when one gets confused with the many choices available and is unable to buy with the number of choices available and avoids the risk of not buying the best.

Post purchase dissonance occurs when the product is not upto one's expectations and does not match with the need. This arouses anxiety and dissatisfaction with the product. This is known as post purchase dissonance, because it is experienced after the purchase.

Problem Recognition

Problem recognition occurs whenever consumption situations exist. Many situations prompt a consumer to buy. Some situations are common and can't be recalled. Some are special and can be recalled. This depends on the degree of involvement. Some purchases are recognised and concluded on the spur of the moment. These are impulse purchases.

Threshold Level

In problem recognition, this refers to the minimum amount of tension, energy or intensity which is necessary for the feeling or "need" to occur. Tension can be increased by enhancing peer comparison.

Explanation of Problem Recognition

Problem recognition is a perceived gap between existing and desired consumer position. Existing consumer position is how one feels presently about the product.

Desired position is his expectation and anticipation about the products. The gap then results in a natural fashion. As the consumer grows financially, physically and psychologically, a perceived gap is created between the existing and desired position, e.g. growing child first needs a tricycle, then a bicycle, and then a motor cycle. Marketing stimuli influences the current or desired state of mind or both.

An overview of problem recognition

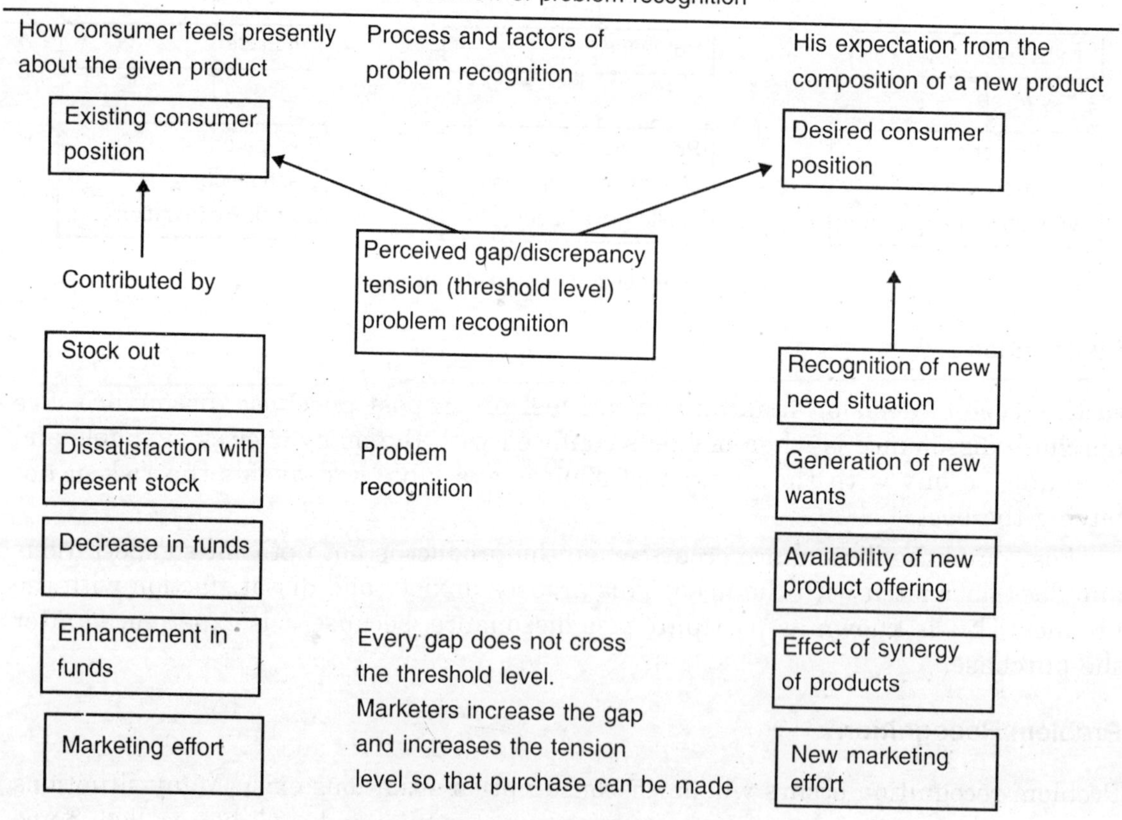

Fig 10.3 An overview of problem recognition.

At the current state of mind, the marketer may induce dissatisfaction in a current in use product or, project their obsoleteness of style and technology. Most efforts are made to condition the state of mind so that the new products are desired and bought.

Desired consumer position is achieved by advertising a new use of the product or, introducing new accessories or promising his satisfaction. The consumer gets tempted to buy new products, i.e. picture in picture television, bike with gears, easy credit facility, etc. These new attributes and facilities lure and, customers fall for the effective marketing strategies, and use the advertised products to their satisfaction and delight.

The gap between the existing and desired state of mind is provided by the marketing stimuli. Every gap will not lead to a purchase but, has to cross a threshold level to become a felt need, which will lead to purchases.

The marketing effort is not only to increase the gap between the existing and desired state of mind, but also to increase the tension level where need recognition is ensured. Marketers therefore make efforts to provide easy payment facility (credit), or through bank loans and other financing companies. They also try to compare the consumers with their peers. All these tactics of marketing lead to problem recognition, which leads to felt need and then to purchase. Without problem recognition there is no need for a decision process. Problem recognition occurs when there is a discrepancy between the actual and the desired state. The degree to which it is out of alignment is also important. The desire to resolve a problem depends on the (a) magnitude of discrepancy and (b) the relative importance of the problem, e.g. if the discrepancy is small, a decision may not be made. Sometimes the discrepancy is large but the importance is small, so a decision may not be required, because of budget constraints, time constraints, or both, or other more important problems like housing utilities, etc. e.g. if an individuals using a Bajaj Scooter for a long time and has been recommended an LML, which may have some advantage on driving comfort or on mileage, which may not be very substantial. The discrepancy may not be large enough to prompt him to change to a new scooter.

Also, if an individual has to change his scooter which is already serving his purpose but he has other more pressing problems which may concern the house or his children. He may tend to ignore the scooter problem and give greater preference to more pressing domestic engagements and other more important work which would be given preference in comparison to his own scooter problem.

The desire to resolve a recognised problem is therefore of relative importance. An individual tries to resolve a problem when it is convenient for him in terms of money, involvement, nature of the problem to be solved and the advantages in changing over to a new situation or a new product.

Types of consumer problems may be active or inactive. Active is one in which the consumer is aware or will become aware of, in the normal course of events, e.g. consumer is aware of the gas lighter but insists on safety measures. A consumer may be aware of the advantages of flying, yet is scared to do so.

Inactive Problem

When the consumer is not yet aware of the gas lighter or he may not be aware of the advantages of a cell phone. The marketer must activate the problem recognition.

Marketing strategy and problem recognition

Marketers are concerned with the following:

1. What problem consumers are facing.
2. Managers must know what market mix to develop to solve the problem.
3. They actually want the consumers to recognise the problem.
4. Sometime managers suppress problem recognition.

   (i) Managers get to know the problem by intention and determine what improvements can be made but, the problem identified by managers may be of low importance to the consumer, therefore, the problem is found by survey, focus group interviews, product analysis, problem analysis or activity analysis, human factor research, or emotion research.

Activity Analysis focusses on a particular activity—maintaining a lawn, preparing dinner, lighting the fire place.

Product analysis deals with the use of product, e.g. lawn mower, microwave oven.

Problem analysis takes an opposite approach. It states the problems and asks respondents to associate a product brand or activity with it.

- ➢ Packages are hard to open.
- ➢ Does not pour well.
- ➢ Packages of_______do not fit in the frigidaire.
- ➢ Packages of________waste too many resources.

Human factor research attempts to determine human capabilities in area of vision, strength, response time, fatigue.

Emotions research marketers find the role of emotions in decision-making, i.e. emotions associated with certain products or brands.

Developing Marketing Mix

Once the problem is recognised, a marketing mix be offered to solve the problem—product development or alteration, modifying channels of distribution, changing pricing policy, revising advertising strategy. Many people want to remain slim or away from diabetes, yet want to enjoy sweets. Sugar free is their solution.

Weekend stores and night stores provide more shopping time. When you are financially independent you are exposed to insurance and credit cards to solve your future problems.

Activating Problem Recognition

By increasing the importance and magnitude of discrepancy, advertising benefits promote a sense of excitement and personal freedom, questioning the perception of the existing state (are you satisfied with the present offer?).

Consumers often realise a problem when it has already occurred, and they can not do much about it, e.g. becoming aware of insurance after the accident

- ➢ Want emergency medicines when they are seriously ill and cannot do much.
- ➢ Want flowers and forgot to plant them.

Marketers help solve such problems after they arise. Pharmacists can make home deliveries. They should try to trigger the problem recognition in advance of the actual problem.

Suppressing Problem Recognition

In case of tobacco selling, they undermine the role of cigarettes as injurious, with such advertisment as “Alive with pleasure”. They minimise problem recognition of it being injurious.

Thus, problem recognition plays an important part as the first step in decision-making. The marketers learn of the problem of the consumer, their needs and accordingly formulate a strategy.

Questions

1. What are the stages in the decision-making process? Explain briefly.
2. When does problem recognition occur? Explain the perceived gap and the threshold level.
3. Suggest a market strategy for problem recognition.

11

Information Search

The cost is long forgotten but the quality is remembered forever.

Information search is required for gathering information about products/services to be able to make a correct choice.

The students must understand:

- The sources of information
- High and low information search
- Market strategies

INTRODUCTION

Information search starts the moment a need is recognised. It is a deliberate attempt to gain appropriate knowledge about products. Knowledge of brands and their important characteristics, and knowledge of stores from where to purchase the goods is gained. Optimum amount of information is required for making a proper choice. Consumers gather information, they then understand (perceive) by selecting, organising and interpreting it.

Acquisition process	*Type of involvement*
On going search....................................	Enduring involvement (computer)
Purchase specific search.......................	Situational involvement
Passive acquisition................................	Low involvement.

Questions faced by Marketer

1. What are the types of information search, and what are their determinants?
2. What is the appropriate information load that can be handled by customers?

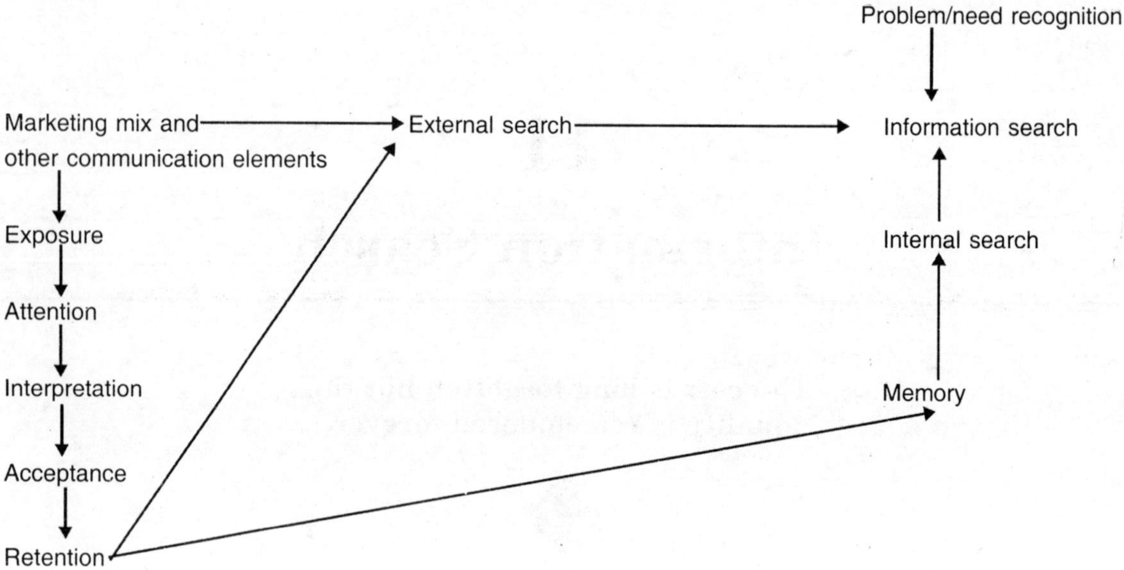

Fig 11.1 Information search for high involvement consumer durables.

3. How can marketers help facilitate the information search?
4. Which source of information is used by the customer?

Types of Information Search

- *Internal search:* It is sufficient in case of loyalty decisions and impulsive purchases. Internal search is also done for routine response behaviour and limited problem solving.
- *External Search:* It is a mediated, planned and rational pursuit of information for high involvement purchase decision, i.e. extensive problem solving.
- *Passive Search:* Low involvement—use repetitive advertising use T.V. Emphasize Price Promotion and in-store marketing stimuli.
- *Active Information Search:* Marketer must vary message content frequently. Use Print Media. Emphasize advertising and emphasize marketing before customer enters store.
- *Hedonic Search:* In this sensory stimuli dominates. There is ongoing information search. Personal sources are more important symbols and imagery is most effective.
- *Utilitarian Search:* Product attributes are more important for purchase. There is specific information search. Non personal sources are more important. Product information is more effective.

Information Overload

Jacob Jacoby and associates developed this concept, which cautions marketers against the popular assumption "If some information is good, then more information must be better".

Too much information confuses the consumer, and with more information, often poor decisions are made. Increasing package information adversely affects the ability to choose best brands.

Sources of Information

(i) *Controlled by marketers:*

(a) *Advertising:* Provides about 35 per cent to 50 per cent information sought. It is the most important sources of information.

(b) *In-store promotion:* e.g. display prices, danglers, brochures, technical reports, summaries.

(c) *Information on distribution support:* Yellow pages.

(d) *Package information:* Colour, design, ingredients and mode of using.

(e) *Sales personnel:* Consumer durables, furniture, electronic, clothing indigenous products.

(f) *Samples and demonstrations* (most important): Create a favourable impact for marketers.

(ii) *Outside marketer's control:*

Personal friends, independent consumer reports, new articles shopping columns.

Some sources are face to face, others are non-personal in nature. (advertisement and publicity, etc.)

There are many situations which lead to high or low information search.

Factors Leading to High Information Search

1. If one feels that there will be more benefit by undertaking a search—search is high.
2. If there is greater involvement in the product, i.e. a camera bought by a professional photographer or, a racket chosen by a professional tennis player.
3. If one likes shopping and enjoys it—search is high.
4. If more time is available—high search.
5. If one is mobile and can go from place to place, i.e. his movement is not restricted—high information search.
6. If one can process the information easily about the product one wants to buy. It leads to high information search.
7. If many attributes are to be evaluated and one is interested in many attributes and their mix—high information search.

8. If there is little product knowledge & experience it leads to high risk. Therefore more information search is required.
9. If there is more product differentiation high price is charged.

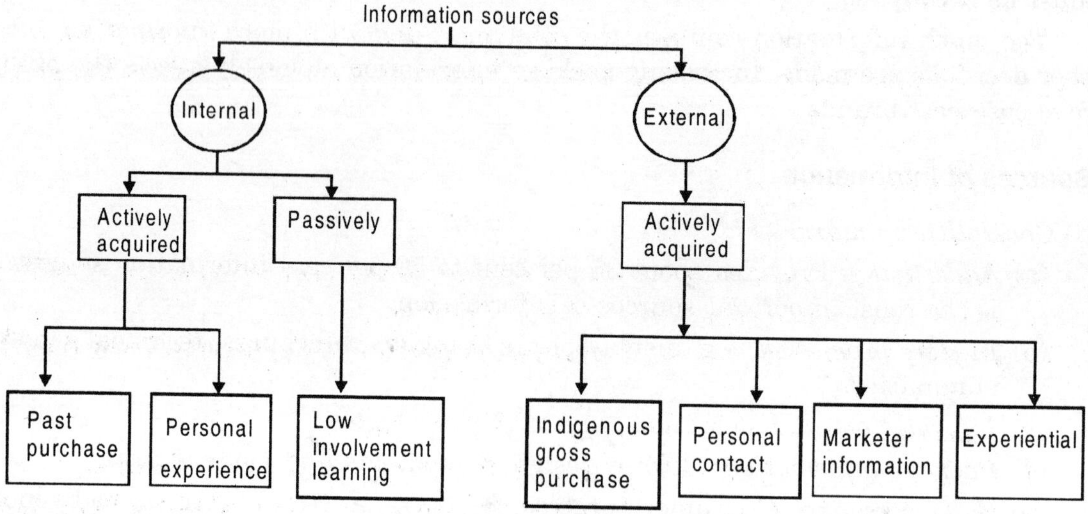

Fig. 11.2 Information sources.

Factors leading to low information search

1. If the cost of the information search is high—it leads to low information search.
2. If one relies on his past experience of purchases—low information search.
3. If one is satisfied with existing brands he is using he will go for—low information search.
4. If there is social pressure of friends and relatives to buy a particular product—low information search.
5. If one has low confidence in dealing with information or, cannot process much information—low information search.

For external information search, certain measures are taken.

1. Number of stores visited
2. Number of alternatives considered
3. Number of personal sources used
4. Overall or combination measures

Consumers can be classified as:

1. Non searchers
2. Limited information searchers
3. Extended information searchers.

Cost vs Benefit Analysis

Benefits can be (a) tangible, i.e. lower price preferred style, more quantity, better quality; (b) Intangible—reduced risk, greater confidence even providing enjoyment.

It has been observed that 50 per cent of the appliance buyers do little, or no external search as they do not perceive enough benefits from it.

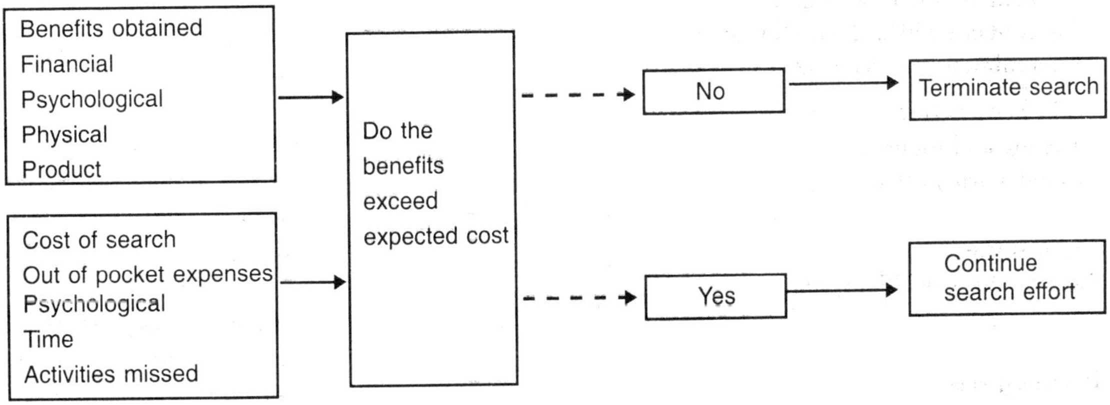

Fig. 11.3 Cost and benefit guide.

Cost

No search is also done because of the cost incurred. It can be both monetary and non-monetary, i.e. money used in transportation, lost time, lost wages, lost opportunities.

Non-monetary may include psychological and physical cost, frustration cost, conflict between search and other activities fatigue, etc.

Table 11.1 Factors that Influence Cost and Benefit

Influencing Factor	*Effect of increasing the influencing factor*
Market character	
Number of alternatives	Increases search
Price range	Increases search
Store concentration	Increases search
Information availability (This includes—advertisements, point of purchase, sales personnel, packaging)	Increases search
Product character	
Price	Increases search
Differentiation	Increases search

Influencing Factor	*Effect of increasing the influencing factor*
Positive products (These are products which the customer enjoys buying like a camera, tennis racket, good food, etc. Negative products, negative reinforcement which the customer avoids; i.e. inoculation, medicine, etc.)	Increases search
Consumer Character	
Learning and experience	Decreases search
Shopping orientation	Knowledge of consumption about existing product
Social status	Increases search
Age and household lifecycle	Age inversely proportional to search. Also new stage of L.C. requires more search.
Perceived risk	Increases search
Situation Character	
Time availability	Increases search
Purchase for self	Decreases search
Pleasant surroundings	Increases search
Physical/Mental energy	Increases search
Social surroundings	Mixed search
Pleasant surroundings tends to Increase search.	

When a consumer undertakes a search, he comes across various brands and has to choose from them. Some brands are considered out of the total set of brands available.

We thus have:

Total set: All the brands available in the market.

Awareness set: Brands potential buyer is aware of.

Inept set: Not suitable/rejected.

Considerations set (Evoked set): Brand to be considered.

Choice set: In contention with final choice.

Choice: Ultimate choice.

Total set	*Awareness set*	*Input set*	*Consideration set*	*Choice set*	*Choice*
Godrej	Godrej	Voltas	LG	LG	LG
Samsung	LG	Samsung	Videocon	Videocon	
LG	Videocon	Godrej	Kelvinator		

Contd.

Kelvinator	Kelvinator	BPL
Videocon	BPL	
Allwyn		
BPL		
Voltas		

Table 11.2 Marketing strategy based on information search process

Brand Position	*R.R.B.*	*Limited D.M.*	*Extended D.M.*
Brand in evoked set (consideration)	Maintenance Strategy	Capture Strategy	Preference
Brand not in evoked set (consideration)	Disrupt Strategy	Intercept Strategy	Acceptance Strategy

To design market strategies, the nature of search is to be considered, i.e. R.R.B., L.P.S., E.P.S. and the nature of the evoked set. (This influences the direction of search). This gives rise to six strategies.

Maintenance structure

If the brand is purchased habitually, the strategy is to maintain that behaviour. Attention is to be paid to product quality, avoiding out of stock situation, reinforcement, advertising. Also defend against the competitor's move which might be disruptive to the brand. Maintain product development, give rebates, P.O.P. displays, etc.

Disruptive structure

If the brand is not in the evoked set and the decision is habitual, we must disrupt the existing decision-making process. It is a difficult task. A major product improvement must be made. Attention attracting advertising should be done. Free samples, coupons, rebates and tie-in-sales can disrupt habitual decision-making.

Capture structure, limited decision-making and evoked brand

Limited decision-making involves few brands which are evaluated on price or availability. Information search is mostly done at P.O.P. and through available media prior to purchase. Strategy is to catch as much of the market share as possible/practical. In limited search, the marketer tries to supply information of his brand by cooperative advertising. He must also maintain product quality and adequate distribution.

Intercept structure, limited decision-making and not evoked set (consideration set)

Marketer has to intercept the consumer during a search on brands in evoked set. Emphasis will be on local media with cooperative advertisement, P.O.P. displays, shelf space, package design. Consumer's attention is to be drawn as the brand is not in the evoked set. Coupons can also be effective. Low involvement learning, product improvement and free samples can also be used.

Preference structure, extended decision-making and evoked set

Extended decision-making involves several brands, several attributes and many information sources. We have to have a campaign that will result in the target market preferring our brand.

We should be strong in the attributes preferred by the target markets. Extensive advertising campaigns must be undertaken to impart information to groups. Groups be encouraged to test the brand. Extra motivation be given to salesmen. Pamphlets be provided.

Acceptance structure

It is used in extended decision-making and for the brands that are not in the evoked set.

Similar to preference structure brand is not in evoked set, therefore, the customer is not seeking information about the product. Motivate customer to learn about the brand and visit showrooms. Besides preferred strategies, effort should be made to bring the brand in the evoked set by extended advertisement and imparting information.

Marketing implications of research behaviour are broad ranging

It makes marketers aware of how customers search for information. They can help the customer and facilitate the search process to match with their marketing stimuli. Marketers influence search process by advertising product and packaging and pricing policies.

Marketers' influence on information search

Through areas of advertising, product and packaging policies and pricing.

Advertising: Complex due to selective reception and perception. With time, audience erosion occurs, constant review is important. Audience may not be attentive to the advertisement.

Review is the key word: To present an attractive packaging, one should vary the packaging and design of the product.

Product and packaging: Use words like 'new', 'improved', 'better', or 'power' packed. Change in package design and colour, periodically helps to push information through. It stimulates the consumer and, pushes the information through the threshold level. These adjectives help the consumer to break the threshold level faster, so that the purchases are expedited.

Pricing: Review pricing permutations and combinations to convey desired price quality perception. Most people are sensitive to price variations. This strategy is commonly used.

Questions

1. What are the various types of information search, and what is marketer's role in information search?
2. What are the sources of information and the factors leading to high and low information search?
3. What are various sets for making the choice of a brand?
4. How are marketing strategies based on information search?

Note: For more examples see Chapter 13.

12

Outlet Selection and Purchase

Customer satisfaction is affordable and profitable because the customer becomes your salesman forever.

The selection of outlet is given due importance by the customer.

The reader must understand:

- The importance and dimensions of the outlet
- Customer characteristics and risks involved
- Influences altering brand choice
- Store atmospherics

INTRODUCTION

As the number of products and brands are increasing in the market, so are the retail outlets, and it becomes very confusing for the customer to choose the retail stores. The selecting of a retail store also involves almost the same process as selecting a brand. A retail outlet relates to a service or a product which caters to the consumer. The retail trade occurs from the stores, but it also occurs from catalogues, direct mail via print media, television and radio. Retailing is also done in weekly markets which are put up in different areas of a city on different days. It is also done from consumer to consumer, by means of various media. It has become very challenging and exciting, both for consumers and marketers. The consumer may give first preference to the store or the product or, he may give equal importance to both. Sometimes one prefers a store first, where he can get friendly and logical advice to buy the product, and prefers to buy a product/brand of second priority, if he is assured of proper service and proper guidance, rather then buying a product of his choice on first priority and missing out on other important aspects of purchase.

The selection of retail outlet therefore, can be made considering a number of factors. These are: outlet image, advertising, outlet location and size consumer characteristics.

Outlet Image

It is the perception of the consumer about the store. It concerns all the attributes associated with the store. It can be perceived on the following dimensions.

Table 12.1

Dimensions	*Components*
Merchandise Service	quality, selection, style, price, place, sales personnel, easy return, credit and delivery.
Clientele	types of customers frequenting the store.
Physical facilities	cleanliness, store layout, shopping ease and attractiveness.
Convenience	location and parking
Promotion	advertising, P.O.P. displays.
Store atmosphere	atmospherics, ambience, fun, excitement, comfort, etc.
Institutional	store reputation
Post-transaction	satisfaction

The table gives dimensions of store image. Marketers make extensive use of these dimensions to formulate retail strategies. First they try to project a favourable image; secondly they try to group customers with similar wants, and they try to coordinate the two together, to be effective as a retail store. Some stores which try to be "everything to all customers" fail miserably, as their image is not focussed in a proper manner. The target market must be well defined. There can be junior stores, senior stores, veteran stores, feminine stores, low priced stores, elite stores, etc. Some stores concentrate on providing service when it is not available easily. They provide service all round the clock, and give a lot of importance to service. All these aspects create image in the minds of the consumer.

Advertising

Retailers use price advertising and attract people to stores. People usually come to buy the advertised items and also end up buying other products. Sales of additional items is known as spillover sales. Price is also an important factor for purchasing the product and, at least three decisions in this regard are necessary:

1. How much discount should be given?
2. How long should the discount last?
3. How should the information be given to the target customer?
4. Should preference or comparison price be used?

Consumers perceive price advertisement as reduction in price. Many advertisers project the regular price, as well as the offered price, showing a discount or a substantial savings. Reference price is the price compared with other products on sale. Other factors like product category, brand, initial price level, consumer group and retail outlet is also to be considered in price advertising.

Outlet Location and Size

For the location of the store convenience is the important factor. The consumers tend to buy from the store that is closest to them. All other things being equal, larger stores are preferred to smaller stores. People will go to smaller stores or nearby stores for minor items, but for purchasing items of high value, or speciality items, people will take the trouble of going to distant places and choose the best.

Location creates an impact on the consumer. Travel time to reach the store is an important factor. If it takes more than 15 minutes to reach the store and if there are traffic jams in the way it is a hinderance or a barrier in the way of shopping for many consumers. The square feet of floor space is also an important factor. Consumers like ample space to move around and want to see the displays and the products closely. Location of the store may not be of so much importance to many as may be other variables like the price, the variety, store quality and cleanliness and the ambience of the store. Stores in attractive surroundings are preferred to those in unattractive surroundings.

Consumer Characteristics

Consumer characteristics must be studied because it gives an idea of the consumer. Different consumers have different reasons and different desires for shopping. Some buy for convenience others for an image. Others for fulfilling obligatins, etc. In this connection, perceived risk and shopper orientation are quite important.

Perceived risk

The risks that are perceived by the consumer are of various types. They are social or, economical risk, and these differ from consumer to consumer. Economic risks are concerned with monetary aspects. Whereas, social risk is concerned with the approval of the society. The way one does one's hairstyling, the choice of clothes, jewellery. Some products can have both big social and economic risk. These can be living room furniture or automobiles. Some products may be low in both economic and social risk, e.g. items of low value such as pencils, pens, socks, kitchen appliances, etc. Perceived risk therefore comes under both consumer characteristics and product characteristics. These give a lot of information to retailers for formulating a retailing strategy. Following risks could be involved.

Financial risk → paying more.

Social risk → does not meet the approval of social group.

Psychological risk → loss of self esteem. Others buying at cheaper rates.

Performance risk → not performing.

Physical risk → bodily harm, faulty brakes adulterated food etc.

Table 12.2 Social and Economic Risks

Social risk	*Economic risk*	
	Low	*High*
Low	Wine (home use)	Personal computers
	Socks	Auto repairs
	Kitchen supplies	Clothes washer
	Pens/Pencils	Insurance
	Gasoline	Doctor/Lawyer
High	Fashion accessories	Business suits
	Hairstyles	Living room furniture
	Gifts (inexpensive)	Automobile
	Wine (entertaining)	Snow board
	Aerobics suits	Skin suit

Source: Taken from Hawkins, Best and Coney, covering p. 495.

These risks are to be reduced in a number of ways. In traditional stores, quality products and famous brand names must be kept for the consumer. Toll free service may be provided, other facilities like 24 hour service may be provided with trained staff and 100 per cent satisfaction guarantee. Economic risk can be reduced through warranties and other price policies. Social risk is harder to reduce and skilled sale force and known brands should be used.

Shopping Orientation

There are many reasons for shopping. It may be for acquiring a product, or for making social interaction, or for exercise, or just for looking around and gaining more product knowledge. It can also be for exercising the physical parts and mental faculties. These motives may be different for different individuals and the purpose for shopping may also vary.

Thus, by shopping orientation we mean, what emphasis is put on various activities or, the reasons we have for shopping. Shoppers are therefore categorised into seven different categories, as given below:

Inactive shoppers

They do not enjoy shopping and are not concerned much with price, product selection, etc. They have a restricted lifestyle and restricted interest in shopping.

Active shoppers

They enjoy shopping, and like to find out about various products. They are knowledgable and balance price with quality, fashion, attributes, etc.

Service shoppers

They give importance to service by the shopkeepers. Both in-store and after-sales service is their main consideration.

Traditional shoppers

They are active shoppers and engage in outdoor activities. They are knowledgable and not price sensitive.

Price shoppers

They are price conscious. They make a lot of search and find the lowest price available. They take the help of the media for this purpose.

Dedicated fringe shoppers

They are catalogue shoppers, and have little interest in television and radio. Not store loyal. They are not heavy socialisers and do things by themselves.

Transitional shoppers

They are experimental and keep changing stores and products. They do not go for low price and buy products that interest them most.

There are also a number of influences that alter brand choices, as shown in Fig. 12.1

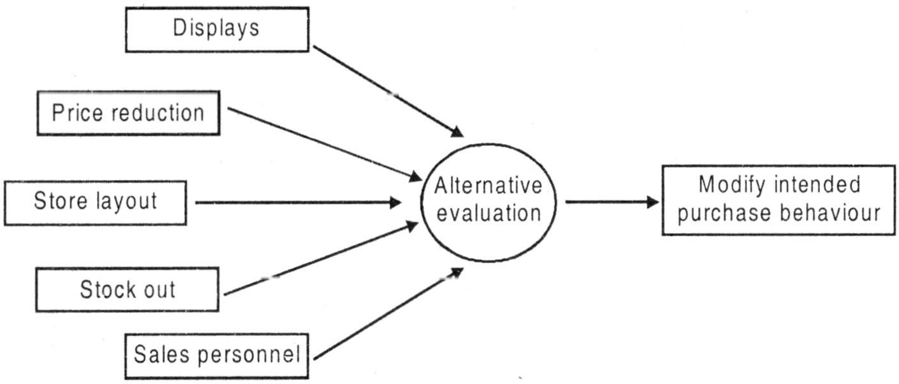

Fig. 12.1

Sometimes unplanned purchases take place. These are purchases which have not been planned from before. These are also known as impulse purchases which the consumer had not planned or thought or, before entering the store. This can mean a lack of rationality in decision-making.

Point of Purchase Displays

These are important influences in helping the customer to make a decision. They become very effective in case of snacks, foods, etc. and the impact of these displays is tremendous and can be enhanced when combined with advertising.

Price reductions

Price reductions can be in the form of discounts, coupons, gifts. When price reduction is given to the consumer, the preference for these brands becomes more enhanced and the brand moves faster than the competing brands. This is a great motivation which acts in multiple ways. The consumer may buy the product because he is getting it cheaper, and may stock the product in a greater quantity than is desired. This is known as stockpiling. The users of competing brands may switch to the low price brand for the time being and, may or may not become permanent buyers of the brand. The price reduction may induce the non buyers to visit the stores and strike a bargain. It is not necessary that all householders and consumers may respond to price reduction.

Store layout

This is an important factor in store retailing. Prominently displayed products with good lighting and visibility, attract greater attention of buyers and have more chances of being sold. The store layout should not be monotonous, and be changed after intervals of time to give it a more innovative look. The principle of store displays and various types of displays must be practised.

Store atmosphere

A congenial atmosphere influences a person psychologically, and good environment makes the customer stay a longer time in the shop, which enhances the chances of sales. In atmospherics we give importance to lighting, floor layout, presentation fixtures, colours, sound dress, behaviour of salesman. The atmospherics apply to a number of services, such as banks, hospitals, restaurant, etc. The types of racks used, and the way the merchandise is displayed on them, also influences the atmosphere. It is the setting which is enjoyed by the consumer. The consumer feels happy in a good atmosphere which also constitutes the type of clientele visiting the store.

Table 12.3 Store atmosphere and shopper behaviour

Store Atmosphere	*Individual characteristics of the consumer and sales personnel*	*Response*
Ambient conditions	*Sales personnel*	*Sales personnel*
Temperature	Career objectives	Mood effort
Air quality	Training	Commitment
Noise	Personal situation	Attitude
Music	Social class	Knowledge skill
Odor	Stage in HLC	

Store Atmosphere	*Individual characteristics of the consumer and sales personnel*	*Response*
Physical conditions Layout Equipment Colours Furnishing Space		
Social conditions Customer Characteristics Number of customers Sales force Characteristics	*Consumers* Lifestyle Shopping orientation State in HLC Situation	*Consumers* Enjoyment Time in store Items examined Information acquired Purchases satisfaction
Symoble Figures P.O.P. displays Décor style		

Source: Adapted from Hawkins, Best.

Stock out

If a product or a brand is out of stock, i.e. not available at an appropriate time, the consumer gets tempted to switch brands, or delay the purchase. This is detrimental to the product and the manufacturer. It is therefore necessary for the retailer to order the inventory in good time, and also to ensure that stocks are always available, or replenished in time. If the stocks are not available when required, it influences the purchase behaviour of the consumers in many ways.

- He may purchase a substitute product or brand.
- He may delay the purchase.
- Forego the purchase entirely.
- Purchase the desired brand at another store.
- He may make negative comments about the product/brand
- He may praise the substitute product and adopt the new product/brand permanently.
- He may develop a poor opinion of the store he had been patronising.
- He may visit alternative stores quite often.

All these behaviour patterns or outcomes are detrimental and negative to store in question.

Sales personnel

It is the sales person that educates and enlightens the prospective customer. A competent, smart and intelligent salesman can change the entire perception of the consumer, i.e. retail owners having adequate knowledge can convince a consumer that Britta which is much cheaper has a better purifying affect. It retains the bacteria away from drinking water, better than Aquaguard. They can also explain the convenience of Britta and its cost effectiveness and ease of handling which makes it quite competitive in the market. Therefore, many retail stores train their salesman both in the selling process and in closing the sales to the prospective customer and ensuring consumer satisfaction. The salesman also emphasises after-sales service, which is a part of good salesmanship. A good interaction may take place in case of high and medium involvement products which are costly and risky to buy. The salesman in this case plays an important role.

Purchase

This is the final step in a transaction. Unless the purchase is made, all efforts of layout, atmosphere, effort of the sales man are a waste. Closing the sales is important. The trend these days is shifting to credit sales, which can be done by using various credit cards—various types of credit can also be given. Marketers are competing to provide credit facility. In fact, credit has also become a product. Firms want to sell their credit facilities to the consumer.

Questions

1. How do outlets influence purchase behaviour of the consumer?
2. What are the dimensions of outlet image?
3. What is meant by shopping orientation.
4. Describe briefly the influences that affect or alter brand choices.

13

Attitude Development and Alternate Evaluation in Buying

**Good attitude does not result from good positions or wealth.
The fact is that people get good positions
because of positive attitude.**

One's attitude plays an important role in buying.
The student should understand:

- The meaning of attitude
- Attitude component
- Multi attitude choice model
- Basic choice heuristics
- Marketing inferences and action

◆ INTRODUCTION

Consumers of all products are engaged in low, medium and high involvement information search. There are various questions to be considered.

- ➢ How do consumers choose among brand alternatives?
- ➢ Do they use any choice rules?
- ➢ Do they select best alternatives or reject bad ones?
- ➢ How do they find their way amidst many brand alternatives with different attributes?

People have different attitudes (bent of mind) for different products, e.g. many consumers think of plastic to be cheap, artificial, weak, breakable non-degradable, environmentally harmful and not desirable. They have a negative attitude and discourage the use of plastics.

Plastics also create positive attitudes, as it is light unbreakable, easy to carry, handy. People do not dislike plastics, but do not know what to do with it after using it.

Attitude is the way we think, we feel and act towards some aspect of the environment.

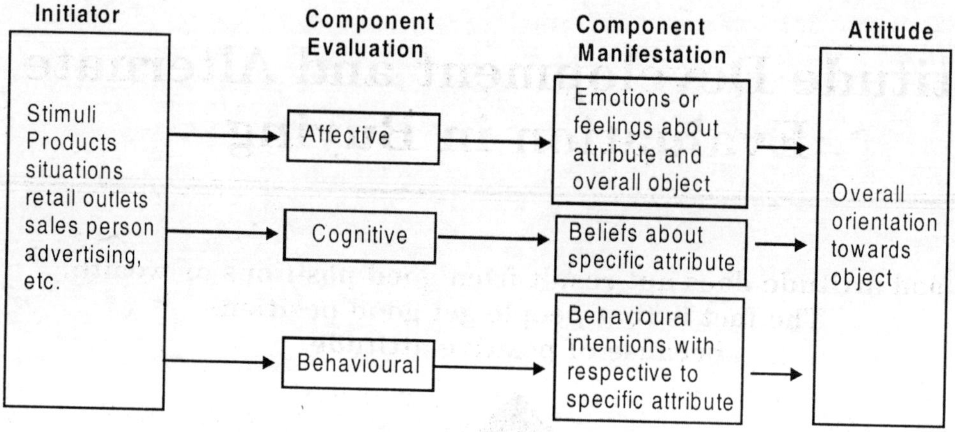

Fig 13.1 Attitude component and manifestation.

Key variables that surpasses all variables in alternative evaluation, is consumer attitude.

Consumer Attitude and Alternative Evaluation

It presents a summary evaluation of the consumer environment around them.

Definition

Attitude is a learned predisposition to respond in a constant favourable or unfavourable manner, in respect to a given object.

Marketers try to bombard consumer with information. These may have a positive or negative effects.

Schematic conception of attitudes has three components:

An attitude provides a series of cues to marketers. They predict future purchases, redesign marketing effort and make attitude more favourable.

Attitudes indicate, knowledge, feelings and intended action for the given stimulus.

Utilitarian Function

In building a favourable attitude towards a product, utilitarian function plays an important part. It guides consumers in achieving their desired needs and avoiding failure and disappointment, e.g. desire for hi-tech products or after sales service may

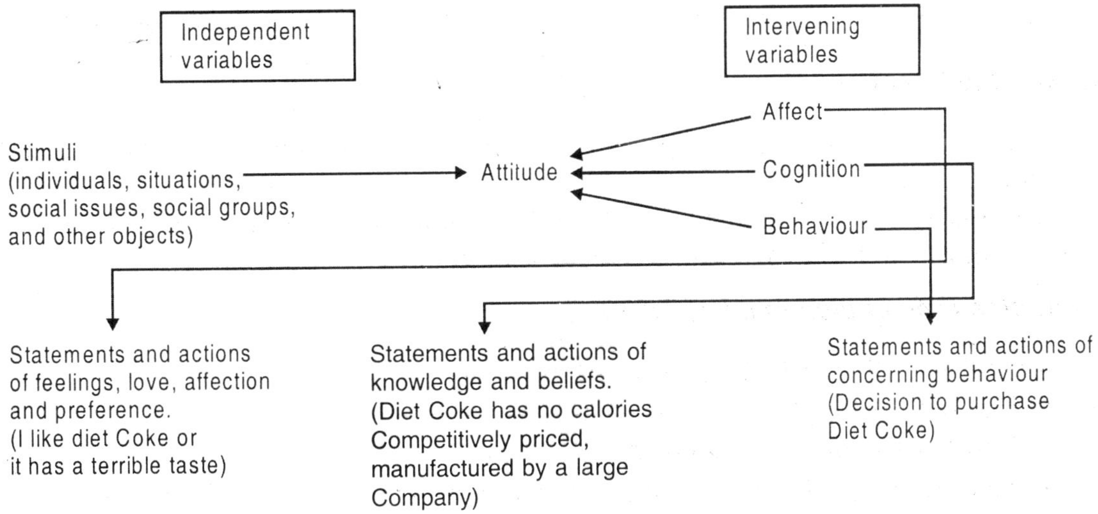

Attitude indicates knowledge, feelings and intended action for the given stimulus

Fig. 13.2 Schematic conception of attitudes.

be the priority of the customer. Customer builds a favourable attitude if he is satisfied with the function, e.g. safety, image etc.

Criticism
1. Assumption that attitude influence specific and overt behaviour
2. Attempts to minimise importance of multiple attributes of the stimulus object

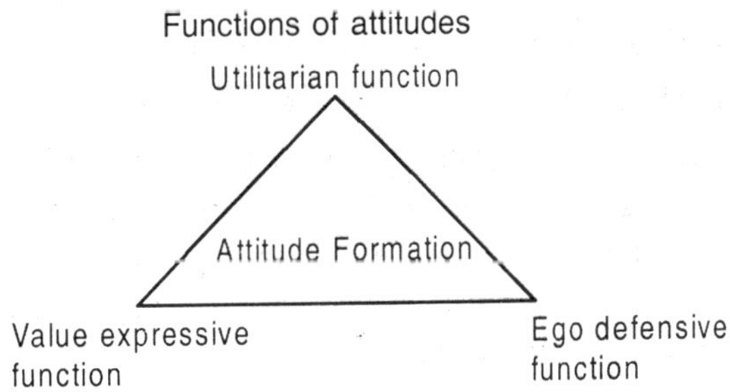

Fig. 13.3

Ego Defensive Function

Individuals are attracted towards products that give them protection and enhance their image in a society. It protects consumers against internal and external anxieties and environment. Here marketing stimuli and more particularly products become an instrument of the protection process, e.g. visible prestige products, mouthwash, deodorants, perfumes, make an individual more acceptable in a gathering, e.g. Mouthwashes are used to avoid anxiety producing situations. Creams are used for removing pimples from the face.

Value Expressive Function

This helps to maintain self-identity among consumers and lead them to expression and determination, e.g. Gandhian followers—select handloom and khadi clothes.

Consumers openly express opinions that reflect their belief and self concept.

Knowledge Function

The knowledge that listerine stops bad breadth. The knowledge that high cholestrol food is not good for health.

Consumers want to uphold the values they stand for. As a member of a club one has to conform to the attire prescribed by that club.

Heuristics (The choice making rules)

The advantages of choice rules to consumers are:

- Guidance while decision-making.
- Short-cut to decision-making.
- Help to integrate and arrange information to enable quick decisions.
- Helps them to take complex decisions.

After recognising the problem and completing information search, the consumer combines and integrates various attributes to facilitate choice making.

Marketers must know what criteria is available to consumers which may be used and why? How can marketers affect choice rules? Purchase decisions may be:

R.R.B.—Routinised Response Behaviour.

L.P.S.—Limited Problem Solving.

E.P.S.—Extended Problem Solving.

The above three types of behaviour have already been discussed in the earlier section of the chapter. For extended problem solving a multi-attribute choice model is used. In this model if the choice is to be made between various brands of products, their attributes are listed and weightages on these attributes are given by the customer according to the importance of attributes. These attributes are rated on a scale (1 to 5) and the total is found out. The higher is the total of ranking, more suitable may be the brand. This is illustrated in the following example.

Consumers use different evaluative criteria in different situations, despite the product being the same. A plethora of evaluation processes are available. There are complexities of evaluation of attributes. A buyer of a computer may look for many attributes. This is a very involving process.

Product Attributes

Product=bundle of benefit expressed through its attributes desired by its target consumer. These vary with customers and are determined by their needs, e.g. for a female lipstick buyer, range of shades, packaging, price and prestige factor are the desired attributes.

Car—styling, low maintenance, fuel economy, price are the desired attributes.

Types of information sought in search behaviour for fulfilling product needs.

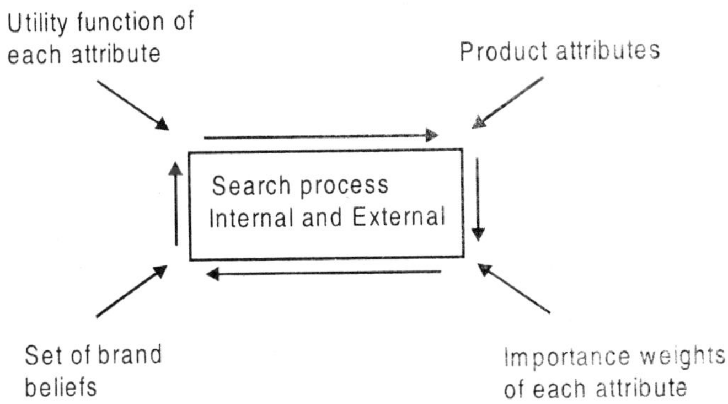

Fig. 13.4 Attributes vary with consumer and are determined by consumer needs.

Importance of Weights

All attributes are not equally important to different buyers of similar products, e.g. lipstick buyer may conclude that price is more important than prestige factor, or vice-versa in brand evaluation. For a car, fuel economy may be more important than styling or vice-versa. Importance of attributes helps a consumer to reach a balanced evaluation.

Brand Belief

The brand image helps consumers, i.e. believing which brand is more likely to have a particular attribute, based on consumer perception, and may be at variance with reality, e.g. what a consumer believes about a brand may not be true.

Utility

By combining the performance levels of salient attributes, consumers can determine utility and make-up what is called in 'ideal brand'.

In evaluating it has to be decided how many brands will be considered. For a mixer/grinder, a large number of brands are available. This is known as the total set.

Awareness set

The brands one is aware of, as given in Column II.

Marketing gains are many

1. *Marketers find* where their brand ranks in terms of consumer knowledge.
2. It indicates the limits of consumer awareness and recall for the number of brands.
3. *Marketers know* how to reinforce their efforts to push their brands in the consideration set.

Table 13.1 How many brand alternatives to consider?

I Total set	*II* Awarenes set	*III* Inept set	*IV* Consideration set	*V* Choice set	*VI* Choice
***Example I** Selection of a mixer/grinder*					
Singer	Singer	Maharaja	Singer	Singer	?
Phillips	Phillips		Phillips		
Inalsa	Inalsa	Kanchan	Inalsa	Inalsa	Ultimate
Solac			Gopi		Choice
Whiteline					
Maharaja	Maharaja				
Sumit	Gopi				
Bajaj	Kanchan				
Gopi					
Jaipan					
Kanchan					
***Example II** Selection of a washing machine*					
IFB	IFB		IFB	IFB	?.
Whirlpool	Whirlpool	Videocon	Whirlpool	Whirlpool	
BPL	BPL	Maharaja	BPL	BPL	Ultimate
					Choice
LG	LG		LG		
Videocon			Sumit		
Maharaja					
Sumit	Sumit		Godrej		
Godrej	Godrej				
Brands Available in the market	Brands potential buyer is aware of	Brands rejected not suitable not available	Brands meeting initial expectation and evaluative criteria	Brands in contention with final choice	Ultimate choice

4. Prevent from going into inept set.
5. Provide information to meet expectation of consumer.

◆ MULTI-ATTRIBUTE CHOICE MODELS

They explain how consumers may combine their beliefs about product attributes to form their attitude about various brand alternatives. A brand which forms the best attitude is chosen. Consumers go through a standard hierarchy of effects sequence. (awareness-interest-desire-action).

Attitude-Towards-Object (ATO) Model

- Seeks information on importance of brand attributes.
- Belief about the presence or absence of those attributes in brand alternatives.
- Information on their combined effect in alternative evaluation.

$$A_0 = \sum_{i=1}^{n} Bi\,ai$$

A_0 = Overall attitude towards object 'O'.

Bi = Belief of whether or not object 'O' has a particular attribute.

ai = Importance rating of the attributes. Rated on a 1-5 scale in the example shown.

n = Number of beliefs.

Process: To choose between the 3 cars (Premier, Ambassador and Maruti). First the attributes are choosen then the weightages are assigned to them then the importance of these ratings are decided on a 1 to 5 scale as shown then a × b gives the value for each attribute. This is then added for all the attributes, and the final score gives the ratings of the car for the choice.

Table 13.2

0 1 2 3 4 5

Rated on A 1--5 scale

Attribute	*Weight*	*Premier*		*Ambassador*		*Maruti*	
	a	B	$a \times B$	B	$a \times B$	B	$a \times B$
Designing	3	3	9	2	6	5	15
Low maintenance cost	2	3	6	2	4	2	4
Fuel efficiency	1	3	3	3	3	5	5
Total			18		13		24

Maruti = Best car

Premier = Average

Ambassador = Worst of the lot.

This model fails to consider that often consumer attitude does not equate with behaviour.

Heuristics—rules that guides the search into areas of high probability.

Basic choice heuristics

Used for mainly limited problem solving and routine response behaviour.

Broadly speaking, there are five basic choice heuristics as shown:

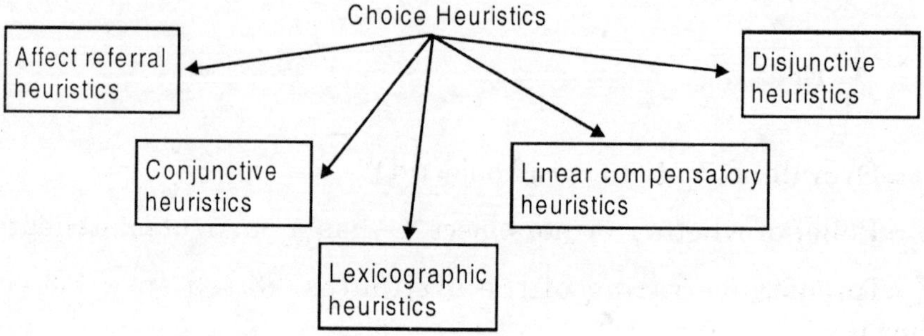

Fig. 13.5

Most consumer try to satisfy their purchase goals instead of optimising them. Most products require low to mild involvement.

· Suppose you want to choose a refrigerator out of the three shown in the example below. Choices can be made by applying various heuristics as shown in Table 13.3.

Table 13.3

Attributes	*Weight*	*Godrej*		*Kelvinator*		*Allwyn*	
		Rank	*Max. 10*	*Rank*	*Max. 10*	*Rank*	*Max. 10*
Styling	30%	3	9	7	21.0	5	15.0
Economy	25%	5	12.5	2	5.0	7	17.5
Low maintenance	45%	5	22.5	4	18.0	3	13.5
	100%		44		44.0		

Affect referral heuristics

Consumer uses earlier experiences and memory in brand evaluation. Holistic approach is used, e.g. for salt, tea, cigarettes. This is the simplest of all rules. Brand that fulfilled earlier requirement will be chosen.

Conjunctive heuristics

This is negative in nature. Many brand alternatives are available with distinct attributes. Consumers set minimum cut-offs on each attribute, which each brand alternative must passes to prevent rejection. Minimum cut off is three. Then Kelvinator will be dropped, i.e. 2/10 on economy. Weighs negative information.

Lexicographic heuristics

This is positive in nature. Brand attribute scoring the highest on most important attribute according to the customer is chosen. Godrej will be chosen. It scores five on low maintenance.

Linear compensatory heuristics

Consumer permits strength of a particular brand attribute to compensate for the weakness of another attribute. Choose the best—Allwyn. It scores the maximum of 45 marks, and if linear compensatory heuristics is used, the automatic choice will be Allwyn.

Disjunctive heuristics: Used infrequently, also sets minimum cut-off points for every brand attribute. But here only salient brand attribute (on basis of weights) is considered. Brand must clear minimum cut-off on dominant attributes.

Godrej clears the minimum criteria of three points. It has at least three points for each attribute, and it also scores the maximum of five points on the most salient attribute, that is low maintenance. So if disjunctive heuristics is applied, Godrej will be chosen. Similarly, by giving weightages to various brands and scoring on 1 to 5 scale, brands can be chosen. This applies to extended problem solving where the involvement is high, the risk is high, cost is high and a rational choice is to be made.

Choice for Personal Telephone Scrvice Decisions

Compensatory: Personal telephone selected by balancing the good ratings against bad.

Conjunctive rule: Selected the one that had no bad features.

Disjunctive rule: Sclected the one that excelled in atleast one attribute.

Lexicographic rule: Chose that one which ranked highest on the most important attribute.

Affect referral rule: Everything the company does is out-standing so. I bought their telephone.

Table 13.4 Examples of attributes.

Personal computer	*Shaving cream*	*Watches*	*Air conditioners*
Processing speed	Frangrance	Wrist Band	BTUS
Price	Price	Alarm piece	Efficiency
Type of display	Size	Water resistent	Quietness
Disk size	Smoothness of shave	Quartz movement	Warranty
Popular Russian Software	Consistency	Size of face	Price
Laptop or desktop			

Marketers may modify their products according to consumer ratings.

Marketers may modify consumer beliefs through proper communication.

For competitive evaluation alter the consumer belief, either by running down competitive products, or by a positive role to give new focus on neglected attributes. This can also be done by manipulating the product.

The acid test for marketing effectiveness is whether the consumer is led to an actual purchase action or not.

Table 13.5 Areas of marketing inferences and action.

Area	*Inferences*	*Actions*
Market Identification	Segment the market on the basis of product attributes, beliefs, attractive benefit, beliefs and product benefit belief.	Market product on basis of lifestyle and benefit segmentation
Competitive Analysis	Possibility of attractive beliefs and benefit manipulation	Change product attributes
	Positioning the product	Contingency review product positioning with proper consumer support
Marketing Mix	Sources of ideas of new product	Use consumer perception and attitude to design new product
	Communication has impact on comfort and earning	Enrich consumer with fresh and distinct information
	Impact of price evaluation matrix	Price perception should be made in line with brand image
	Dist. outlet about product image	Encourage dist. in consumer evaluation
Making positive opportunity analysis	Need to keep an eye on demographic and social changes	Create exclusive segments of consumer demographics
Attitude formation and measurement	Attitude is an indicator of brand preference and behaviour	Strengthen the positive attitude and modify unsuitable ones by a variety of means
	Continuous feel of the market is essential	Develop regular attitude checking system.

Questions

1. What is meant by consumer attitude? What are its components and functions?
2. "Attributes vary with consumer and are determined by consumer needs." Elaborate and explain the above statement.
3. What is an ATO model? How does it help you to make choices of products that require extensive problem solving?

4. Illustrate the method of choosing between various cars by the ATO model with the information given:

   Cars: WagonR, Santro, Indica, Zen, Matiz.

   Attributes: Fuel economy, Cost, Comfort, Style, Utility.

   Assign weightages to the attributes and choose on a 1 to 10 scale.

   Note: Refer example given in Table 13.2.

14

Purchase Behaviour (Situational Factors)

Out of the small orders of today grow into the long orders of tomorrow. Put yourself in your customer's shoes.

The goals of this chapter are to impart an understanding of:

- Purchase behaviour
- Basic situational factors
- Non-store buying

INTRODUCTION

We have seen that in many products, decision-making is a very lengthy process, and takes a very long time. The problem is recognised and a lot of information is gathered. After this is done, the last two stages of decision-making, that is, the purchase and post purchase come into play. Purchase is very important as it generates revenue, and dislikes of the consumer. Post purchase behaviour also establishes a link between the marketer and the target market segment. Purchase is important to the marketer as the product was planned, produced, priced, promoted and distributed after a lot of effort. If purchase does not take place, the marketer has failed in his marketing effort. He then needs to change the marketing mix. He has to change the entire strategy, as the ultimate aim of the marketer is to float a product which will generate revenue and bring satisfaction to the customer. Purchase is important to the marketer for his success, for achieving his objectives, and far formulating competitive strategies against the competitors. Similarly, the customer pays money and expects certain benefits and satisfaction from the product. It marks the end of his search, end of his efforts and chooses the brand of his choice for expected benefits.

Need aroused ⟶ Consumer information processing ⟶ Brand evaluation
↑ Feedback ↓
Post purchase behaviour ← Purchase ← Instrumental action ← intention to buy
out side consideration
No purchase ←

Consumers delay a decision because

- They are too busy.
- Do not like shopping.
- Fear of making wrong decisions.
- Price may decrease or better item may be available.
- Social risk (Not meeting approval of society).

For purchasing, the customer has to consider the (a) selection of outlets, i.e. where tɔ buy from. A product may be available in a number of stores of different types and different sizes. Where to buy form is an important decision that has to be taken by the customer. He further has to think about the quantity of product that he has to buy. Should he buy in small quantities or in bulk. Should he take advantage of the discount facilities which are offered only for a short period of time, or should he ignore them, and buy his usual requirement for a month or for a week. This also depends on the amount of discretionary income that is available to him. There is another choice with the customer, (b) How should he make the payment. Should he buy in cash or in credit, or hire-purchase or any alternative offered by the dealer.

While taking a decision on these issues, a number of factors are to be considered, and these factors influence the decision-making process or the purchase process. The two sets of factors necessary for purchase are the buying intentions and the situational factors. Both these factors exert a joint influence on the purchase process. One without the other may not be sufficient to effect a purchase. The buying intention is a must for the purchase to come through. No matter how congenial the situational factors, the purchase may not take place without the customer having intentions to buy. He has to be motivated to buy the product by exposing him to the product and instilling into his mind that the product is needed by him and will satisfy his long felt need.

Situational factors can be very many in number, but for all purposes, five basic situational factors are considered. These are:

1. Physical surroundings
2. Social surroundings
3. Task definitions
4. Temporal decisions
5. Antecedent conditions.

A situation is the prevaling conditions at a certain time. When related to purchases, it can be linked with the situations given above.

Buying intentions }
Situational factors } Purchase

Fig. 14.1

Store choice influence brand choice

- When store loyalty is high—It influences brand choice.
- When Brand loyalty is Low—Customers first make the store choice.
- When Brand information is inadequate—Customers should rely on Sales Personnel.

Physical Surroundings

As soon as a consumer enters a shop with the intention of purchase, the most important things that he observes is the decor, style, cleanliness, etc. of the shop. These are known as physical surroundings, and they include:

1. Location of the store.
2. The sound (music and other noises present in the store).
3. Aromas (smell of the place).
4. Lighting—how well lit are the products, how well lit is the store and the show windows.
5. The decor (Decoration is done with great fineness and the displays are eye catching).
6. The colour (The colour of the store and of the walls and the railings or any other show cases, etc.).
7. The merchandise itself (a merchandise of high value, quality, high in demand, etc.).

These physical aspects are eye catching and the most visible part of the purchase situation. The surroundings act as a stimuli for the consumer, and influence him through his five senses of sight, hearing, smell, touch and taste. The presence of these elements is not enough. They have to be present in the right mix to create an atmosphere which is congenial to all consumers. This is the concept of atmospherics, where not only the physical surroundings but, the music and the handling of the crowd in the store is also emphasised. Since the consumer is exposed to a proper blend of these stimuli, he responds in a particular manner. He sometimes responds emotionally, and shows his pleasure or displeasure and may go in for a purchase. These physical surrounds also control the time he spends in the store. How he responds to purchase. The customer also tries to affiliate with other customers and also with the people in the store. If all circumstances match, a purchase is on the offing. This is illustrated in the Fig. 14.2.

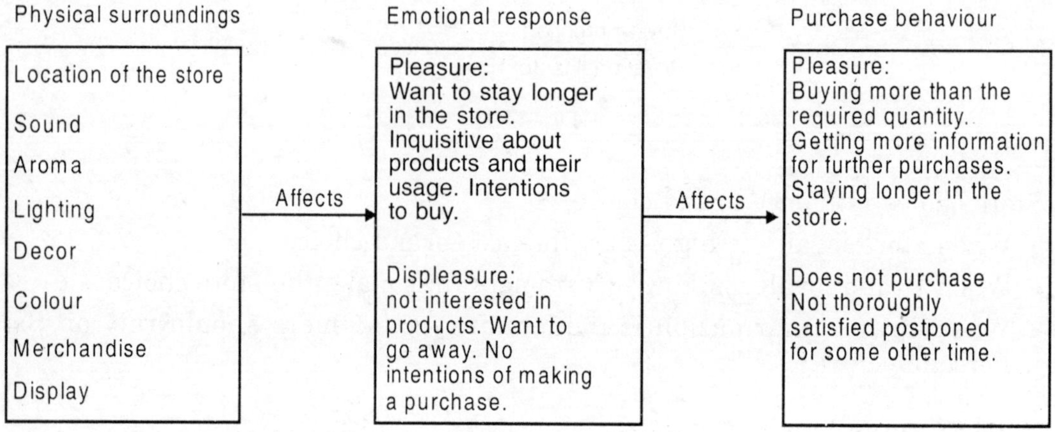

Fig. 14.2 Physical surroundings purchase process.

Social Surroundings

Purchase is affected by the presence of other members of the society and their opinion about the purchase and use of products. A consumer is a social being. He lives in society, and is affected by the opinion of society members. If a customer is ambitious to spend time with high society members, his purchases are influenced, and he goes in to buy premium and branded items. Shopping is a social experience, and consumers are influenced by society members and sometimes blindly purchase things approved by trusted members of the society. There are some general observations that when a consumer is shopping with friends he tends to visit many more stores and makes many unplanned purchases. This is because he thinks that his wise companions are giving him sound advice which he is getting for free, and that the opinion of a handful is better than his own judgement. While with friends, he likes to spend more time with them, and feels more confident of going from store to store and visiting the shops with new displays, new products, new variety and new items.

Salesmen have also observed that it is easier to sell to individuals rather than customers in groups. Unaided buyers can be convinced much easily than those with friends. Individual buyers sometimes give into the persistence of the salesman. It has also been observed that buyers who are with friends, comply to the request of the group of friends, even though they know that the product is not to their liking or, that they would rather buy some other brand.

Task definition

By task definition is meant, the buying intention or motive. Why is the purchase being made. Is it for self consumption or is it for a gift, or is it for a special occasion like a marriage gift and so on. Purchase task is decided by the above factors and what will be the reaction of the person to whom the gift is being given.

Buying flowers or a piece of jewellery on your wedding anniversary. The situatin also defines the task. Titan watches are advertised for giving as a present. A bigger present as a Godrej Storewell may be given for a marriage to a friend. Sweets or chocolates to be given to children visiting your house. Marketers use these techniques of selling products, and use the occasion based marketing opportunities to push their products. The task or the purpose and intentions must be known to the marketer to make his job easy.

Temporal factors

By temporal factors we are referring to time. It may be the time allotted for shopping. It may be the time of the day, shopping in the morning, evening or afternoon. Time of the season, time of the year, time of festivals, etc. Some ladies shop in the afternoon as they can be given more attention by the sales person. They can see a variety of products. The time which the sales man has is also ample, and he can pay more attention to customer's needs. Some buy or do shopping during festival seasons only, and their main shopping takes place during the festivals or when there is a function in their families. Some are regular buyers and are in the habit of buying regularly. These are the people with high discretionary income.

The time of buying also varies from product to product. An item of high value will require much more time than buying cosmetics. A high value item may take several days. A much higher value item like a flat or a house may take days and months together.

It also depends on the availability of time with the consumer. A busy executive may have very little time compared to a house-wife. The time available with them is different, hence the degree of involvement in the purchase also differs. With the involvement, the information search also varies from product to product, from situation to situation. If a buyer is buying regularly, he spends lesser time in purchasing, than a buyer who buys at greater intervals of time.

Antecedent conditions

There are other factors that also play an important part on purchases. These are the availability of resources (money) for buying the product of your choice. Other factors like the mood, the attitude, or the bent of mind for purchasing a product. If the purchases are made for a future period of time, they can wait or can be made at any convenient time. If the purchases are urgent, and you have used up your product and need to replenish the same soon, then the purchases are finalised quicker. The availability of the product is another factor for purchase. If one visits a few stores and does not find the product or the brand of his choice, he may develop a negative attitude towards the store or even towards the products.

When the buyer is in the mood, he is more likely to purchase goods, than otherwise. Therefore, marketers try to create a positive mood, by advertising appeals to get a positive response from the buyer.

A proper marketing strategy is to designed to get a positive response from the customers. All the five situational factors described above should be kept in mind and a process be followed. This can be done by identifying the situational factors and the buying process of the consumer, and also to find the impact of these variables by research techniques. The market has to be segmented in a proper manner, and the product positioned according to the need of the target segment. Needless to say that the marketing mix needs to be developed appropriately.

Non-Store Buying

This type of marketing is gaining importance in advanced countries where a shopper does not want to go to a store, and avoids the difficulty of finding parking space. Wants to avoid loong queues for payment or does not have the time to drive down to a store several miles away. Has a higher discretionary income, pays greater importance to consumer life style. Non-store buying or direct marketing is one in which products and services are offered to a prospective customer by telephone, mail or other accesses.

In the purchase process, non-store buying also plays an important part. The non store buying is prevalent where there is general economic development, availability of long stores and infrastructure facilities, consumer is aware of advanced technology. Where the marketer desires to reach untapped markets.

Many compaines have a list of prospective buyers, and send them catalogues, brochures, discount offers almost every week. They get a lot of busines and give a lot of facility, and offer products at competitive rates. This also increases the knowledge of the consumer, and he also feels important and regularly places orders with these companies. There are many routes to non-store buying and the buyer can buy in a number of ways. Known buyer is one who places the order from the home by telephone, catalogue, brochure or mail. The consumer can avoid an extra trip to the market. This type of order on telephone is becoming very popular for items like rations for the whole month. A consumer gives the order over the telephone to his supplier, who notes down the order, and supplies it by reaching the goods to the desired destination.

Tele marketing

This is similar to the above, and prepaid telephones are provided or toll free telephones are provided, so that the orders can be placed without any charge to the customer. This is used mainly by ladies, and is of western origin.

Video-tax or interaction video

In this the buyer seller interaction can occur through TV sets and computer terminals. He can type his requirements on the computer, and through video-tex facility can interact, even see a portion of the store where his product is kept and all the variety of products that are available in that category.

These methods are gradually gaining importance and with the increase in population, and congestion of the cities these methods are becoming popular in advanced countries.

We have therefore seen that the purchase is an important part of the consumer behaviour, and purchases are the backbone of marketing activities. If the purchases are good, and the goods are moving fast, a company can rest assured of revenue, otherwise the marketer has to keep thinking of ways and means to find out the reasons for the shortfall in purchases.

Significance of Non Store Buying

The non store buying is becoming popular because working women and others have less time to shop. They can see more items on T.V. than a single store can display. By this method speciality products are easy to get. Non store innovations are becoming popular e.g. Mail order catalogues, pay by phone etc.

Some customers prefer the older methods of store buying and oppose the new techniques because they like to see the products and feel them. They like to go out to shop and get tempted to buy the products they do not need. They feel that being hooked on a computer may invade their privacy.

However more innovations are expected in the future and that the customers will get the feeling of shopping in store by just sitting at home and can do everything sitting at home that they can do in a shop.

Questions

1. What are the main considerations for the purchase of products?
2. Discuss the situational factors in buying.
3. What is non-store buying? Elaborate on the methods of non-store buying.

15

Post Purchase Behaviour

"A dissatisfied customer is like a spark that spreads fire"
"A dissatisfied customer should not be taken as an unwanted nuisance".

Post purchase behaviour is very important to the marketer. It gives a feedback about the success of failure of a product/service:

- Expectations and actual performance
- Evil effects of dissatisfaction
- Marketer's role to satisfy the consumer

INTRODUCTION

It is important for the marketer to know whether his product is liked by the consumer or not. He wants the feedback about his product so that corrective action, if necessary, can be taken, and the marketing mix be modified accordingly. Post purchase behaviour is the reaction of the consumer, it gives an idea of his likes and dislikes, preferences and attitudes and satisfaction towards the product. It indicates whether or not the purchase motives have been achieved. Purchase is the means, and post purchase is the end. Post purchase behaviour indicates whether or not repeat purchases will be made. Whether the customer will recommend the product to others or not. It indicates whether long term profits can or cannot be expected. All this can be found out by the post purchase behaviour of the customers. Post purchase is the last phase in the decision-making process as indicated by the Fig. 15.1

The customer while making a decision goes through three phases:

1. Pre-purchase activity which consists of;
   Problem recognition → Information search → Evaluation of alternative
2. Purchase process → {Intention to buy; Situational influences}
3. Post purchase behaviour → {Maintenance; Repair; Usage cost}
4. Feedback to the marketer → {Improves the products; Changes the marketing mix; gives more facilities to the consumer}

Fig. 15.1

After purchasing a product, a customer is either satisfied or dissatisfied and his satisfaction or dissatisfaction depends on his expectation and the difference between the performance. Expectation gives the degree of customer's satisfaction/ dissatisfaction with the product. This is shown in Fig. 15.2.

Customers experience with prior proeduct

Expectation of the performance of the product/brand → Discrepancy between the expected and actual performance

Actual performance of the product As evaluated by the consumer → Discrepancy between the expected and actual performance

Dissatisfaction	**Expectancy confirmation**	**Satisfaction**
Performance is below expectation	Performance almost as expected–not different	Performance of the product is better than expected

Fig. 15.2

The figure illustrates that if the performance is below expectations the customer is dissatisfied. However, there can be a match between the two, i.e. performance is in line with expectation. In another position is the product which surpasses the expectancy level, and performs much better than expected. This is a source of satisfaction and delight to the consumer.

Satisfaction or dissatisfaction cannot be generalised, i.e. there is no accepted definition of satisfaction or dissatisfaction. It depends on a number of factors outlined below:

(a) The presence of a particular factor may cause dissatisfaction. If the same factor is removed, it may not unnecessarily lead to satisfaction, i.e. greasy snacks may lead to dissatisfaction but, the absence of greasiness in the same snacks may not lead to satisfaction.

(b) It is a cumulative effect of many factors put together. The effect of individual factors cannot be gauged easily.

(c) Dissatisfaction may as such not lead to any complaint, but the dissatisfaction of a high degree may lead to complaint making of a complaint and, handling of satisfaction or dissatisfaction is a logical process. A person will not complain if he sees no use of doing so or, feels that the complaint will not entertained. Also, consumers complain if it is convenient for them to do so. They may not go out of their way to make complaints. Complaining also requires resources, i.e. time, money, knowledge, expertise, etc. which one may not possess. The dissatisfaction by a consumer towards a product may lead to:

   (i) *Discontinuing purchase* of those products or brands by which a customer is dissatisfied. If he had been patronising that product which has led to his dissatisfaction, he may change to a new brand or a new product.

   (ii) *Negative Word of mouth* He speaks negatively about the product to his friends, peers and associates. Instead of propagating the positive aspects, he starts defaming the product/brand and shows his dissatisfaction openly.

   (iii) *Lodges a complaint* to the concerned authorities. Consumer Forum is one such agency that entertains such complaints. It may be a time consuming process and difficult for all dissatisfied customers to resort to.

   (iv) *Complains directly* to the seller and gets his claim settled or, the product/brand changed according to his liking or, agrees for any such settlement.

It is the effort of every firm to produce satisfied customers. This is essential to fight increasing competition. Some dissatisfied customers however remain repeat purchasers, as they do not find a suitable alternative or, find that brand readily available and buy it due to force of habit or, because of low price. These purchasers may not be brand loyal. A brand loyal or a committed customer is attached to the brand emotionally. He believes in the firm and trusts the brand. Brand loyalty increases if the performance of the brand is more than the expected performance. In case of committed customers, they believe and have faith in line extension and brand extension of the firm. Committed customers also promote the product by positive word of mouth.

Role of a Marketer

The marketer has to watch that the customer is not dissatisfied. Through dissatisfaction, a lot of customers or clientele is lost and the marketer suffers losses.

To avoid this, a marketer has to be on the look out for causes of dissatisfaction and maintain and build consumer satisfaction. This can be done by regularly monitoring consumer reaction. It can be done by interviewing the consumer or serving questionnaires and analysing and interpreting them carefully. Besides this, a strict vigil is to be kept on the quality of the product. The quality should be the joint responsibility of marketing and production. If necessary, other departments should also be involved, and an integrated marketing procedure be followed.

In case of complaints, they must be given proper attention and redressal be made as soon as possible. All complaints must also be acknowledged to satisfy and assure the customer that appropriate action will be taken as soon as possible. While registering complaints, due courtesy should be shown to visiting customers and their complaints be entertained in a proper manner. To avoid dissatisfaction of the consumer, only realistic claims be made—i.e. advertisement of a scooter giving 55 km. per litre may be unrealistic when it can give a maximum of 40 km. This unrealistic claim made by the manufacturer may lead to dissatisfaction of the consumer. The marketer must also help train the consumer for the proper use of the product. If the product is not used in the way it is meant to be used, it gets spoilt, and does not perform upto expectation leading to a discrepancy between the actual and the desired which leads to dissatisfaction of the consumer. A marketer must also assure after sales service and keep in touch with the consumer even after purchase, to give him the promised after sales facility, as well as, importance to the consumer. A marketer must also sell solutions instead of the product. He should emphasise upon the felt need and fulfill it, rather than emphasise the product. He should take care of the marketing concept. If this is not taken care of, it becomes injurious in the long run.

In case of dissatisfaction post purchase dissonance occurs which creates anxiety and the consumer feels psychologically uncomfortable. The consumer reduces the negative information received by the following methods.

- Ignoring the dissonance information.
- By selectively interpreting the information.
- By lowering the level of expectation.
- By seeking +ve information about the brand.
- By convincing themselves that the purchase was right.

If the disparity between performance and expectation is not great an assimilation effect occurs and consumers ignore the product's defects and their evaluation is +ve. If the disparity is great a contrast effect takes place and repeat purchase does not take place.

Product v/s Service Consumption

Products are tangible while services are intangible and the consumption experience is more variable while travelling one trip can be pleasant, other trips may be unpleasant. Once the service can be courteous then it can be discourteous. It is therefore difficult for consumers to assess services rather them products. Therefore marketers must reduce service variability and build a long term customer relationship. (Relationship Marketing)

Re Donald stresses on uniformity in service, training etc. Products are bought for their utility, feeling of independence, self image etc.

Questions

1. What is satisfaction and dissatisfaction? How is it formed?
2. What are the factors leading to satisfaction and dissatisfaction and, what are the responses of a dissatisfied customer?
3. How should a marketer try to do away with the dissatisfaction of the consumer? What should be his role?

16

Family Buying Influences, Family Life Cycle and Buying Roles

Help your children to take and make decisions, educate them with examples and stories. The road to success is filled with women pushing their husbands along.

A family is a cohesive social unit, and the members have a great influence on each other and play an important role in decision-making. The goal of this chapter is to make the student understand:

- Reciprocal influence of family members on each other
- Family buying influences
- Intergenerational influence
- Family life cycle
- Consumption pattern

INTRODUCTION

A family is two or more people living together who are related by blood or marriage. It is a part of a household which consists of individuals living singly or together with others in a residential unit.

Consumer behaviour is influenced not only by consumer personalities and motivations, but also by the relationships within families (family is a familiar social unit).

In a family, members must satisfy their individual and shared needs by drawing on a common and shared, relatively fixed supply of sources.

The individual family is a strong, most immediate and most pervasive influence on decision-making.

The husband, wife and children influence each other and are influenced by others.

A consumer is influenced by many factors as shown below:

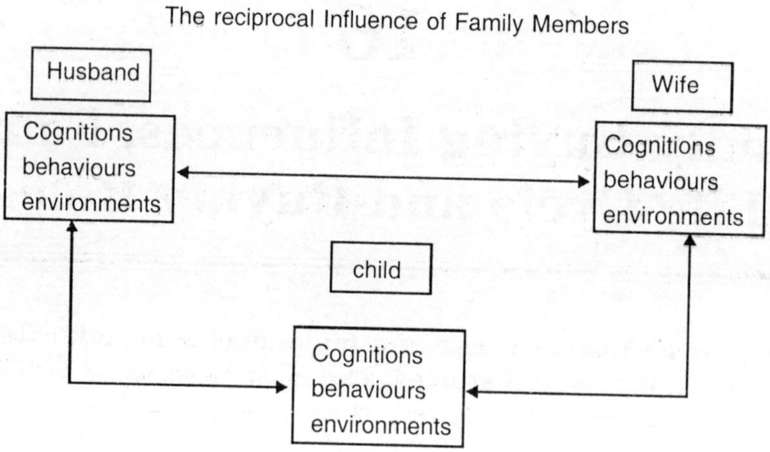

Fig. 16.1 The reciprocal influence of family members.

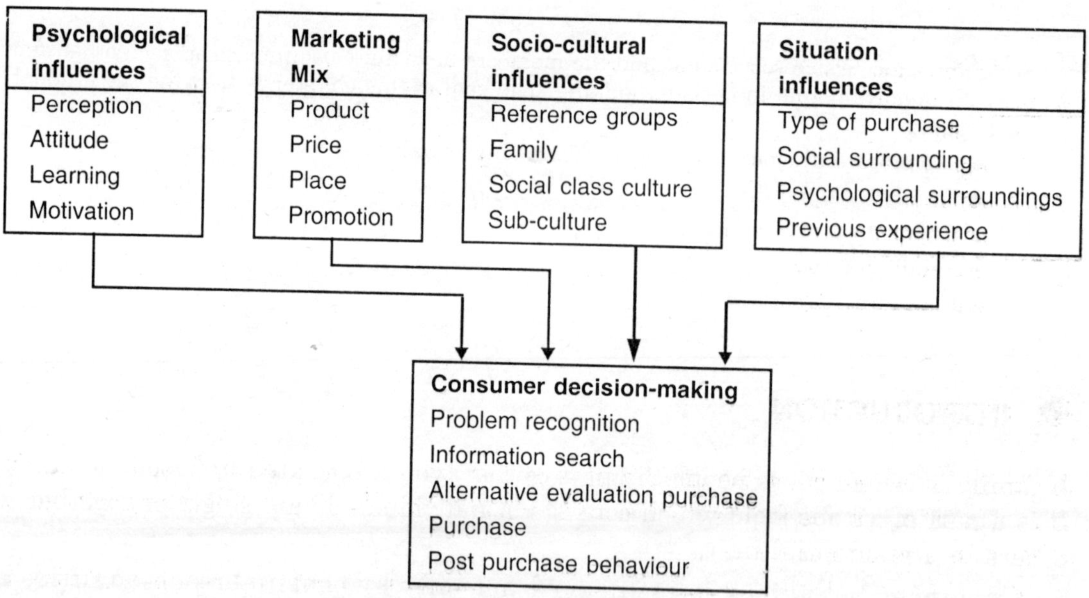

Fig.16.2 Factor influencing a consumer.

Family Life Cycle and Buying Roles

It is important for a marketer to know the family structure and its consumption characteristics. He should be able to understand the family which is a subset of a household. A household is made up of persons who live and occupy a housing unit.

These include both, nuclear and extended families. A household is a basic consumption unit for most consumable goods. Major items such as housing, automobiles, electrical appliances, washing machine, etc. are used more by households than individuals. In a household, many items can be shared and possessed, whereas individuals some times do not posses many such items individually.

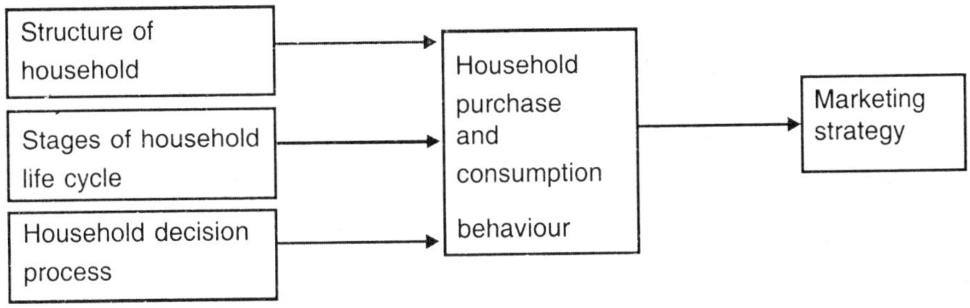

Fig. 16.3

Family types

Nuclear family: It consists of two adults of opposite sex living in a socially approved sex relationship with their children. It consists of husband, wife and their offspring.

Joint family: It includes a nuclear family and other relatives such as parents of husband/wife, aunts, uncles, and grandparents, also.

Consumption Decision and Household Influence

Family buying Influencces

Family is a social group. It is also an earning, consuming and decision-making unit. All purchases are influenced by family members. Family is a closely knit unit, and the bonds in a family are more powerful than in other groups. A reciprocal influence operates in all family decisions. There are three main influences which are father, mother and other family members. Every member has his own motives, beliefs and predisposition to the decision process. Every member is influenced and influences other family members. There is a reciprocal influence exerted in the decision process which is shown in Fig. 16.4. It becomes important for a marketer to sort out all family influences, and formulate a strategy for effective marketing.

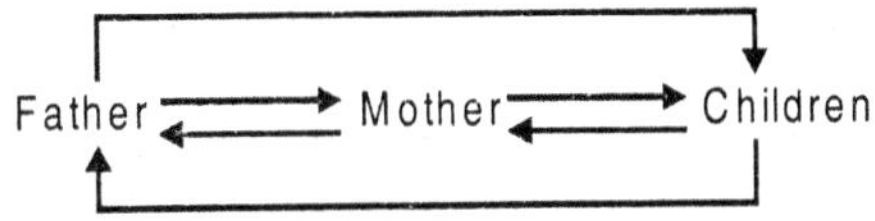

Fig. 16.4 Reciprocal influences in a family.

Consumer socialisation is the process by which young people acquire the skills, knowledge and attitudes relevant to their functioning as consumers. Interactions take place in a family which develops tastes, preferences, shopping styles, choice of clothes to wear. How much money to spend, where to buy from, what to use at which occasions. The figure shows how a consumer is socialised. There are a number of background factors like the age, sex, social class, etc. Then there are the socialising agents from whom they learn. These as media, family members, peers and teachers.

These influence the learning mechanism and the result is a socialised consumer. Advertising and promotional activities have a strong influence on consumer socialisation. It can also be done by the family members through:

(a) *Instrumental training:* In this the parent teaches the children the value of food, which to consume which to keep away from. What choice is to be made for clothes, what products to refrain from. How to avoid dysfunctional behaviour.

(b) *Modeling:* When a child learns the behaviour by observing others. It can be consciously or subconsciously learnt. One such example is smoking.

(c) *Mediation:* To make the children realise the facts by discussion, or by demonstration, or by any other method available.

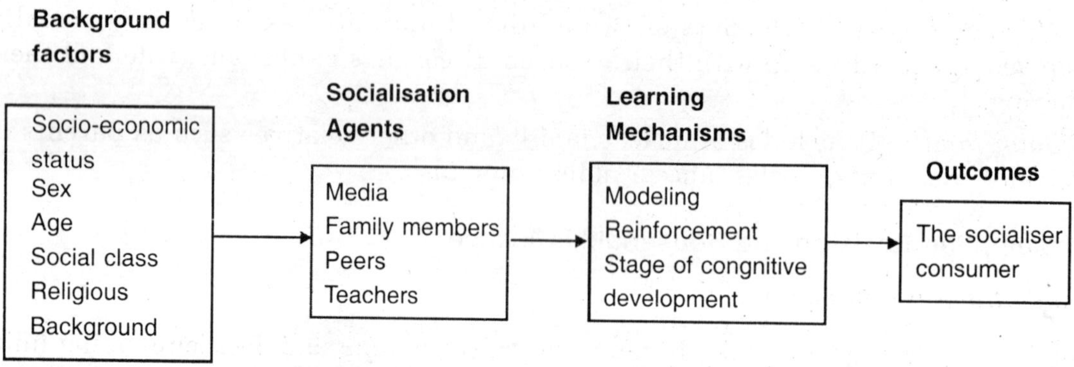

Fig. 16.5 A model of consumer socialisation.

Inter-generational influences

By this we mean that children learn from their fathers and forefathers. A child is influenced through generations, which develop religious and cultural values. The attitudes are developed towards sports, leisure, education, social life. This is known as the intergenerational carry over. Children learn to use products and services used by their family members, mostly parents and grand parents and some take pride in it too.

Family Decision-Making

In a family there is the

Instrument role: Taken by the head of the family for the achievement of special goals.

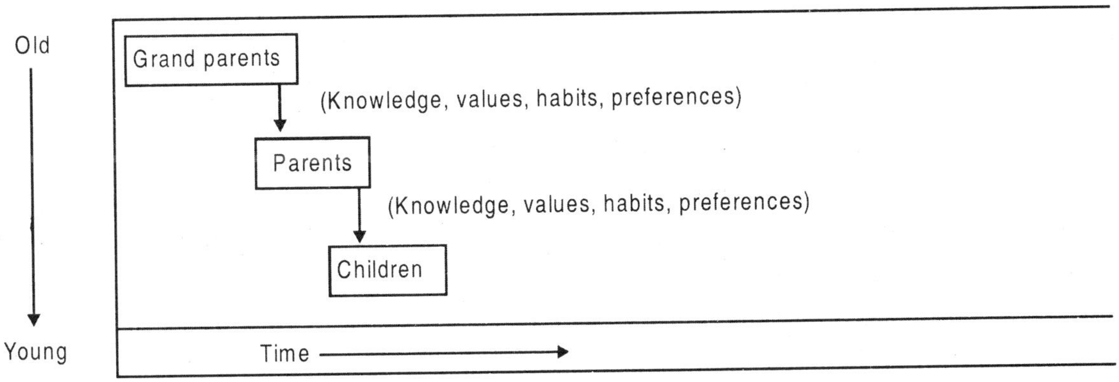

Fig. 16.6 The concept of intergenerational carry over.

Expressive role: Undertaken by the wife and other family members to provide emotional support.

Important buying roles are:

1. *The instigator* (initiator): Person who first suggests the idea of a product/service and initiates the purchase process.
2. *The influencer:* Person having direct/indirect influences, on final purchase decision.
3. *The decider:* Person who makes the final decision.
4. *The purchase* (buyer): Person who actually purchases the product, pays for it, takes it home.
5. *The consumer:* User of goods/service.

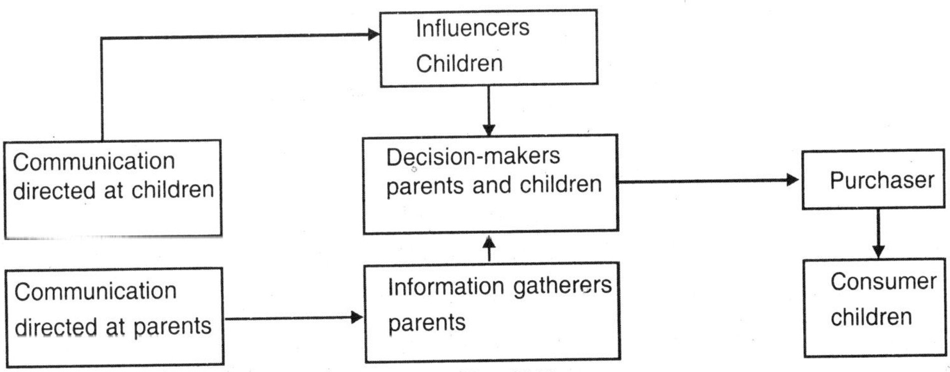

Fig. 16.7

Family Decision Stages

1. Problem recognition
2. Search for information

3. Evaluation of alternatives
4. Final decision

Husband-wife influence studies, classify consumer decisions as:

Wife—dominant decisions, e.g. food, purchase of groceries.

Husband—dominant decisions, e.g. automobiles, life insurance.

Syncratic decisions (joint), e.g. vacations, choice of schools for children.

Automatic decisions (unilateral)

Decisions may either be:

Consensual: Everyone in the family may agree with the desired outcome.

Accommodative: Need conflict resolution by persuasion or bargaining.

Element of power within the family is obtained from:

Economic resources: Persons making greater economic contribution have more economic power.

Cultural norms: In a male dominated society—husband has greater powers.

Expert power: More knowledge a person possess. Husband may know more about cars—wife my know more about household items.

Legitimate power: This depends on the role the family members play.

Bargaining power: Power through give and take method.

Reward/referent power: Giving rewards to others which are liked and appreciated.

Emotional power: Purchase decisions are influenced by emotions, sentiments and feelings of one partner.

The family life cycle stages

1. The bachelor stage—young and single.
2. The newly married couples—young, no children.
3. Full nest 1—young, married, with child.
4. Full nest 2—older, married, with children.
5. Full nest 3—older, married, with dependent children.
6. Empty nest—older, married, with no children living with them.
7. Solitary survivor—older, single, retired people.

1. *The bachelor stage:* Young and single is characterised by being young which can stretch upto 35 years of age and not married. Some singles live with their family, others live independently. They have an average age of about 24 and are free from worldly cares, live an active and carefree life. They do not have financial obligations. They manage their affairs themselves, and are fond of sports and other recreational activities.

2. *Newly married couples:* Young no children (empty nest). After getting married, the life style changes slightly. They lead a joint life style. They share new

experiences and responsibilities. Start spending on furnishing and household goods. They also tend to have a dual income and spend heavily on outings, vacations, luxury, restaurants, meals, etc.

3. *Full nest 1:* Young married with child. With the addition in family, purchases are concentrated on baby foods, clothings, medical care, health products. A change is brought about in the lifestyle and most activities revolve round the care of the child. Discretionary funds are also reduced.

4. *Full nest 2:* Older married with children. More children lead to more expenses. Children start going to school and there is more expenditure on books, stationery and college fees. Toys, bicycle, insurances also become a part of the expenses, parents start spending less on themselves.

5. *Full nest 3:* Older married with dependent children. Income is high at this stage. Parents grow older. They become experienced buyers and are less interested in new product purchases. Expenditure high due to replacement buying luxury products.

6. *Empty nest:* Older married with no children living with them. Financial position stabilises and there is no expense on children. The couple is free to enjoy their own pursuits and spend on luxury or self improvement items and medical care.

7. *Solitary survivor:* Older single retired people. Retired people living alone, after the death of a partner. Life becomes lonely and income may reduce due to retirement. This again changes the consumption pattern and living style of old people.

Another point to note, is that the family life cycle concept segments the families on the basis of demographic variables, and ignores the psychographic variables (families interest and opinions) of family members. Family life cycle is also related to the spare time and the available income, education, etc. A marketer has to take these elements into consideration.

The stages at which families find themselves, affect the nature of the goods and services required, their wants and consumption patterns, as well as the volume of consumption on specific products.

Table 16.1 Consumption patterns of families in life cycle strategy.

	Stage	*Consumption patterns*
1.	Young single (Bachelor)	Outdoor sporting goods, sports cars, fashion clothing. Entertainment and recreation services.
2.	Young married with no children	Recreation and relaxation, insurance, home furnishings, travel, home appliances, high purchase rate of durables.
3.	Yound married with child	Baby food, clothing, and furniture, invests in housing insurance, washer-dryers, medical services/supplies for children, toys for children.
4.	Middle aged with children at home	Children's lessons, large food purchases, dental care, higher priced furniture, auto and housing, fast-food restaurants.

5.	With no children at home	Luxury products, travel, restaurants, condominiums, recreation, make gifts and contributions, high discretionary income, solid financial position.
6.	Older (married or single)	Health care, home security, specialised housing, food products, recreation geared to the retired, general cash poor.
7.	Solitary survivor	Money-saving products, frozen foods, rental house, child care, time-saving appliances and food, cash poor.

The traditional view of the family life cycle has been criticised for failing to recognise that a single family unit may not exist throughout the life of an individual. Families may be created by second marriages, and these may involve children from prior marriages. The traditional model also ignores the existence of single parent households. The modern family life cycle which takes into account the existence of working women, is a more complex and more useful model than the traditional model.

Marketing strategy for family decision-making

It is realised that various purchasing tasks are performed by various members of the family. The products are bought for joint use of the family. Refrigerator, TV, sofa set, car, etc. The product is to be purchased by family funds where more than one person may be contributing to the fund. Sometimes the funds are not enough and other products may have to be sacrificed to own an expensive product. Some family members may not be agreeable to the choice made for the product, and may consider it as a profligate expenditure. These are the main influences in the family decision-making, which are the outlets preferred by the family members for the purchase of the product. All the above considerations are important, and once all this is known strategy can be formulated in a better manner.

Questions

1. How is consumer behaviour influenced by relationships within families? Discuss with context to various family types.
2. Discuss the family lifestyle stages and the changing consumption patterns?

17

Lifestyle

It is your attitudes, interests and opinions that project your lifestyle.

Our lifestyles or patterns of living are changing fast and are determined by our activities, interest and opinions, and this affects our consumption pattern.

This chapter imparts knowledge about:

- Lifestyles and their characteristics
- VALS lifestyles classification
- Segmentation strategies

INTRODUCTION

It is defined simply as how one lives, and spends money. It is determined by our past experiences, innate characteristics and current situations. The products we consume are related to our lifestyle. Lifestyle marketing establishes a relationship between the products offered in the market and targeted lifestyle groups. Lifestyles segmentation is based on activities and interest and opinions of groups. These are psychrographic segmentations, and lifestyles are derived from psychographics. Lifestyle is a unified pattern of behaviour that determines consumption and, is also in turn determined by it.

Demographic and psychographic lifestyles are complimentary and work best together. Demographic variables help marketers "locate" the target market, and psychographics provides more insight into the segment by taking into their activities interests and opinions.

An idea of AIO studies is provided as above on next page:

Table 17.1

Activities	*Interest*	*Opinions*	*Demographics*
Work	Family	Themselves	Age
Hobbies	Home	Social issues	Education
Social events	Job	Politics	Income
Vacation	Community	Business	Occupation
Entertainment	Recreation	Economics	Family size
Club member	Fashion	Education	Geography
Community	Food	Products	City size
Shopping	Media	Future	Life cycle
Sports	Achievements	Culture	Dwelling

Source: Joseph T. Plummer—The concept application of lifestyle dimensions journal of marketing.

Activities: Activities can be described as how one spends his time.

Interest: Interest are a person's priorities and preferences.

Opinions: It is how one feels about a wide variety of events.

Marketers try to find out the activities, interests, and opinions of people by questions to be answered on a rating scale. This is done to find out how strongly one agrees or disagrees with the question.

Characteristics of Lifestyle

1. Lifestyle is a group phenomenon which influences others in the society. A person having a particular lifestyle can influence others in a social group.

2. Lifestyle influences all areas of one's activities. A person having a certain lifestyle shows consistency of behaviour in other areas as well. You can always predict that a person shopping from elite or speciality stores, would not shop from common places. The same applies to eating habits and other habits as well.

3. *Lifestyle implies a central life interst:* A person may have interest in education, leisure, adventure work, sexual exploits, etc. which may become their main interest in life.

4. *Social changes in society affect lifestyles:* For example, as the society becomes more affluent, lifestyles of people change, sometimes drastically. As one would become richer ones lifestyle changes accordingly.

Lifestyle Segmentation

This is known as value and lifestyle segmentation and was introduced in 1978 by Arnold Mitchell. It provides a systematic classification of American adults into nine segments. These were widely used. Despite its popularity, some managers felt that the nine segments given by VALS are not appropriate, as two of the sements cover one-third of the entire population, leaving the rest to be divided into 7 segments, which become too small to be of interest to many firms. These nine segments are shown in Fig. 17.1.

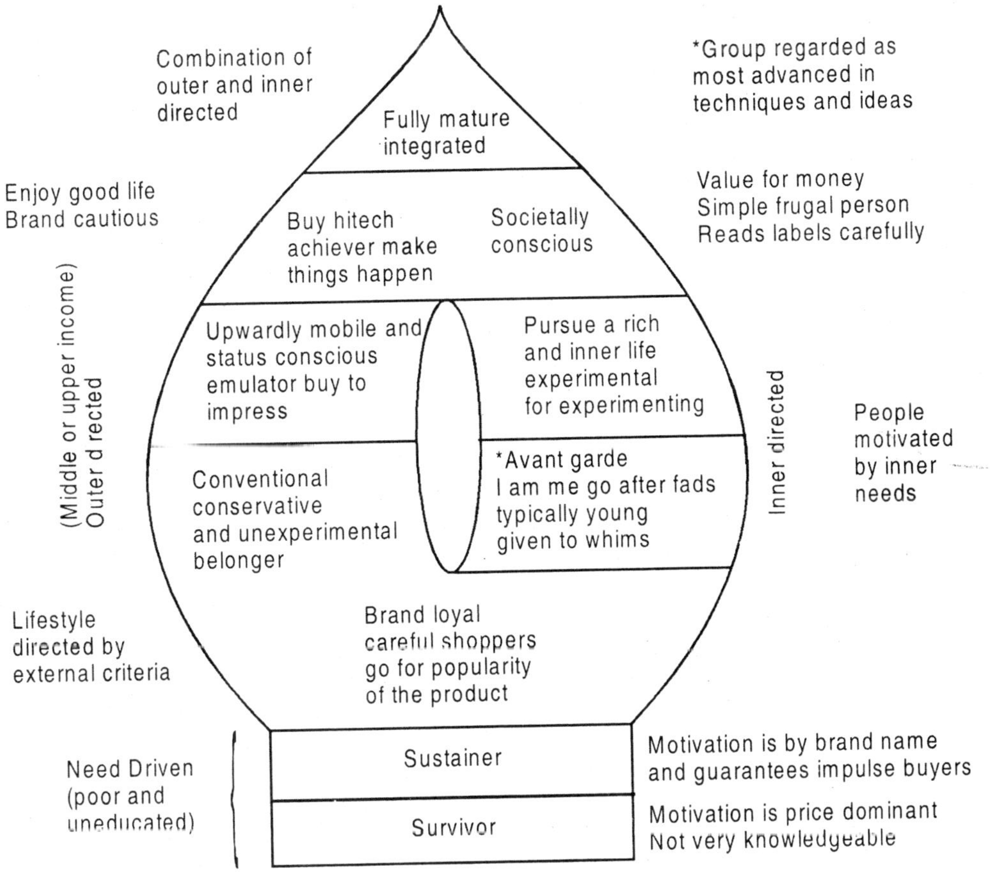

Fig. 17.1 Values and lifestyle segments (VALS).

The figure shows four major groups or classification:

(a) *Need driven:* (poor and uneducated).

(b) *Outer directed:* (middle or upper income class consumer whose lifestyle is directed by external criteria).

(c) *Inner directed:* (people motivated by inner needs rather than by the expectation of others).

(d) *Integrated:* (this group combines the best of outer and inner directed. They are fully matured).

A further break-up of these groups is shown in the figure, and their characteristics can be described as given below:

1. *Survivors:* They are disadvantaged people, who are poor, depressed and withdrawn. Their purchases are price dominant, and they like to buy products which are economical and suit their pocket. They are not very knowledgeable.

2. *Sustainers:* They are motivated by brand names. They look for guarantee and are impulse buyers. These people are disadvantaged and want to get out of poverty.

3. *Belongers:* They buy products which are popular. They are careful and brand loyal shoppers. They are people who are conventional, conservative, and unexperimental.

4. *Emulators:* They are status conscious and upwardly mobile. They emulate others, and buy products to impress other people. They have high aspirations in life.

5. *Achievers:* They buy top of the line products. They are brand conscious and loyal. They are leaders and make things happen. They want to enjoy a good life.

6. *I am me:* These people are typically young, self engrossed and given to whims. They go after fads and do not mind taking the lead.

7. *Experimentals:* These people pursue a rich inner life and want to directly experience what life has to offer.

8. *Societally conscious people:* They are simple, frugal persons, who read labels carefully and seek information. They are conscious of society and social responsibility. They want to improve conditions in society.

9. *Integrated:* These are fully matured people and constitute the best of outer and inner directed.

These segments did not appeal to many marketers and therefore, VALS 2 was introduced in 1989. This system has more of a psychological base than the original, which was more activity and interest based. VALS 2 is based on attitudes and values. It is measured by 42 statements with which the respondents state a degree of agreement and disagreement.

It has identified three primary self orientations:

Principle oriented: They are guided by their beliefs and principles.

Status oriented; These individuals are heavily influenced by actions, approval and opinion of others.

Action oriented: They desire social and physical activity, variety and risk taking.

These three orientations determine the types of goals and behaviours that consumers will pursue, and the goods they will get interested in.

VALS 2 segments, consists of eight general psychographic segments as shown in Fig. 17.2

This classification is based on Maslow's hierarchy of needs. At the bottom are the people with minimal resources and, on the top we have people with abundant resources. This divides the consumer into 3 general groups or segments. Each of these segments have a distinctive lifestyle, attitude and decision-making. The figure shows their characteristics as well. The eight segments also differ in their resources and orientations. The resources possessed by those at the bottom are very little and as we move upwards the resources increase. Besides money and physical resources, people at the bottom lack in education, social resources, psychological resources and

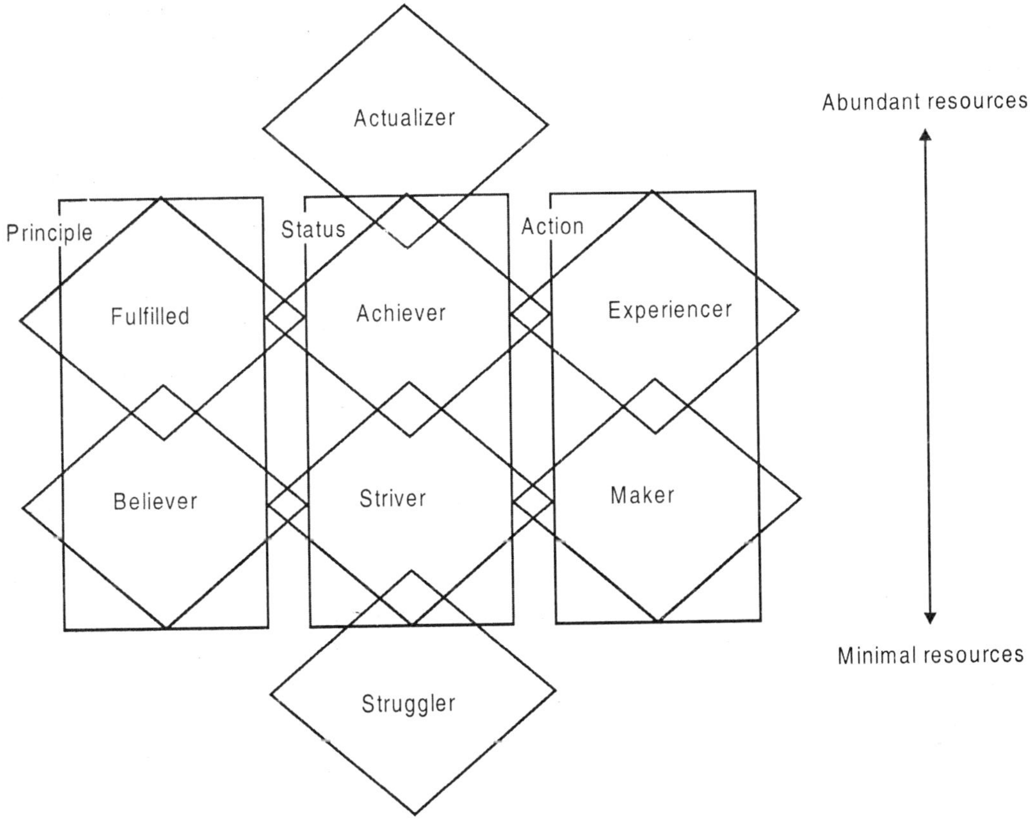

Fig. 17.2 Values and lifestyle segments (VALS)

in self confidence. These studies were made on American people. The demographic characteristics like, age, income, occupation, role, religion, sex education, marital status can easily be identified. However, it is more difficult to identify psychographic characteristics of attitudes, beliefs interests, benefits, lifestyle, etc. This can be done by VALS segmentation.

For a segment to be worthwhile, it must have a proper size, i.e. enough number of people in the segment to make it feasible. It must be stable, so that the people belonging to a segment not only remain there, but the segment must also grow in size. The segment must also be accessible, so that the marketer is able to reach the segment in an economical way. They can be reached through various media. Marketers also are on the lookout for new media that can reach the audience with minimum waste, circulation and competition. The segment should be such that profits can be gained. By catering to a segment, profits must be ensured. Profits are the backbone of any organisation. The target segment has to be profitable.

Strugglers

These are poor people, struggling for existence. Education is low, low skilled, without strong social bonds. They are despairing and, have a low status in society. Their chief concern is to fulfil their primary needs of physiological security and safety needs. They represent a modest market and are loyal to their favourite brands.

Makers

They are in the action oriented category. They have construction skills and value self sufficiency. Makers experience the work by working on it. They are people engaged in construction work and work with their hands and in the industry. They are politically conservative, suspicious of new ideas, they buy stuff which helps them in achieving their purpose. They buy tools, pick up trucks and, all that helps them in practical work.

Strivers

They are a status oriented category, but have a low income as they are striving to find a secure place in life. They are low in economic, Social and psychological resources. They are concerned about the opinion of others. They see success with money. They like to be stylish. They wish to be upwardly mobile and strive for more.

Believers

They are in the principle oriented category. They are conservative, conventional people, with their needs, strong faiths, and beliefs. Have modest resources sufficient to meet their needs. They are conservative and predictable. Use established brands.

Experiencers

They are action oriented, young, vital, enthusiastic, impulsive and rebellious. They have enough resouces and experiment in new ventures. They indulge in exercise, sports, outdoor recreation and social activities. They are avid consumers and spend much on entertainment, clothing, food, music, videos, movies, etc. This pattern of behaviour changes, as they are enthusiastic to new ideas.

Achievers

They are also placed high in the Maslow's hierarchy of needs and are career and work oriented. They make their dreams come true. They are workaholics. Work provides them with a sense of duty, material rewards and prestige. They live conventional lives, authority and image is important to them. They also favour established products and show their success around.

Fulfilled

As the name suggests, they are satisfied and mature people who are well educated, value order, knowledge and responsibility. They are practical consumers and conservative. They look for products which are durable, have value and function properly. They are well informed about the world, and are ready to increase their knowledge. Prefer leisure at home.

Actualisers

They have abundant resources and are sophisticated in their taste and habits. They are active, and have high self esteem. They develop, explore and express themselves in a variety of ways. They have taste and are leaders in business, and in government. They have wide interests and are concerned with social issues and are open to change.

While designing a marketing strategy, a company can employ a concentrated marketing strategy or, a differentiated marketing strategy or, even a counter-segmentation strategy, depending on the need and requirements.

Concentrated Marketing Strategy

In this there is one segment with a unique marketing mix designed for that particular segment.

Differentiated Marketing Mix

Each target segment receives a special designed marketing mix, that is, for each market we have a special mix consisting of product, price, promotion and place. Here we target several markets with different marketing mixes. This is called differentiated marketing. This is used by firms which are financially strong and well established in a product category and compete with other firms, that are also strong in the same product category (soft drinks, automobiles, detergents). For a small company concentrated marketing is a better bet.

Counter Segmentation

When a firm practices differentiated marketing strategy in different target markets, some segments tend to shrink, so that they do not have enough size and promise, and are not worthwhile to be worked upon separately. They are merged together or recombined for better handling. This is known as counter segmentation strategy.

Lifestyle marketing is being used extensively these days for developing new products, positioning new products and, creating new product opportunity. Lifestyle research helps in selecting media, formulating media and promotional strategies, and improving retail performance.

Questions

1. What is lifestyle marketing? Explain its characteristics?
2. Explain VALS segmentation. Why importance was given to VALS 2 segmentation?

3. Explain VALS segmentation given by Arnold Mitchell and explain the various categories.
4. Explain VALS 2 segmentation with a diagram.
5. Differentiate and explain concentrated marketing, differentiated marketing and counter segmentation.

18

Diffusion of Innovation

Do not wait for the best idea, implement the better idea, still better, and the best will follow.
God grant me the serenity to accept the things I cannot change, change the things I can, and the wisdom to know the difference.

This chapter gives an understanding of:

- Diffusion and its process
- Types of innovation
- Classification of adopters
- Diffusion enhancement strategies

◆ INTRODUCTION

Diffusion is process by which a new product is accepted and spreads through a market. It is a group phenomenon, in which first an idea is perceived, then it spreads through out the market, and then individuals and groups adopt the product.

Definition

Diffusion is a process by which the acceptance of an innovation/new product, a new idea, a new service, is spread by communication to members of a social system over a period of time.

◆ INNOVATION

An innovation is an idea, practice, or product, perceived to be new by an individual or a group. A product is said to be an innovation when it is perceived by the potential market as a change, and not by a technological change brought in it.

New products or new services have been classified as under:

Firm Oriented

If the product is new to the company, it is said to be new.

Product Oriented

It focusses on the features inherent in the product and the effect it has on the consumer's established usage pattern. This leads to three types of product innovation—continuous, dynamically continuous, discontinuous innovation.

Market Oriented

It stresses on how much exposure consumers have to the new product:

(i) It can be new if purchased by a small percentage of consumers in the market.

(ii) It is new if it has been for a relatively short period in the market.

Consumer Oriented Items

It is based on the consumer's perception of the product. If he judges it to be new. For example, the Polaroid camera can be considered as an innovation, because a whole lot of people who constitute the market, use it, and can get photographs in minutes. Microwave oven for example is an innovation. It does wonders for cooking and warming of foods. Similarly, mobile phones (cell phones) can be considered an innovation. Not only are they popular, but they were unthinkable a decade or two back. Innovation can be of various degrees. For instance, a microwave oven is more of an innovation than sugar free cola. In innovation, behavioural changes take place. These behavioural changes can be small, modest, or large. The innovation can be continuous or, dynamically continuous or, discontinuous.

Continuous innovation

In this type of innovation, minor behavioural changes are required for adoption of the product, from ordinary cookware to Teflon coated cookware, where minor behavioural changes are required. A modified product, e.g. a new scuba watch, new car model or, low fat yogurt, etc.

Dynamically continuous innovation

Communicator behavioural changes are required for the adoption of the product. Products in this category include compact disk players, cellular phones, erasable ink pen and disposable diapers.

TV has led to related innovation

Table 18.1 TV has led to related innovation.

Discontinuous Innovation	→	*Dynamically continuous Innovation*	→	*Continuous Innovation*
Black and white TV ↓ Video cassette recorder ↓ Video camera	→	Colour TV Portable pocket TV Stereo TV Giant screen TV Cable ready TV Picture in picture TV ↓ Video walkman	→	Remote control various cabinet styles instant on flat screen Electronic tuning Stereo sound

Discontinuous innovation

Here the adoption of the product requires major behavioural changes and the product is new, and requires high involvements of the user, alongwith extended decision-making, which consists of the following steps;

Table 18.2

Stages in adoption process	*Steps in extended decision-making*
Awareness	Problem recognition
↓	↓
Interest	Information search
↓	↓
Evaluation	Alternative evaluation
↓	↓
Trial	Purchase
↓	↓
Adoption	Post-purchase evaluation

Diffusion process

Diffusion process is the manner in which innovations spread throughout the market. Spread refers to the purchase behaviour where a product is purchased with some continuing regularity. Spread of innovation can be of three types as shown in the Fig. 18.1 on next page 155.

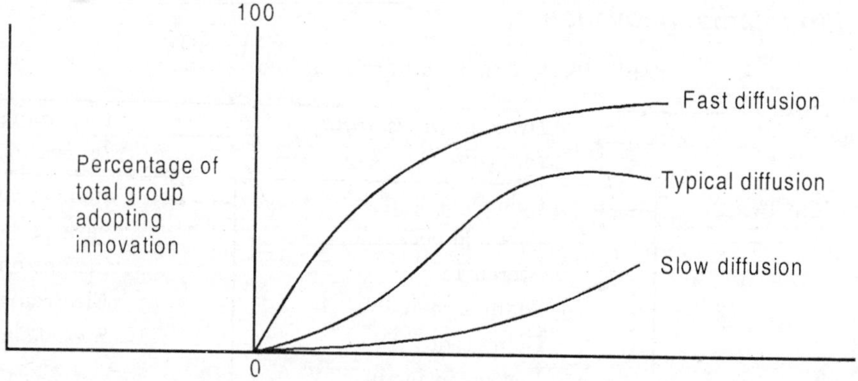

Fig. 18.1 Three types of innovation spread.

The diffusion process follows a similar pattern, overtime, irrespective of the social group or innovation. *The typical diffusion* process shows a slow growth or adoption. It later rises rapidly, and then a period of slow growth is noticed. In *fast diffusion* process, the product clicks immediately. The spread of innovation is very quick. People patronise the product immediately, and later on there is again slow diffusion.

In *slow diffusion* process, the product takes a lot of time to diffuse or spread, and the consumer follows a pattern of adoption slowly by getting acquainted with the product.

These studies show that the products take a certain amount of time, from when it gets introduced to its saturation. The marketer therefore has to understand what determines the spread of innovation in a given market segment, and how do the early buying consumers differ from those of late purchasers.

The rate of *spread of innovation* depands on a number of factors listed below:

1. *Type of group:* Some groups who are young, affluent and highly educated, accept changes faster than the old, traditional and poor groups. This shows that the target market is an important determinant of the rate of diffusion.

2. *Perceived risk:* The more the risk associated with changing to new innovation, the slower is the rate of diffusion. The risk consists of the product not performing as expected, the risk of the consequences of change-over, and the risk of reverting back to the old product, if not satisfied with the innovative product.

3. *Type of decision:* An individual, vs a collective decision. Individual decisions lead to faster diffusion than collective ones.

4. *Marketing effort:* This also affects the diffusion process. More aggressive marketing effort, consisting of high and continuous advertising expenditure, diffuses faster than otherwise.

5. *Trial:* The trial can be taken at low cost and low risk, the diffusion is faster. Some products can be borrowed, rented or, their trial can be taken at retail outlets. These products like medicines, and other low priced items have faster diffusion.

These days even car outlets are giving free trials and rides to prospective customers, to make their new models of cars diffuse faster.

6. *Fulfilment of felt need:* The faster a need is satisfied or fulfilled by a product, the greater is the rate of its diffusion.

7. *Compatibility:* The more the product is compatible with the beliefs, attitudes and values of the individual or group the faster the diffusion—vegetables soup for vegetarians, ordinary microwave no roasting

8. *Relevant advantage:* The advantage could be of price, quality, ease of handling, product quality. To have quick diffusion, the product must offer either a price advantage or a performance advantage. Washing machine is expensive, but a labour saving device.

9. *Complexity:* If the product is complex (difficult to understand and use) the diffusion is slower. The product may be complex but its use must be easy. Complexity may be because of many attributes (attributes complexity which are difficult to understand). The other complexity may be trade off complexity. The trade off takes place between cost of purchase and economy. Convenience vs space or speed of cooking, vs quality of cooking, as in microwave ovens.

10. *Observability:* The more easily the positive effects of the products can be observed, the more discussion takes place and faster the diffusion process, e.g. cell phones.

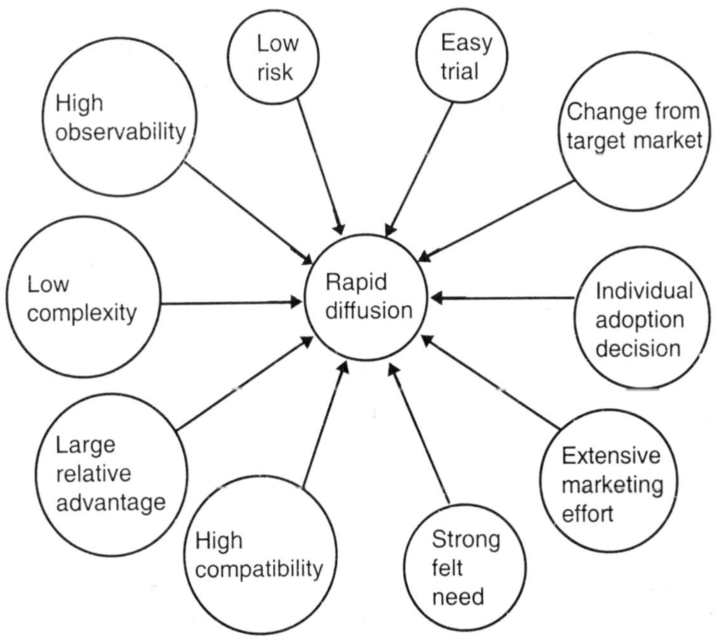

Fig. 18.2 Rapid rate of diffusion.

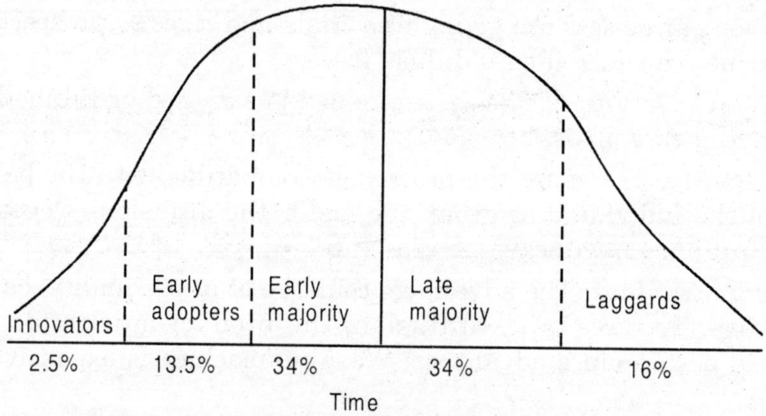

Fig. 18.3 Slow diffusion.

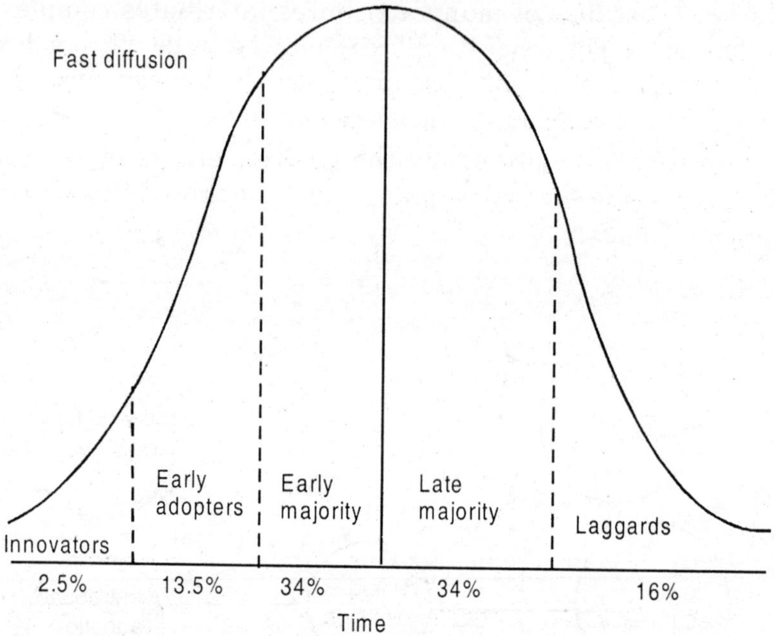

Fig. 18.4 Fast diffusion.

Classification of Adopters

Adopters can be classified into five groups based on the time when they adopt.

Innovators: The first 2.5 per cent to adopt innovation.

Early adopters: The next 13.5 per cent to adopt.

Early majority: The next 34 per cent to adopt.

Late majority: The next 34 per cent to adopt.

Laggards: The final 16 per cent to adopt.

nnovators (2.5%)

nnovators are venture some risk takers. They are younger, more educated and ocially mobile. They have the capacity to absorb risk associated with the new roduct. They are cosmopolitan in outlook, are aware and make use of commercial nedia, and eager to learn about new products, are progressive, ready to use new roducts.

arly adopters (13.5%)

hey take a calculated risk before investing and using new innovations. They are pinion leaders and provide information to groups, but they are also concerned about ailure. Therefore, they weigh advantages and disadvantages of the product before lunging in for a purchase.

arly majority (34%)

hey tend to be more continuous and use the product after the innovators and early dopters seem to be satisfied with it. They are elders, well educated and less socially nobile. They rely heavily on inter-personal source of information. They constitute 34 er cent of the consumers.

ate majority (34%)

They are doubtful and sceptical about the innovation of new products. They tend to se the product not so much because of innovation, but because of other pressures— on-availability of the product and social pressures. They have less social status, and re less socially mobile than previous group. They are average in age, education ocial income. They make little use of media (Magazine etc). They rely heavily on nformal sources of information.

Laggards (16% of a Market)

They are more traditional. They possess limited social interaction and are oriented to he past. They adopt the innovations with great reluctance. They constitute a small portion of 16 percent of the consumers. They have the least education, lowest social status & income. They possess no opinion leadership and are in touch with other aggards and donot subscribe to many magazines.

Market strategy related to diffusion

There are differences in the early purchasers or innovators and late purchasers (Laggards). The strategy for the target market adopted, is a "moving target market" approach. First the general target market is selected, and then the focus shifts to innovators, early adopters, early majority, late majority and laggards. This takes place as the product keeps getting acceptance from the consumers. There is then a change in the media and advertising themes for different target groups.

Diffusion enhancement strategies

The idea is to find out the diffusion inhibitors and to eliminate them for the enhancement of diffusion. For this the diffusion determinants are analysed, and diffusion strategies framed, as given in Table 18.3.

Table 18.3

	Diffusion determinant	*Diffusion inhibitor*	*Diffusion enhancement strategies*
1.	Type of group	Conservative traditional	Try other markets modern and consumer
2.	Perceived risk	High	Give guarantees, reduce risk by endorsing with credible sources
3.	Type of decision	Group decisions	Choose media to reach all deciders and provide conflict reduction themes
4.	Marketing effort	Limited	Extensive and aggressive marketing effort
5.	Trial	Difficult	Distribute free samples to early adopters. Use high service outlets
6.	Fulfilment of felt need	Weak	Show importance of benefits use extensive advertising
7.	Compatibility	Conflict	Stress attributes consistent with values and norms
8.	Relevant advantage	Low	Lower the price—redesign the product
9.	Complexity	High	Use extensive marketing effort. Use skilled sales force. Use demonstration of product
10.	Observability	Low	Expose the product more through promotion and advertising

These diffusion inhibitors have to be analysed, and strategies formulated accordingly.

Adoption & Diffusion Through Marketing Strategy

Marketers have been trying to influence consumers to adopt new innovations. This is done through free samples and price promotions. Advertising is done extensively, when the results are not found positive by distribution of free samples and promotions. Some time Price Promotions and free samples are backed by advertising techniques. Some times change agents are used to overcome resistance to adoption. For medical products, hospitals, clinics and physicians of repute are used as change agents.

Rate of Diffusion—The rate of diffusion can be low or high. Marketers have 2 options that can infrluence the rate of diffusion.

Skimming Strategy—This strategy used for major innovations and when the product is in great demand. Prices are set high and it has slow rate of diffusion. The strategy aims at skimming the cream of the market i.e. to take advantage and get the profits in abundance. The sigment is small and specific. The segment is price insensitive. It has its own lifestyles and demographic characteristics, awareness and information advertising is used in this case. The distribution is done from selective outlets.

Penetration Strategy—In this there is rapid and widespread diffusion as the product is of low value and is within the reach of many. The product is sold to a General Market by an intensive campaign. The distribution is extensive and the product used is general. It is used in new products which are not major innovations like Cold Drink, health drinks, Coffee etc. The advertising is widespread other means of promotion is also used.

The distribution is extensive and covering as many outlets as possible. The price is low and the product is available. The strategy keeps changing with its position on the diffusion curve. All ececyronic products of major innovation start with the skimming strategy and gradually move down to penetration strategy. The price of computers, Television sets, microwave, ovens etc. start with a high price and as the product is adopted and many more competitors come in the skimming strategy is changed to penetration strategies. Some products start with a penentration strategy and raise their prices with the widespread acceptance of the product in the market.

Marketing Strategies and Rate of Diffusion

Rate of diffusion	*Slow*	*Fast*
Marketing Strategy	Skimming	Penetration
Price	High	Low
Market Segmentation	Target market is specific and small lifestyles and demographics are considered	Target market is large difficult to specify by lifestyles and demographics.
Promotion	Information and Advertising backed by personal selling and sales promotion	Repetitive advertising use of imagery and symbols.
Distribution	Selection through prominent stores	Intensive very large number of outlets.
Product Characteristics	Discontinuous Innovations	Continuous Innovation.

Questions

1. Explain innovation and diffusion. Discuss the stages in the adoption process.
2. What are various types of diffusion? List and explain the factors that are responsible for the spread of innovation.
3. What are the classification of adopters? Illustrate and explain with the help of a diagram.
4. What market strategy must be adopted for the spread of innovation or diffusion enhancement?

19

Organisational Buying Behaviour

Men may come and men may go, but the organisation goes on forever.
If your costs are going up, try lowering your prices by selling more.

Organisational buying behaviour is important as it is done for the organisation by a group of human beings constituting the power centre. One should understand the:

- Difference between consumer and organisational buying
- Characteristics of organisational buying
- Factors affecting organisational buying
- Risk factors and their reduction
- Buying situations
- Selection of a supplier

INTRODUCTION

Organisational buying is a complex process of decision-making and communication. It takes time, involves several members and considerations. Robinson, Faris and Wind have identified eight steps in organisational behaviour.

1. Need recognition
2. Definition of characteristic and quantity needed
3. Development of specification to guide the procurement
4. Search for and qualification of potential sources
5. Acquisition and analysis of proposals
6. Evaluation of proposals and selection of suppliers
7. Selection of an order routine
8. Performance feedback and evaluation.

Example Illustrating the Eight Steps in Organisational Buying Behaviour

Need recognition is the first step while making a purchase decision. The need may be for a machine which could bring efficiency in production or packing. It can be to provide a cool and comfortable working climate in the office. It may be a transportation need or, any requirement which is essential to carry on with the day to day work. The need can be fulfilled by various alternatives. A transportation need can be fulfilled by a scooter, a car, a mini truck or a van or any other way. Working cool climate can be provided by an air cooler or an air conditioner. A packing machine can be manual, semi-automatic or automatic.

Once the need is identified by a purchase committee, which may consist of the purchase officer, general manager, production manager and others, the type and quantity of the item needed are specified, i.e. the number of pieces to be bought. While specifying these, economic consideration are also important depending upon the work and economy of the company or/firm.

Once these things have been decided, quotations are asked for or, tenders are floated and the offers given by various interested parties which are then scrutinised and analysed on a number of criterion. These may be

1. Past reputation of the manufacturer.
2. The efficiency of the machine, the durability, economies of working, the design, etc. are considered.
3. Delivery period.
4. Terms of payment.
5. Guarantees given by the company.
6. Price.
7. After sales service, etc.

On the basis of the above a few firms are short listed and then again reviewed.

In certain cases there are recommendation by very high authorities which cannot be ignored. Although the order may have been decided in favour of a supplier, but recommendations and other factors may change the decision in favour of another supplier. If supplies are to be spread over the whole year or an extended period of time, an *order schedule* is prepared, instructing the suppliers to make supplies at required intervals of time. From the above example it is clear that organisational buying differs from consumer buying in many ways. Organisation buying has its own characteristics, as given below:

Characteristics of ORG Buying (O.B.B.)

1. *O.B. is a multi-person activity:* it is done by a team consisting of some important people in the organisation. These people come from many backgrounds and have different view points and notions which have to be integrated. They have different qualifications and hold different positions in the organisational hierarchy. They can be referred to as the buying centre, and play different roles.

User

The person who actually uses the product, like the person using the typewriter, computer, or the production department.

Influencer

The people who influence the buying like the purchase officer, the production manager, the design engineer, etc.

Decider

The committe appointed for purchases who decides what product and what quantity is to be purchased.

Gate keeper

Those who control the flow of information within the organisation.

Specifiers

These are the consultants or design people who develop the specifications of the product, or of the services required.

It is a formal activity: Unlike consumer behaviour, organisational buying is a formal activity, where rules and procedures are laid down. There is also a formal contract between a buyer and a seller. The terms and conditions of payment are also laid down. The time of supplies are also specified.

There is a larger time lag as compared to consumer buying:

As all procedures are to be followed, it takes much longer. The deciding of the purchase, quality, quantity and adherence to rules and regulations, the delivery of product, etc. may take quite some time.

2. *It is a formal activity:* The purchases are made according to certain procedures, rules and regulations. Some times quotations are asked for, and for higher amounts of purchases, tenders may be floated. These have to be given proper importance by advertising in news papers or by proper publicity. These are formally opened before a committee constituted for the purpose. Many aspects are looked into, but an important consideration is also the money or, the cost that is quoted for the product. All the activities are carried out in a judicial manner and with the consent of the committee.

3. *It is a rational but emotional activity:* By this we mean that we are dealing with people who are human beings and those who are dealing are also human beings. This gives rise to emotions and no matter how rational we tend to become, it is the human element that also comes into play, and many a time the order goes not to the most deserving candidate, but could tilt in the favour of somebody who may have connections, which may be political, or on the basis of friendships and relationships.

4. *There is a longer time lag between efforts and results:* In individual buying, th sales and the purchase may not last more than a dew minutes, but in industria buying, a lot of procedures have to be followed. These procedures lead to time delay It takes long to ask for quotations and tenders—once all the tenders have bee submitted, a date is fixed for opening the tenders, which is intimated to the partie concerned. Later the order is placed. The order takes a long time to complete as it i mostly a bulk order. Once the order is supplied, many times in instalments, th payment also takes time, and may get held up for many reasons. Thus, there is time lag between the effort and the results.

5. *Uniqueness of the organisation:* Every organisation is unique in some way o the other. Some are partnership firms, others could be private limited and publi limited companies. They have their own structure and their distinct culture. Thei objectives, resources and nature of buying is different.

Some firms like to pay cash, some always ask for credit. Others also pay i advance, some have limited resources, some have abundant resources. Thes influence the nature of buying as well. The objectives of a company could be to kee in tune with the modern times. Others may stick to traditional methods, some ar willing to change and welcome it, others resist change. These and other difference of the company influence organisational buying in a big way.

6. *There are fewer industrial buyers than individual buyers:* For example, a firr produces medicine which is bought by many individuals, or a firm making cosmetic is used by thousands of individuals.

7. The industries buy in bulk and in huge amounts, whereas, individua consumers buy in lesser and in smaller quantities.

8. Most industrial buyers are geographically concentrated in an area. We hav industrial estates or industrial houses, where most industries are concentrated.

9. *Reciprocal buying:* In this we follow the principle of "you buy from me, I bu from you".

The manufacturer buys raw material from the suppliers who sell his products a well.

10. *Middlemen role is reduced:* In organisational buying, the manufacturer mostl sells directly to the user or, the channel path is very small as compared to consume buying.

11. *Demand* of industrial goods is dependent on the demand of the consumer. I could be called derived demand. When there is a baby boon (more children are born the demand for baby products increases.

12. *Inelastic demand:* Price changes do not make much difference in the demand If the cost of cigarettes increase, smokers will buy cigarettes any way. Similarly people need to fulfill their genuine requirements irrespective of the change of price

Organisational Customers

We need to understand the organisational market. For making a car, many components are required, to market help of a distribution channel is required. It is a chain.

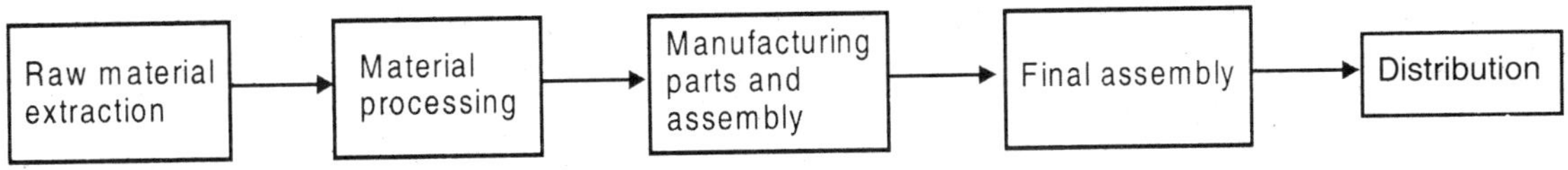

Fig. 19.1

The area is very vast and heterogeneous. Organisational marketing or "ghost" organisational customer, as the customer is huge and unlimited. There are many types of organisations with different classifications. These require different types of raw materials. In manufacturing a car one needs all types of material. Iron sheets to wires, to screws, bolts, iron strips. Elcctrical gadgets, battery, glass windows and screens, rubber goods, aluminium goods and, hundred of other materials. The suppliers of these materials also require raw materials for their use. Hence, there is an endless chain of suppliers of raw materials. What is a finished product for an industry, can become raw material for the other industry.

Organisation can be classified as *Industrial*—industries are scattered all over the country, and they constitue all organisations involved in manufacturing, assembling, fabrication, etc.

Institutional

These organisers cover universities, hospitals, distribution firms, advertising firms.

Government organisation

Like the PWD, the DGS and D organisations several collecting organisations, several boards and government administrative organisations.

Public organisation

Post, telegraph, and telecommunication, water works, health organisations.

Private organisation

There are many other firms in which the organisation exists. These are:

Mining and extractive industries: These include Coal India ONGC, Hindustan Copper Limited, industries involved in extraction from are.

Material processing industries: Tata Steel, Steel Authority of India, Bharat Aluminium Company (BALCO), Hindalco, etc.

Manufacturing of parts and assembly: General Electric Company, Larsen Turbo, Kirloskar, MICO, Bharat Forge and many other industries involved in making parts and assembly.

Final assembly: Local brands of cooler manufacturers, shelves, cupboards, trays, tables, chairs, TV manufacturers, truck manufacturers, computer manufacturers.

Distributors

These firms undertake the distribution of various goods, and many products are marketed by them. These include consumable goods, office goods, food products, bearings, tubes, electrical appliances. They may be in the form of marketers, distributors, agents, middleman or agents.

Factors Influencing Organisational Buying

There are a number of external and internal environmental factors that directly or indirectly affect organisational buying behaviour. Economic factors are considered very important for organisational buying. Strong personal relationships also play a very important role in organisational buying. Other factors are political influences that are dominant. Organisational buying is also situational and situations play an important role. Most thinkers feel that these influences can be grouped under four major headings.

1. External environment factors

Under this heading we have social, political, legal, cultural, economic factors that interact with each other, for example they could be power shortages, credit squeezes, political and economic changes, which govern many of the rules regulations. The shortage of raw materials. Excessive tariffs and taxes on a particular item. These affect the buyer behaviour and the industry has to adapt itself to these changes. Competition in the market has to be studied, and strategies designed to outdo or fight the competition in a proper manner.

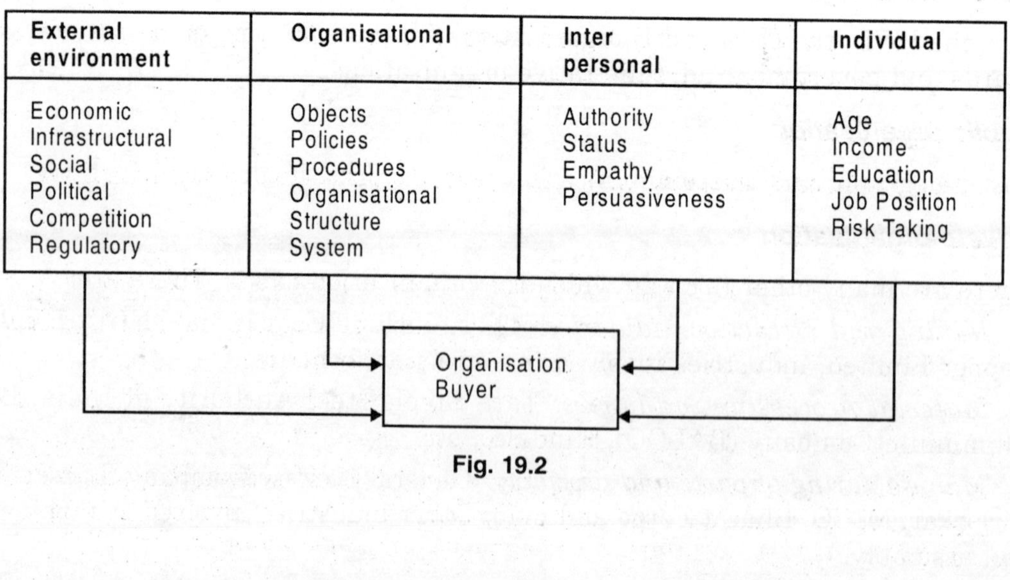

Fig. 19.2

2. Organisational factors

An organisation is purposefully created and deliberately structured to attain specific objectives. These objectives and policies differ in every organisation. Every organisation had a climate and culture of its own. The organisation is interested in selling its products to the industries who have a "buying centre" or, a group of people who have the authority to buy. The marketer of industrial products thus wants to know who constitutes this "power centre." How many people are involved in it. What are their specific requirements. What is their bent of mind or attitude towards the products. What are their likes and dislikes and, what is their criteria of evaluation and, what are the company's policies and procedures, for placing bulk orders.

3. Interpersonal factors

The buying centre consists of a number of persons who are involved in buying. It is an inter personal activity. Those people come from various levels of the organisation. They have different backgrounds, different expertise, different values and considerations. They play different roles and make the buying more complex. In some cases this leads to a conflict, which has to be solved, and a uniformity and harmony is made to prevail between different members involved in buying. This can be done by

(a) *Problem solving* approach where various alternatives are considered and discussions and deliberations take place. This should be done in a rational manner and, them conflicts can be resolved.

(b) *Persuasive:* In this method of conflict resolution, the parties are persuaded to take a different view by reducing the importance of a criteria over the other. The objectives of the organisation are given more importance than the objectives of the departments. It is the overall objectives that must be considered, and the objectives of the various departments and members be unidirectional.

(c) *Bargaining:* This is another method of resolving conflict amongst members. In bargaining, a little give and take is required i.e. in new buying situations there arises a lot of difference in goals and objectives. In this method, the decision of a party is agreed upon with the promise of reciprocity in the future.

(d) *Politicking:* This is a negative approach of resolving the conflict. Here parties spread false charges, or cast aspersions on others. They resort to unhealthy tactics. This is considered as a non-rational method to resolve a conflicting situation.

(e) Each member has a unique personality and experience. His own perception depends upon his age, income, expertise, job position and his attitude towards risk. With more experience, one takes more distinguished and mature decisions. Organisational buying is big buying, which involves risk and the perception of risk is very important.

Factors that affect risk

(a) *Characteristics of the purchase problem*

- ➢ Size of the expenditure (rupees)
- ➢ Degree of novelty contained in buying
- ➢ Degree of product essentiality
- ➢ Factors provoking purchase

(b) *Characteristics of the buyer (general and specific)*

Buyer's self confidence and experience, degree of technical and professional affiliation.

(c) *Organisational environment*

- ➢ Size and financial standing of customer
- ➢ Degree of decision centralisation
- ➢ Degree of decision reutilisation

(d) *Management of perceived risk:* There are two types of risks involved:

Performance risk: When the products fail to perform. A rolling machine not able to perform on the specified thickness of metals. A life pump not performing upto expectations. An aerosol spray not functioning satisfactorily.

Psychological risk: This risk arises when a person is held responsible and accountable for the decision taken by him. Performance and Psychological risk are associated with the wrong choice.

This leads to four types of risks as shown in Fig. 19.3.

External uncertainty	External consequence
Internal uncertainty	Internal consequence

Fig. 19.3

These risks can be reduced by purchasing from familiar suppliers. Risk can also be reduced by placing orders on high credibility suppliers in new buying situations. It is necessary that industrial marketers must understand the perceived risk, and methods to minimise them. This is necessary to formulate effective sales strategies.

Organisational Buying Situations

An organisation buys a variety of products and services. These may include a variety of items, some of these are mentioned:

Raw material: Steel, Aluminium, Iron ore, etc.

Major capital items: Machinery, Plant, etc.

Minor Capital items: Pumps, valves.

Fabricated components and parts, and auto assemblies: Castings, forgings, small parts of iron, rubber, plastic, etc.

Processed chemicals: Fluxes for melting, powders, chemicals.

Consumables: Lubricating oils, electrodes, fuel, gas, etc.

Office equipment: Paper, copier, typewriters.

Services: Transport, travel, touring, etc.

Basically there are three types of buying situations, according to Robinson, Fari's and Wind.

Straight rebuy situations

In this routine orders are placed for office supplies, raw materials, other items of daily use, where the supplier is known and a procedure is already laid down, which is followed in a routine manner.

Modified rebuy situations

Buyers may change or modify the product according to the situation, e.g. Nylon rope for ordinary rope. Plastic washers in place of steel or brass washers, aluminium instead of copper, hydraulic in place of mechanical. This may be done for economic consideration, or for the ease of procurement, or to modify or change the product. The change may also be due to external or internal environmental changes.

New task

When a new task is performed, items may be bought without previous experience and for the first time. These could be new machines like computer or Fax machines. The need for such a product may not have occurred previously. For a new task, a new set up and new items are necessary, which may not have been purchased before.

Fisher gave a model and identified two factors for buying decisions. These are product complexity and, commercial uncertainty. This gives a combination of four situations as shown:

Commercial uncertainty ↓ / Complexity →	Low	High
Low	Buyer Emphasis (1)	Technological emphasis (3)
High	Policy maker Emphasis (2)	Total involvement (4)

Fig. 19.4 Fisher's model.

Table 19.1 Product complexity and commercial uncertainty can further be shown as under:

Product complexity low	*High product complexity*	*Low commercial uncertainty*	*High commercial uncertainty*
Standard product	Different product	Low investment	High investment
Technically simple	Technically complicated	Small order	Large order
Established product	New product	Short term commitment	Long term commitment
		Small effect on profitability	Consequential adjustments required
Previously purchased	Not purchased previously	Easy to forecast	Large effect on profitability
Easy to install	Difficult to install		
No after sales service	After sales service required frequently		Hard to forecast

The four quadrants shown above require different emphasis as shown:

In quadrant (No. 1): There is low complexity and low uncertainty, in such a situation Buyer emphasis must be given.

In quadrant (No. 2): There is high uncertainty and low complexity, in such a situation policy makers emphasis is required.

In quadrant (No. 3): There is low uncertainty and high complexity, in such a situation there should be technological emphasis.

In quadrant (No. 4): When both uncertainty and complexity is high, there should be emphasis on total involvement with the product.

Selection of a supplier

In industrial buying, there are many considerations for selecting a supplier. Some suppliers are old suppliers and already listed and registered with the establishment. Other suppliers are also considered. They are considered on a number of criteria. These are:

1. Price
2. Reliability of delivery dates.
3. Quality of the product and maintenance of quality.
4. Suppliers reputation in the market.
5. Quick response to the needs of the customer.
6. Capability of the supplier to supply regularly on increase on demand.
7. Supplier's flexibility.
8. Consistency in dealing with supplies.
9. Rejection rates.

All these attributes are considered and the supplier is very carefully chosen. If the supplies are delayed the business fails, which is not tolerated by any organisation.

Questions

1. Outline the steps in the organisational buying behaviour. How do these differ from customer buying?
2. Illustrate with an example the organisational buying highlighting the characteristics of organisational buying.
3. Discuss the main characteristics of organisational buying.
4. What do you understand by an organisational customer? Why is it called a Ghost?
5. Describe the factors affecting organisational buying.
6. What is meant by risk in organisational buying? How can you reduce these risks?
7. Describe the various organisational buying situations.
8. Describe Fisher's model of product complexity and uncertainty in organisational buying.
9. What are the considerations for selecting an organisational supplier?

20

Customer Delight

We must adjust ourselves to the customer—
Never the customers to ourselves.

After going through this chapter the student should be able to:

- Distinguish between satisfaction and delight
- Understand how companies are trying to delight the customer
- Understand the need for delight
- Correlate expectation and delight
- Suggest methods of delighting the consumer

INTRODUCTION

While discussing consumer behaviour, it is seen that the process of decision-making consists of five steps. These are:

1. Problem Recognition
2. Information Search
3. Alternative Evaluation
4. Purchase
5. Post Purchase Behaviour

In the last step one is concerned with the satisfaction or dissatisfaction of the customer. The aim is to satisfy the customer. However, in pursuit of satisfaction the marketers and the manufactures have gone a step further and they now not only want to satisfy but delight the customer. By delighting the customer we go far beyond satisfaction, and by innovation, augmentation and value addition, we improve the product greatly, so that the customer is looking for a special feeling, which is far beyond his expectation. Delight dazzles the customer and gives extra benefits which he had never imagined. We can define delight from the following statements:

(a) The fulfilment of latest needs that a customer is not aware of.

(b) A quality of service or an unexpected benefit from the marketer.

(c) Personalised standard service of a product/service.

(d) Solutions of the problem offered at the personnel initiative of the company's employees.

For example, the very entry into a room hired by a customer at the Le-Meridian Hotel, delights the customer. He is welcomed with a caption on the computer screen.

"Welcome to the hotel"

"Mr and Mrs. Johnson and family"

"Have a nice day".

Delight to need (↑)	
	Customer delight
	Customer satisfaction
	Augmented product
	Branded product
	Basic product that fulfils a need

By delight we mean that extra facilities are provided in terms of fruit trays, fridge full of drinks, a cake with the inscription, "Welcome to Le Meridian" Information about the contents of the food and the calories of the meal is provided. Any other information is readily available and can be had at the press of a button. This delights the customer, and the company also benefits as they get a premium on the price which justifies the investment made for delighting the customer.

Many companies are offering products and services to delight the customer, to try to retain the existing customer, and also to attract new customers. Given below are the practices adopted by various companies.

Wipro delighted the customer by delivering the computers to the clients at a much earlier date than promised, thus generating unexpected benefits to the consumer.

Arvind Group of Mills are trying their best by improving the quality of cotton, and for this they are ready to import the best technologies. The improvement in the quality of cotton will delight the customer and supplier, and build lasting relationships with them.

Maruti Udyog Limited has given a number of choices to the consumers for their cars with special attributes, so that the customers of different income groups can choose from various cars available. This includes Maruti 800, Maruti Van, Zen, Esteem, Wagon R. Alto, Baleno. Special features are built in to give the customer extraordinary benefits in terms of comfort, economy, durability, smoothness, space, etc.

Other car companies are also engaged in the same pursuit. Airline services, rail and bus services, tour operators and manufacturers are also trying their best to do whatever they can in this regard, to delight the customer.

Need for Delight

The millennium is witnessing dramatic changes in the market place, change in lifestyle of the consumers and a radical revolution in information technology. The behaviour of the new generation customer has seen drastic changes. His expectation has increased, he has become more knowledgeable, is aware of multiple options to satisfy his needs, and switches over to newer brands for more value for his money. There are increasing number of competitors, both domestic and global, offering higher value-added products and processes through innovation. This has led to a change in the marketing mix. The consumer has greater purchasing power, he is more educated, uses ultra modern tools—E-commerce and E-business to get more information about products, prices, features, attributes and can make a better choice.

(a) The customer has become more demanding.
(b) There is greater economic liberalisation.
(c) There is increasing competition.
(d) The costs are rising.
(e) There are lower margins.
(f) Markets are splintered.
(g) Greater choice of customers.

The marketing concept is being followed in its entirety.

(a) All marketing efforts are directed at the customer.
(b) Companies allow customers to dictate their specifications and standards.
(c) Marketers track customer's needs continuously and respond to them instantly.
(d) Corporate strategy is aimed at delivering greater customer value than their rivals.

Figure 20.1 shows the customer surrounded by the functional areas of management, i.e. marketing, finance, production and personnel. All the functional areas are working together in an integrated manner, following the marketing concepts, and this leads to customer driven mission, customer driven vision, customer driven rewards, customer driven appraisals, customer driven goals, customer driven strategy and customer driven values. All activities are centred round the customer and the customer is supreme.

Expectation and Delight

Before a company or a marketer can delight the customer, it must have an in-depth knowledge of the customer's expectations, so that not only are they able to meet, but exceed the expectation, to delight the customer. For this a knowledge of the core elements of the products and services are essential.

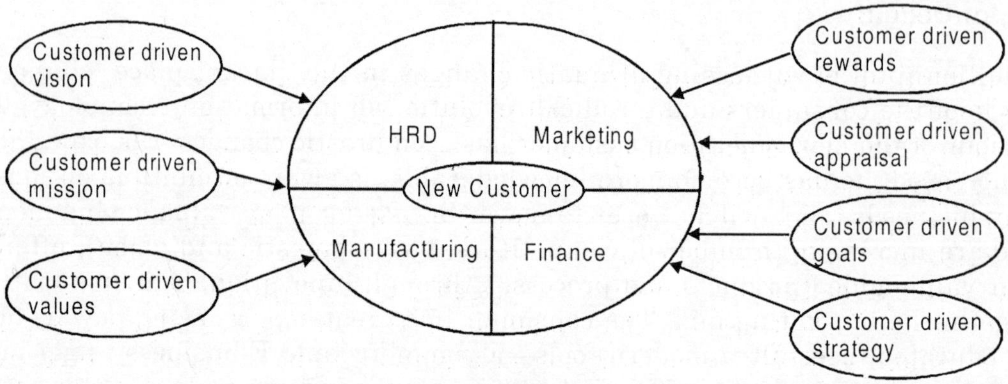

Fig. 20.1

The core elements of a product are its shape, quality, colour, quantity, packaging, price, brand name differentiation, etc. While the core elements of service are reliability, usefulness, responsiveness to specific needs assurance and acceptability, etc. from the service provider.

In case of a product (tangible), the customer should be provided what he expects and the core elements remain almost the same. However, services being intangible and their characteristics which are intangibility, inseparability, perishability, etc. must be kept in mind. The core elements given above can be manipulated to exceed the expectations of the customers, as the human touch is also involved, and this can give unexpected positive elements to delight the customer and have a competitive edge as well. A study conducted by Parsuram, Berry and Ziethmal in 1991 came out with some conclusions given below.

- A customer expects fundamental benefits, not fancies.
- A customer expects performance and not empty promises.
- A customer expects competency.

In case of automobile repair

- A customer wants competency (job done right, the first time).
- A customer wants things to be explained.
- A customer wants to know why you have suggested repairs.
- A customer wants to be shown respect.

In case of hotels

- A customer wants a clean and secure room to be provided.
- A customer wants to be treated as a guest.
- A customer wants the promises to be kept.

In case of insurance

➢ A customer wants up to date information.

➢ A customer wants to be treated fairly in case of claims, etc.

➢ A customer wants to be provided with prompt service.

For other services and products

➢ A customer wants reliability which is the ability to perform the promised service, dependably and accurately.

➢ A customer wants tangibility or the appearance of physical facilities, equipment, personnel and other materials.

➢ A customer wants responsiveness—the responsiveness to a query or to a call, e.g. telephone enquiries. Sometimes nobody picks up the phone for a long time, which irritates and turns off a customer.

➢ A customer wants assurance—the knowledge and courtesy of employees and their ability to convey trust and confidence.

➢ A customer wants empathy—the caring individual attention provided to customers. Salesman putting himself in the customers' shoes.

Reliability is more concerned with the service outcome, whereas the other factors of responsiveness, assurance, tangibility and empathy are more concerned with the service process. With the help of these guidelines and their implementation, the customer cannot only meet his expectations, but be delighted to the core of his heart.

Generating Delight

To generate delight is not an easy job. Companies are vying with each other for competitive advantage. A customer gets most satisfied when he least expects it. The company also delivers at the doorstep of the consumer which generates unparalleled value and satisfaction. For this one must:

(a) Strive constantly to provide additional customer value in every transaction.

(b) Try to provide surprise benefits.

(c) Constantly express the expectations that the customer has built around your product.

(d) Treat the customer exclusively.

(e) Look for expectations and performance gaps in order to identify opportunities to delight.

The delight chain shown in Fig. 20.2 starts with measuring the customer satisfaction through customer satisfaction indices, and by market research and consumer researches, and through direct contact to understand the latent needs of the consumer. Once the needs have been recognised, quality management is practised and implemented to provide better service than competitors. For this it is essential for the management to give a lot of power to employees to take proper decisions and initiative. The customer is delighted when the service or the product gives a touching feeling. It is also essential to over deliver (deliver more than has been promised), and also to come out with newer methods of service and techniques to give creativity and innovation as much as possible.

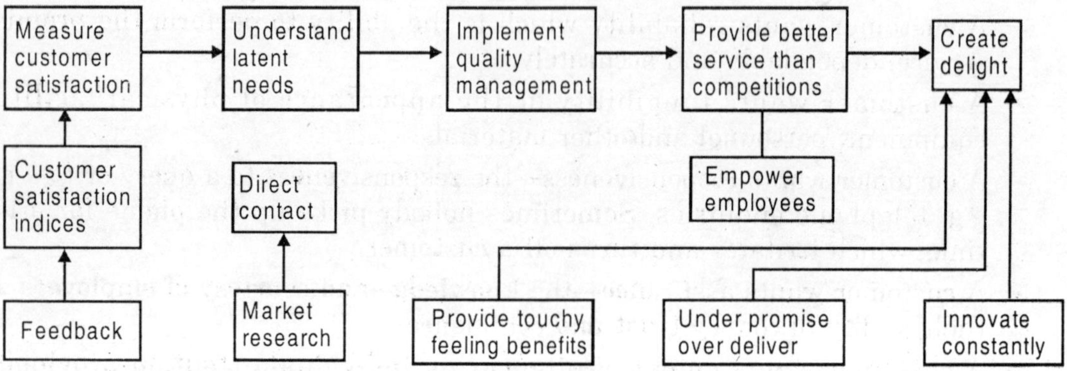

Fig. 20.2 Customer delight chain.

Questions

1. What is the need to delight the customer?
2. Give examples of companies who are delighting the consumer and how?
3. If you were running an automobile workshop, what steps would you take to delight the customers?

21

Public Policy and Consumer Protection

Consumer protection is the duty of the government and the society. Consumer must be protected against all exploitation.

◆

The chapter gives an insight into:

- Need for consumer protection.
- How consumer is exploited.
- Public policy to safeguard consumer.
- Consumer rights.

◆ INTRODUCTION

In the earlier decades the consumer was unorganised and was generally taken for a ride. Today, the consumer is aware of his rights and is highly educated and experienced.

He was earlier being exploited in many ways. These were the adulteration practices of the manufacturers and middlemen. Variations in the contents of the pack, misleading and deceptive advertising which led even the educated consumer to buy unwanted and unnecessary goods to a large extent. Consumers also complained and criticised the factors like price, quality, advertising, packing, distribution, after-sales service etc. There were many unfair trade practices prevalent in India, some example are given below:

Advertising of scooters and cars claiming a much exaggerated average per litre than the actual. The sale of magic rings for the cure of diseases like blood pressure and diabetes.

The sale of medicines claiming to increase the height of children, and other unbelieveable claims. Adulterating the food with cheaper stuff to increase the weight of the product, like adding papaya seeds to black pepper to increase the bulk and weight. Adding animal fat to Ghee, water to milk, supplying poor quality products that did not last long, etc. many other practices which harmed the consumer considerably—amputating the wrong leg of a patient by oversight in a government hospital. Patients losing their sight because of negligence of doctors using infectious surgical instrument in the operation theatre. Doctors leaving scissors or radio-active elements in the body of the patient. A patient was operated upon for the removal of an ovarian cyst, when actually there was none, and other practices which were injurious, unhealthy and unfair to consumers.

The examples show that the attitude of business towards consumers have been very indifferent. This mostly happens in a sellers market, but where there is competitive selling or sellers are many, the needs of the consumer is the first priority, and the marketing concept is being practised.

The exploitation of the consumer has led to the creation of the consumer movement also known a consumerism. Consumerism is the range of activities of the government, business, and independent organisation that are designed to protect the consumer from the unlawful practices of the business that infringe upon there rights as consumers. There has been an awakening in the consumer and the government has passed many laws and statutory obligations that must be adhered to, by companies.

The subject of the present chapter is to highlight how far a consumer is safeguarded by the existing legal provisions, and what were the reasons for the passing Consumer Protection Act, 1986. Consumer is a person who has the ability to pay for the product, who possesses the power to make the buying decision. Therefore, consumer is designated *asking of the market.*

Inspite of existing enactments like the Weights and Measures Act, 1956, Essential Commodities Act, 1955, Prevention of Food Adulteration Act, 1954, MRTP Act, 1969, Sale of Goods Act, 1930 and others having bearing on consumer's right, the consumer's rights were being violated. Under law of nature or, law of the jungle, big fish eats the small ones. The persons in power if not put under legal limitations, will repeat the system in which big fish eats the small one. An orderly society where rule of law prevails, brings peace and prosperity.

The consumer protection Act, 1986 has provided a legal umbrella to safeguard the interests of consumers and to give them cheap and speedy justice. In order to know the significance of the consumer protection Act, 1986, a bird's eye view of the provisions may be made, and then it can be assessed whether the enactment has really given relief to the consumer.

Aims and objective of the Act: In the statement of objects and reasons it is said that since the Act seeks to provide speedy and simple redressal to consumer disputes, a quassi-judicial machinery is sought to be set up at the District, State and Central levels. These quasi-judicial bodies will observe the principles of natural justice, and have been empowered to give relief of a specific nature and wherever appropriate, compensation to consumers. Penalties for non-compliance of orders given by the quassi-judicial bodies have also been provided. It shall be the duty of consumers councils to promote and protect the rights of the consumers. In Section 6 of the Act, a provision for consumers councils has been made. It provides a list of the rights of consumers. They are:

(i) *Protection against hazardous goods:* This right is generally taken care of under the law of Tort, and since the time of *Donohue vs Stevenson*, where remains of a dead snail emerged from the bottle, and the customer had already taken a part of the content, aggravating her illness, and the manufacturers were held liable to the distant user. Now it has become an established principle that, producer providing goods in the market would be liable to the ultimate user, if his person or property is injured in the normal use of the goods. The consumer is assured by this Act, that if he has been victimised into purchasing goods which have injured his person or property, he will have a speedy and effective remedy under the redressal hierarchy constituted under the Act, for example, adulterated food is dangerous to life and weak cement is dangerous to property, and who-so-ever would supply such items in the market, shall be liable to the consumer.

(ii) *Right to information:* The right to be informed about the quality, quantity, potency, purity, standard and price of goods which the consumer buys, has been given to the consumer to protect him against unfair trade practices. *The case of Consumer Protection Council vs National Dairy Development Board,* (1991) demonstrates the significance of this right. In this case, the complainant wanted to know in what way the Dairy Board was using imported Palmolene oil, and the Board was refusing to furnish the information, on the ground that, Boards were prevented from disclosure in public interest. Without that information, the complainant was not able to make out his case. It was held that the consumer had the right to the requisite information.

(iii) *Right to access:* This right would facilitate the shop-keepers in selecting and stocking goods of choice and variety and at competitive prices.

(iv) *Right of proper hearing:* The Central Council is, in the fourth place, charged with the responsibility of assuring the consumers that they would be heard, as of right, by the appropriate forums and the consumer will receive due attention and consideration from such forums.

(v) *Right to seek redressal:* The consumer has been given the right to seek redressal against unfair trade practices or unscrupulous exploitation. In *M.O. Hasan Kuthoos Naricar vs Joseph K. Thomas (1991)*, where money was deposited in advance for the supply of a car within two months, and the car was actually supplied sometime after two months, the retention of the money beyond the period was held to be an unfair trade practice, entitling the party to 14 per cent interest on the deposit for the period of delay.

(vi) *Right to consumer education:* Education makes the consumer aware of his rights and the chances of exploitation become meagre. Every person is a consumer in one way or the other. When aroused by a proper consumer education, one is likely to be above petty temptations and, therefore, more effective in its mission. This has been a mission of the Consumer Protection Act, 1986 that consumer's education is a must. The Consumer Councils have been charged with responsibility to provide to the people, education in terms of their remedies under the Act. If the consumer is educated properly about his rights and remedies the public servants shall cease to act as public exploiters, and corruption and malpractice's in the public life will be reduced, if nor eradicated.

The implementation of the Act: The National Policy in the sphere of consumerism is the responsibility of the Consumer Council. Consumerism has assured great importance in the field of commerce. The meaning of consumer in relation to the transactions with producers, sellers which affect his day to day life, is explained as under:

Consumer: Section 2(d) of the Consumer Protection Act, 1986 defines consumer in two parts. It provides that consumer is a person (a) who buys goods for consideration and (b) who hires or avails of any services for a consideration. In its explanation, it is made clear that if goods are purchased for commercial purposes, then he will cease to be a consumer, but if the goods are bought and used by him exclusively for the purpose of earning his livelihood, by means of self-employment, he would be deemed to be a consumer.

Thus, consumerism is a result of contract, and for contract, consideration is a must, whether for buying goods or, hiring services. Another important requirement is that a sale in course of trade is necessary. Consumerism deals in buying and selling.

The cause of action arises when there is:

(a) *Defect in good:* The producer or seller shall be held liable only when

(i) the buyer makes it clear to the seller that the goods are required for a particular purpose;

(ii) the buyer relies on the seller's skill or judgement.

(iii) The famous case on this point was decided in 1936.

The name of the case was *Grant vs Australian Knitting Mills.* In that case the plaintiff, a doctor, purchased from the retailer, two woollen underpants manufactured by the defendants. Next day after wearing one of them he became ill. His illness was diagnosed as dermatitis caused by a chemical irritant, which the defendants had negligently omitted to remove in the process of manufacturing. The manufacturers were held liable for the defect in the goods.

The second category of consumer is that of user of services. Deficiency in service was explained by the apex Court in *Lucknow Development Authority vs M.K. Gupt (1994) ISCC 243.* The court held that a housing authority would be liable for any deficiency in service, even if the contract for the service was made before the amendment made in 1993. In *Indian Medical Association vs. V.P. Shantha (1995) 6 SCC 651*, the Supreme Court held that the use of words, potential users does not have the effect of excluding medical services from the purview of the word 'service. However, the services must be of commercial nature, in the sense that they must be on payment, which may be either in cash or kind, and which may be made either at once, or partly on credit. In this category of consumer also, any beneficiary of the service would be included, though he is not the hirer. In this category comes a nominee of an insurance policy who is entitled to the service with the approval of the user.

Unlike other remedies available under various Acts, the Consumer Protection Act does give a new forum which will be comparatively free from all weaknesses. Court fee is not there, lawyers are not needed and, time limit is set for disposal. In a favour case of *Laxmi Engineering Works vs PSG Industrial Institute AIR 1995 SC 1428*, the Supreme Court determined the nature of protection, and held that the quasi-judicial bodies created by the Act are not courts though invested with some of the powers of the court. They are quasi-judicial tribunals, brought into existence to render inexpensive and speedy remedies to the consumers. These bodies are not supposed to supplant but supplement the existing judicial system. The idea was to provide an additional forum, providing inexpensive and speedy resolution of disputes arising between consumers and suppliers of goods and services purchased and availed of by them, in a market dominated by large trading and manufacturing bodies. Indeed, the entire Act revolves round the consumer, and is designed to protect his interest. The Act provides for "business to business" disputes.

Mere provisions of the law are of no use unless the effective remedial measures are there. The Act provides for an effective policy making body, i.e. Central Consumer Protection Council, State Consumer Protection Council to keep an eagle's eye on whether the provisions are being implemented effectively or not. In 1987 the Consumer Protection Rules were framed to give effectiveness to the authorities.

The Minister in charge of the Department of Food and Civil Supplies in the Central Government, is the chairman of the Central Council and same is the case of State Councils. There are a total 150 members and their term is fixed for three years. The Constitution and functions are described from Sections 4 to 8 of the Act. Their role is supervisory.

From Sections 9 to 24, the provisions for constitution and functions and jurisdiction of consumer disputes redressal agencies aer narrated. These are as under:

1. *District Forums:* They are organised at the district level and a retired District Judge is nominated by the State Government to be its president. Two other members, one lady and one gent, is appointed by a committee consisting of the Chairman of State Commission, Secretary of Food and Civil Supplies and Secretary of Law Department. Their term is for five years, or upto the age of 65 years, whichever is earlier. Their jurisdiction is upto 5 lakh rupees. A complaint can be filed by the consumer himself, by a recognised consumer association, by one or more consumers, or by the Central or State Governments. The District Forum cannot

grant interim relief. They can grant only the final relief. They also do not have the power to review their orders. Sections 10 to 15 deal with the composition, power and jurisdiction of the District Forum. The decisions of the District Forum can be challenged only according to the procedure prescribed in the Act itself.

2. *State Commissions:* The composition of National Commission is given in Section 16 of the Act. The President of the commission shall be a retired High Court Judge and two other members. Its jurisdiction is laid down in Section 17 of the Act and it can dispose of the cases upto the value of Rs. 20 lakhs. It can hear the appeal from the District Forum and can also call for the records. Section 18 lays down the procedure, which is the same as is laid down in Sections 13 and 14 of the Act. Section 19 lays down the procedure for original jurisdiction which is limited to monetary value only.

3. *National Commission:* The composition of National Commission is provided in Section 20 of the Act. The President of the National Commission is a Supreme Court Judge, who is appointed by the President of India in consultation with the Chief Justice of India. Four other members are appointed. Original jurisdiction is limited to the case the value of which is more that 20 lakhs and rest of the jurisdiction is appellate. From any decision of the National Commission and appeal lies to the Supreme Court. Thirty days time from the date of the order is allowed for the purpose. Where no appeal is made, the orders of the District Forum, State Commission and National Commission are considered and made final. The period of Limitation for filling complaints is two years from the date of cause of action. Delay, if any, can be condoned by the Forums. The orders of a District Forum, State Commission and those of National Commission are enforceable in the manner of an order or decree made by a court in a Civil Suit. From 26 to 31 Sections provisions are insignificant.

Conclusion

The main purpose for which the Consumer Protection Act, 1986 was enacted, was to impart speedy and inexpensive justice to the consumer. However, with the passage of time these forums have also assumed the same character as is practised by the ordinary court. The delaying tactics, the engagements of lawyers and other legal battles have marred the efficacy of the forums created by the Act. They have been losing their importance gradually, and the purpose for which the redressal agencies were created is slowly being frustrated. The cases are now lost in the pending files lying with the judges.

Suggestions

In order to impart speedy and inexpensive justice only serving judges must be appointed. The retired persons have made it a resting place. No lawyers should be allowed to appear on behalf of the complaint and the time limit must be strictly adhered to. Moreover, since the mission of the Consumer Protection Act, 1986, is "consumers education", concerted attempts should be made in this direction. Apart from Consumer Councils, village Panchayats should be actively associated with the education process. Literature, in the local script, explaining consumers rights and remedies should also be distributed, free of cost, at Fair Price Shops (PDS).

Questions

1. What is the need to protect the consumer?
2. Describe in brief the Consumer Protection Act?

22

E-Consumer Behaviour

Transacting business at the speed of thought.

The chapter gives an insight into:

- E-Business and its importance.
- E-Business application.
- World Wide Web and its advantages.

THE COMPUTER AGE

Consumer can't be seen or met (Cyber consumer). This is the age of information Technology. The computers are being put to wide use. They are being used for business and domestic purposes, for government work, for buying and selling, for recording and retrieving information, for electronic communication with the greatest of ease, and they are used all over the world. Companies have been working towards computerisation, and the first commercial computer was given to the world in 1924 by I.B.M. Computer education started in 1928, and today it has changed the entire concept of business and mankind. Right from railway booking which entailed long queues at the reservation counters, to accessing the latest information, things have become much easier and methodical. In the beginning, emphasis was given to programming in various languages, Pascal, COBAL, FORTRAN etc., then we had the transition to three generation languages, and now the E-Business, which can be described as the method of doing business electronically, which has now become an integrated discipline.

In 1990 online services were started which provided a new form of social interaction, such as Inter relay chat (IRC) and knowledge sharing, such as new groups and file transfer programmes. Social interaction led to the concept of "global village". By using the global Internet, people can exchange information and can communicate with each other at a much lower cost.

In 1990, the WWW (World Wide Web) provided an easy to use technology solution, to the problem of information publishing and dissemination. It enabled more diverse activities in Business.

E-Business

E-Business Marketing is the direct marketing online, and through this media advertisements can easily reach the consumer's door step. It provides information through Internet and online services for buying and selling products and exchange of information. It cuts service cost for the marketing and improves the quality of goods/ services, and increases the speed of delivery.

"E-Business enables business to be transacted at the speed of thought."

Business challenges can be overcome, competition can be met, and strategies can be evolved to meet the competition. E-Business enables business to be transacted globally without any significant barrier.

Voluminous and repetitive documentation can be eliminated. It enables differentiation for competitive advantage.

It provides effective Management information and helps in decision-making. It helps manage the customer chain and integrates it with the supplier chain. There is better management of marketing. It leads to reduction in the cost of doing business.

Benefits

There are no geographical boundaries and targeting individual clients is less costly. There are fewer middlemen, there is quick order execution, faster realisation of money, client has much wider choice and he can choose from products offered globally. It also helps in booking airline/train tickets yourself from your home/office. You can have access to Bank transaction and to billing online.

Advantage to the consumer

E-Business or Electronic Business has brought a revolution in many fields. It has also changed the entire concept of selling and buying. It has changed the thinking of the consumer. It has changed the decision-making of the consumer and the physical activities associated with the decision-making process have been reduced tremendously.

Consumers using the Internet can improve the execution of their business. They can generate and exploit business opportunities with greater efficiency and speed. They can 'generate business value'. It gives the consumer advantage of getting better quality products by using interconnected networks, greater consumer satisfaction and delight and greater economy is guaranteed. It saves time and gives greater speed of transactions and delivery. These change not only the thinking of the consumer, but can bring vast changes in the consumer behaviour.

After all, as has been earlier pointed out in the book, consumer behaviour is the decision-making process and physical activity engaged in, while evaluating, acquiring, using and disposing off goods and services. Information based transactions are therefore creating new business opportunities and new ways of doing business. The need for E-Business arose for better computing, better interaction between sellers and buyers, both inside and outside the business organisation.

The use of it in banks in the transfer of money within minutes all over the globe, not only saves time, but also saves interest on the money which takes days to get transferred from one bank to the other across the globe. Traditional business methods of using paper and post are becoming obsolete and the same transactions now take a matter of minutes. This holds goods for purchase, sales, sending of documents and money to any part of the world. This is known as EDI or Electronic data interchange. The Electonically managed system provides a look into the store. The products are divided into various categories. One can see all the shelves of a grocery store, get detailed information about the ingredients of the product, and order electronically and the payment is also made electronically. It provides a look into the store's display and the arrangement of the shelves. A variety of brands with varying prices, sizes and information about the ingredients of the products can be seen as well.

There are three ways in which we can categories E-Business applications.

(a) Inter organisational (business to business, also known as B2B)

(b) Intra organisational (Within a business)

(c) Business to Customer (also known as B2C).

We are in this chapter concerned with business to customer transactions, the customer is always looking for the ease of purchase, convenience, low prices, good quality and proper service. Electronic Business provides the consumer with convenient shopping from online catalogue, to electronic banking which eliminates costs. It eliminates many intermediary steps. It provides video conferencing for better interaction and information. Consumer cannot be seen nor met. The consumer can conveniently transact the business according to his needs.

WEB; (World Wide Web) WWW

Web, as we all know, is a net made by the spider. In Computer terminology, it is a standard for navigating, publishing information and executing transactions. It is used:

1. To develop ways of linking distant documents (Hyperlink).
2. It enables users to work together (Collaborative authoring).

Companies use the web for communication with customers and suppliers, by publishing contents on their web server for widespread distribution. Many companies are selling their products on the web. A number of functions are performed including advertising, sales, customer service and marketing. Information transfers from bank to bank, bank to customers, business to customer, and even entertainment functions can be undertaken. The web can perform a number of tasks. These include attracting new customers via marketing and advertising.

Servicing existing customers via customer service and support functions, developing new markets and new distribution channels for existing products, developing new information based products. It also includes brand name management, exhibiting product catalogues and sales information and new product announcements. (customer service).

It is useful in handling customer queries that would otherwise be handled by a service representative. It can handle many customer oriented tasks. Software can be delivered from one computer to another, within no time. Customers can check their personal bank accounts. They can know their balances and recent transactions which helps to make better and quick decisions.

They can trace their parcels or packages as to where they are kept, or to what point of destination they have reached and when. The interaction with the government agencies has also become more accessible and useful. Tax information, employment opportunities, changes in rules or tax structure are also accessible with the press of a button.

Application to Customer Behaviour

Consumers keep making decisions to buy the products of their choice. The steps included in decision-making which have already been discussed in earlier chapters are:

1. Problem recognition
2. Information search
3. Evaluation of alternatives
4. Purchase
5. Post purchase behaviour.

The decision-making as we have seen earlier is influenced by the internal determinants which include learning, memory, personality, self concepts, attitude, motivation and involvement. The external determinants consist of cultural and subcultural influences, social group influences, family influences, social influences and other influences. External and internal influences thus, together influence the decision-making process and most customers follow these steps in a logical manner.

E-Business enhances this process, and saves time of the consumer by providing all relevant information on the internet that is required.

Problem recognition

A problem is recognised when there is a gap between the existing and the desired position in the use of a product by the consumer. This gap may be caused by a number of factors, and it has to be reduced for the satisfaction of the consumer. E-Business provides the customer with more information regarding products and services. The customer, therefore, has a better understanding of the solving of these problems and starts demanding products which were earlier not available locally. He has higher aspirations and fulfills his needs in a better way.

For example, microwave oven and automatic dish washers which were not available locally, are now made available to the Indian Consumer.

Information search and evaluation of alternatives

Once the problem is recognised, the customer can find the alternatives to solve the problem on the computer. It gives enough and sufficient information to a consumer to choose. It provides many alternatives which can also be evaluated by mathematical models in the case of extensive problem solving, where more money and time is at stake. The evaluation of alternatives can be done speedily, and the advantages and disadvantages of various brands and products can be recognised. This also depends on the weightages given to different desired attributes in a product and making assumptions on a comparative scale. Internet can give comparative charts for making evaluation easier and rational.

The computer can also help in deciding about the choice heuristics (rule that guides the decision in areas of high probability). Information processing becomes easier and the area of information is enlarged greatly.

Purchase

E-Consumer is a fully informed consumer and is aware of various product offerings by all competitors. His purchase decision cannot be influenced easily. He takes rational decisions and usually decides to go for a product that offers good value for money. He also knows the advantages and disadvantages of when to buy, how to buy, from where to buy, what to buy, and from whom to buy.

Post purchase behaviour

After using the product/service consumers can electronically interact with the manufacture or marketer giving valuable feedback. The critical feedback to the company regarding the improvement of the product. If the customer is dissatisfied, he may communicate his anger against the company to lakhs of people worldwide instantly. This may affect the reputation and good will of the company and tarnish its image. A satisfied customer acts as a best advertising and promotional means of worldwide publicity at no cost.

The theoretical study of consumer behaviour cannot be overlooked and remains an important aspect, in spite of the development of E-Business. The theoretical framework of consumer behaviour has to be understood and applied in the application of E-Business for proper marketing results. E-Business does not replace, but supplements the theoretical foundation of consumer behaviour.

Questions

1. What is E-Business? How does it help the consumer?
2. What is WWW? How can it be used to make better decisions?

23

Consumer Research

Consumer research leads you to do the things today which will keep you in business tomorrow.

The chapter is designed to give an understanding of:

- The importance of consumer research
- Steps involved in consumer research
- Importance and sources of secondary data and primary data
- Purchase behaviour
- Methods of scaling, observation and experiment

INTRODUCTION

Consumer Research is an off shoot of Marketing Research. Both follow the same steps and both are used for making better decisions. Consumer research is carried out to understand the behaviour of consumers. How they would react to promotional messages and how their attitudes change after being exposed to the media messages. These studies and understandings can help the marketer to frame appropriate strategies to woo the consumer, to face competition and to locate target markets.

The consumer research follows almost the same steps as are carried out in marketing research, which is known as research methodology.

I. To define the problem and formulating the objectives of the research.

II. Collecting and evaluating secondary data.

III. Designing a primary research study if secondary data is insufficient.

IV. Collecting Primary Data by means of interviews, questionnaires, surveys etc.

V. Analysing the Data.

VI. Preparing a report.

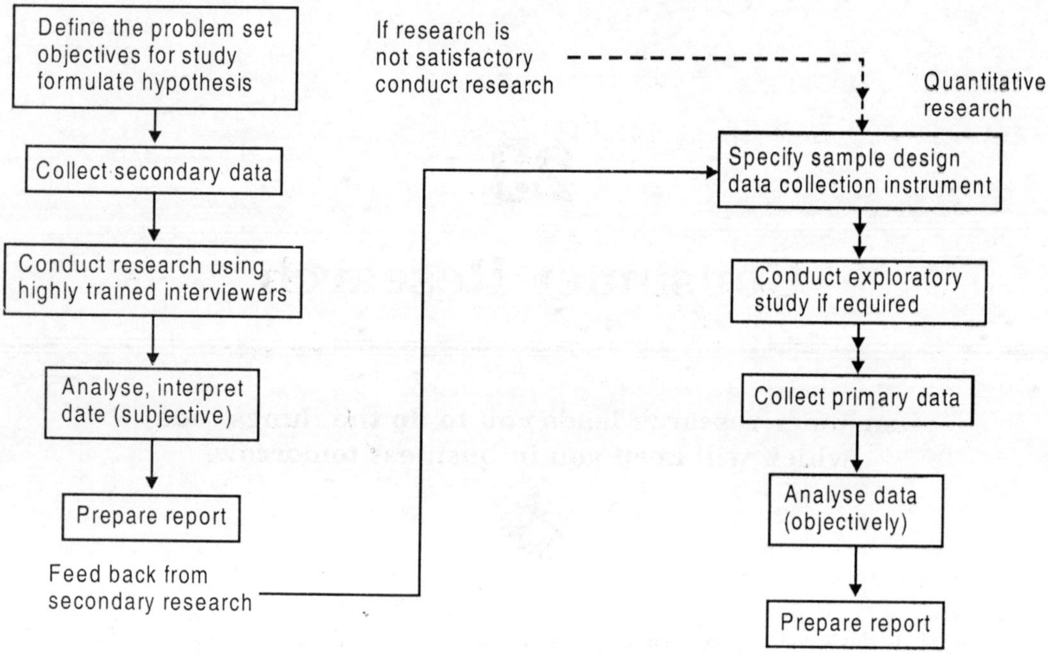

Fig. 23.1 Process of Consumer Research.

The Objectives of the Study

Mostly consumer researches are undertaken to find out the attitudes of the consumer about a product. Their preferences, likes and dislikes which lead to the further modernisation of the sales strategies by the marketer.

Researches can be conducted to find out the percentage of people using a certain product or a facility (a pager or mobile phone).

Researchers may also like to know the types of consumers and their demographic characteristics for a particular product.

They may also like to experiment with new promotional campaigns, and since these campaigns require a lot of expenditure, they may do researches to be sure of the campaign's success, before the final launch of the campaign.

The decline in sales may require the marketer to conduct researches which can give a clue of the changing consumer behaviour.

The objective therefore, must be clearly set and followed strictly. Then only can we decide what type of Research Design should be used. The researches can be quantitative or qualitative in nature.

Qualitative research design is undertaken to come up with new ideas, and in this design, brain storming tools and other face to face techniques with experts are used. This is confined indoors, and is less expensive than the quantitative research.

Quantitative research design is used in the market place where we have to interview people, to find out the number of persons using the product, or how frequently they use the product etc. This can be done by means of a questionnaire, a survey or by observations. This will be discussed later in this chapter.

Secondary Data

After identifying the research problem and determining specific information required to solve a problem, the researcher looks for appropriate data to solve the problem. This can be done by secondary data which is already published and is accessible. If secondary data is not sufficient to solve the problem, Primary Data which is generated by the researcher through questionnaires, surveys and interviews is utilised. We shall discuss here the secondary data first. A problem can be partially solved by the secondary data. It is economical. It saves money and time. In some cases where new products are to be launched or new marketing practices are to be adopted, secondary data may not be adequate or sufficient or may not be of much use. Secondary data is however, an important source of consumer research.

Merits of using secondary data

1. It is economical both in terms of money and time.
2. It has no bias as it is already published and the facts and figures are already collected for some other purpose.

Limitations

1. It has limited applicability.
2. The accuracy of the data is doubtful.

Sources of Secondary Data

Internal data: It is procured from the company itself. It includes orders, shipments, sales, advertising expenditure, detailed statement, inventory records, transportation costs, raw material cost, research reports, profit/loss statements. Some companies have their own data banks where they store, retrieve, analyse and evaluate information whenever necessary.

External Data consists of:

(a) Government sources

(b) Commercial sources

(c) Industrial sources

(d) Miscellaneous sources.

Government sources: Consists of information accessible from (i) Department of Census (ii) State Government (iii) Central Government Census carried out for information on burning issues, i.e. agriculture, population, transportation, manufacturing, minerals and other industries.

The central government can give information on health education and social welfare industries, agriculture and housing. The Central Government Secretariat, New Delhi keeps all this data for records.

Similarly, State Governments and union territories have their secretariat at the capital cities.

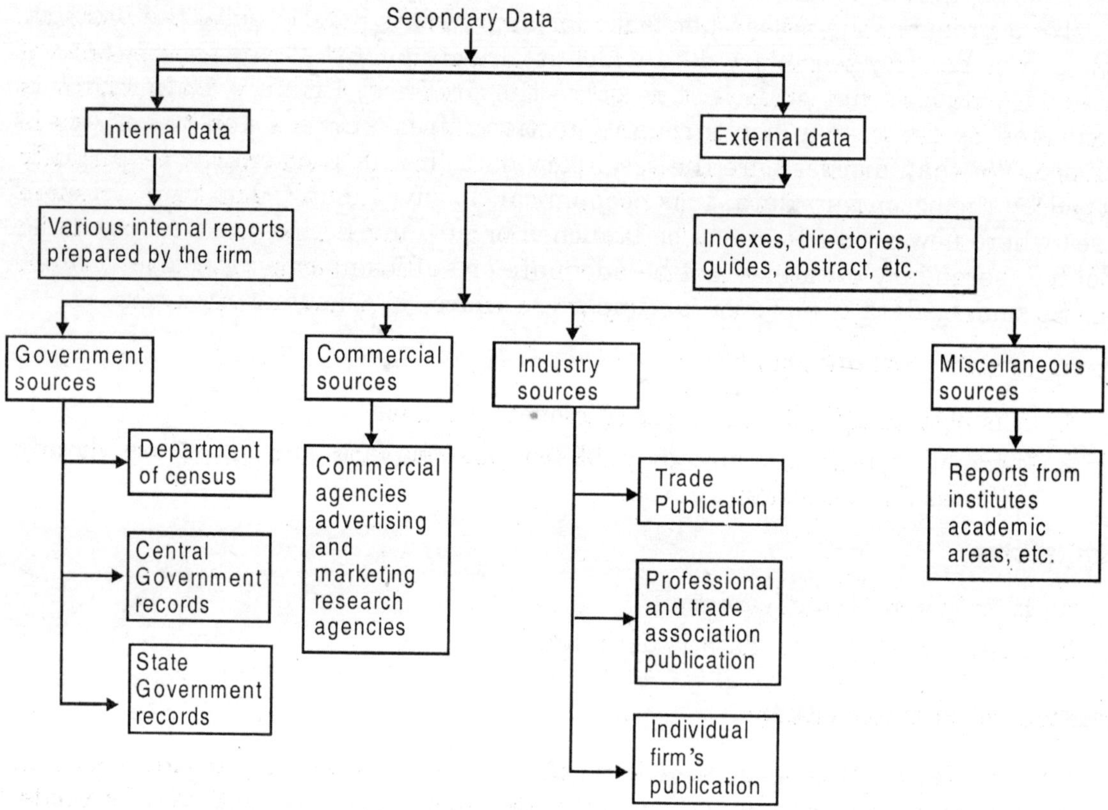

Fig. 23.2

Source: Commercial, industry and miscellaneous sources are illustrated in the above diagram.

Primary data

This is the data collected by the researcher himself and there are many ways of collecting this data. In consumer research we are concerned with the behaviour of the consumer and the behaviour is influenced by the consumers' demographic and socio-economic characteristics as well. Therefore, it becomes necessary to be aware not only of customers demographic characteristics, but also of his attitudes, interests, opinions, knowledge, intentions, motivation etc.

Awareness/knowledge

This is used to find out what the consumers are aware of and what they do not know. This is imparted to them by advertising and by other promotional methods.

This can be done by using awareness approaches of Unaided recall, Aided recall, or by recognition. The idea is to find out whether the consumer is aware of the product:

- ➢ aware of the attributes of the product
- ➢ aware of the availability of the product
- ➢ aware of the price of the product
- ➢ aware of where the product is available
- ➢ aware of the company making the product
- ➢ aware of the use of the product

Intentions

Whether a person is inclined to buy the product. What can be one's purchasing behaviour:

- ➢ Does he have definite intention to buy the product.
- ➢ Does he have a probable intention to buy.
- ➢ Is he undecided.
- ➢ He has no intentions to buy.

However, one cannot freely trust the statement regarding purchases as there is a definite deviation between what is said and what is practised.

Motivation

A consumer researcher wants to find out why people behave as they do. Motives refer to a need, a want or a drive an urge, a wish or a desire that leads to goal directed behaviour. There are various needs that must be fulfilled. A marketer has to know what he can do to fulfil these needs:

1. Physiological needs of food, shelter and clothing
2. Security needs
3. Social needs
4. Aesthetic needs
5. Esteem needs
6. Ego needs
7. Self-actualising needs.

Purchase Behaviour

It is carried out to find what the customer does to fulfil has consumption needs. It involves the description of activities with respect to components of *what, where, why, how, how much* in what situation, and also for instance "what" (one of the components). This what may mean which product or brand.

"Where" : Where to purchase, from which store, which city, which place?
"Why" : To consume himself, or to give as a present?

"How"	: In what manner? To purchase by going himself, by ordering, by cash/credit, etc.?
"How much"	: In what quantity, in bulk or in small amounts?
"What situation"	: Emergent situation; e.g. medicines umbrella, etc.
"Who"	: Who is to purchase, husband, wife children or jointly?

Methods of collecting Primary Data

There are a number of ways in which Primary data can be collected. These can be classified as under:

Questionnaires

Can be open ended, close ended, alternative provided, direct questions, indirect questions.

Observation

Experimentation, surveys and interviews.

Questionnaire

It is a self administered process, whereby the respondent himself reads the questions and answers without the help of an interviewer. They can broadly be classified under four types of questions. These can be on the basis of structure and, disguise and method of communication.

(a) *Structure Undisguised:* The question is framed before hand and is structured. It is undisguised in the sense that the respondent knows why the question is being asked. For Example "Do you feel family planning measures should be given more importance?"

(b) *Unstructured Undisguised:* "What do you feel about family planning in India?

(c) *Unstructured-Disguised:* These questions are for the respondents who hesitate, feel shy, or are threatened to answer the questions. This leads to motivational research. This is also known as projective technique, where the questions are designed to tap the underlying motives of the individuals despite their hiding them. This has been discussed under projective techniques.

(d) *Structured designed questionnaire:* These are least used and they are structured. They do not have the flexibility of the unstructured questionnaire.

Besides this, we also have attitude measurements which can be done by scaling techniques. Attitude is a behavioural disposition of the structure of human perception. In rating scales, respondents indicate their degree of agreements or disagreements. There are various types of scales:

(a) Numerical scales

(b) Comparative scales

(c) Non-comparative scales
(d) Method of comparison
(e) Constant sum scales.

There are also some specific scales for measuring attitudes, and there are (f) Likert scale + (g) Semantic differential scales (h) Rank order rating scales. We shall discuss the last three in brief.

Likert scale

This scale consists of an equal number of agreement or disagreement choices on either side of a neutral choice. A series of statements are given to find out the attitude of the respondents. This can be done on a five or, a seven point scale.

Example: The respondent has to agree or disagree, and the degree of agreement or disagreement has to be marked on the scale.

1. Coca Cola is the best drink for teenagers.
2. Coca Cola is very sweet and contains sugar.
3. Coca Cola gives a good fizz.
4. Coca Cola is very refreshing.
5. Coca Cola is a universal drink.
6. Coca Cola has a very good flavour.

Strongly Agree	Agree	Neither agree nor disagree	Disagree	Strongly disagree
or +2	+1	0	–1	–2

Fig. 23.4

This scale gives the option to the respondent for their responses. The responses can be combined to produce a summated score, and this is done by giving the score of +2 +1 0 –1 –2, to the five options, so that the overall attitudes can be measured.

Semantic Differential Scale

As attitudes are difficult and complex to measure, indirect approaches are used to measure them. One of the methods developed in 1930 by Charles Osgood was the semantic differential scale. This is similar to Likert differential scale, and in this Bipolar adjectives are used to indicate the attitude towards a given subject. It is used to find out the preferences of the consumer for brand and company images. Five to seven levels of intensity are used to separate the Bipolar adjectives.

	1	2	3	4	5	
Expensive	–	–	–	–	–	Inexpensive
Convenient	–	–	–	–	–	Inconvenient
Reliable	–	–	–	–	–	Unreliable

Friendly	–	–	–	–	–	Unfriendly
Modern	–	–	–	–	–	Old fashioned
Wide selection	–	–	–	–	–	Very limited selection.

Semantic differential scale for using the attitude towards a retail store.

This scale is simple and easy to use. It can be used for a variety of subjects.

Rank order scale

Customers are asked to rank items (products) in order of preference, in term of some criterion such as economy or quality or style, etc. Rank the following in terms of your choice on economy, durability, style, comfort, manintenance, etc. giving rank (a) to most preferred and (b) to least preferred.

1. Zen
2. Santro
3. Matiz
4. Alto
5. Ambassador

It produces competition data and is used for ranking only.

	1	2	3	4	
Expensive	–	–	–	–	Inexpensive
Convenient	–	–	–	–	Inconvenient
Reliable	–	–	–	–	Unreliable
Modern	–	–	–	–	Old fashioned

Sampling

For conducting research it is not possible to interview or question each and every customer. Therefore, a sample is chosen which should be representative of the population (all customers). There are many methods of sampling for choosing whom to survey. These can be broadly classified as:

I. *Probability or Random sampling:* Every member of the population has an equal chance of being selected.

(a) Simple random sampling: A sample is drawn from each strata or group.

(b) Stratified random sampling: A sample is drawn from each strata or group of the population.

(c) Cluster sampling: Clusters or groups are formed and samples drawn randomly from these groups.

II. *Non probability sampling:* Every member of the population does not have an equal chance of being selected.

(a) Convenience sampling: Researcher takes a sample from the population convenient to him.

(b) Judgement sampling: Judges and chooses from respondents who can give good accurate information.

(c) Quota Sampling: Researchers form quotas of the population for drawing samples (Men, Women, Children). The numbers of these categories are specified.

We shall now discuss the methods of:

Observation Experimentation, Survey and Interviews

Observation is an important method of consumer research. In this the researcher observes the process of buying and using products. Some companies also make videotapes of consumers while they are in the process of buying etc.

It provides a good insight into the habits of the consumers, and their likes and the preferences they show while in the store.

Observation can be of several types:

(a) Disguised Observation: The customer does not know that he is being observed.

(b) Undisguised Observation: Customer knows that he is being observed.

(c) Controlled Observation: Customer is asked to operate an apparatus (In a shop).

(d) Uncontrolled Observation: They may be observed operating a refrigerator or any other gadget in their house.

(e) Structured: Guidelines are provided to the researcher which he is supposed to follow.

(f) Mechanical: Mechanical devices, automatic counting of entry.

Like a galvanometer, a pupilometer, or an eye camera can be used to register the respondents.

Experimentation

This is a common method to collect the data from customers. An experiment is a process where events occur in a setting at the discretion of the experimenter. Controls are used to register the responses. In this we have an *independent variable,* or a test unit. The *treatment*, which is given, and all *dependent variables* to measure the responses which change with the treatment.

Experiments can be of:

I. Informal Experimental design

(a) Before, after, without, control

(b) Before, after, with, control

(c) After, only, with, control

(d) Ex-Post-Facto design

II. Formal experimental design
   (a) Completely randomised design
   (b) Randomised block design
   (c) Latin square design
   (d) Factorial design
   (e) Four group six study design.

Surveys

It is the systematic gathering of data from respondents through a questionnaire. Surveys can be in the form of personal interviews, mail survey, telephone survey.

Table 23.1

S. No.	*Criteria*	*Personal Interview*	*Telephone Survey*	*Mail Survey*
1.	Cost	Most expensive	Intermediate	Least expensive
2.	Speed	Slowest	Fastest	Intermediate
3.	Accuracy	Most Accurate	Intermediate	Least accurate
4.	Respondent Rate	Highest	Intermediate	Lowest
5.	Flexibility	High	Intermediate	Low
6.	Sample			
	(a) Sample control	Intermediate	Worst	Best
	(b) Interview control	Best	Intermediate	Worst
	(c) Administrative control	Worst	Intermediate	Best

Above data gives the option to the respondents for their responses. The responses can be combined to produce a summated score, and this can be done by giving the scores of +3 +2 +1 0 (–)2 (–)1 to the six options, so that the overall data can be measured. In this case we have + 6 – 3 = + 3 which is the summated score.

Interviews: There are various types of interviews.

Depth, Interview: In this a resondent is persuaded to discuss freely about a brand or a product under the watchful eyes of an expert trained interviewer. It is a lengthy (about half an hour) session, of non-structured interview. The expert may encourage the participants to talk about his own attitudes, habits and interests, in addition to the topic of discussion. Some experts minimise their participation, while others take an active part in the discussion, depending upon the situation. The responses are video taped or recorded, and later studied in detail to interpret the moods, gesture and body language of the participant. Later these are used to formulate better strategies for positioning and repositioning of the products.

Focus group interviews

A focus group consists of eight to ten participants. The moderator or the expert initiates the discussion about a product or a brand. The group talks about the usage of the product and their experiences. They also discuss their opinions, attitudes, lifestyle interest in product category and other aspects. The exercise takes about two hours. While the interview is going on, other experts can also watch the reactions of the respondents sittings in a separate room by the help of a mirror. The proceedings are videotaped and later analysed for the purpose of effective selling and marketing.

Projective techniques

Sometimes respondents do not want to reveal their feelings and they avoid questions that are threatening to them. These techniques are designed to tap the underlying motives of individuals inspite of their concealment. These are carried out be means of unstructured disguised questions that are in the form of Word Association test.

- ➢ Sentence completion tests
- ➢ Story completion technique
- ➢ Thematic apperception test

These reveal the inner feelings of the respondent and how they perceive ambiguous stimuli. The responses reveal their underlying needs, wants, fears, aspiration and motives. The main thing in projective techniques is that the respondents are unaware that they are exposing their own feelings. The picture shows a fat lady and a slim lady with a bottle of milk between them. The respondent has to insert the dialogues of both the ladies in the balloon provided.

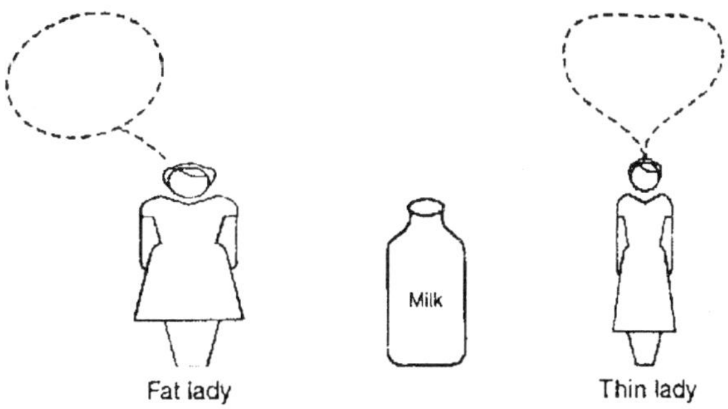

Fig. 23.3

Data Analysis

After all the data has been collected and compiled, the researcher tabulates the data, edits it, and then analyses it by various methods. These could be by means of:

1. Percentages,
2. Averages: Mean, Medium, Mode.

3. Disposition: Range, Mean obsolete deviation (MD), Standard deviation (SD).
4. Statistical methods: Second test, Third test
   chi-square analysis
   Regression analysis, etc.
   Multivariate analysis.

Presentation of the report

After the analysis, the report is prepared and presented. It includes the summary of findings, methodology, sampling techniques, use of Primary and Secondary data, list of tales, recommendations and suggestions, appendices and Bibliography.

Conclusion

Consumer research is therefore an important step to understand consumer behaviour. In this world of competition, consumer research has gained importance as no company can afford to neglect or overlook the changing behaviour of consumers. Consumers want ease, convenience, economy satisfaction, and their needs are changing. They are becoming more intelligent and sophisticated in their buying and, they are equipped to make better and quicker decisions.

Consumer research gives an input to marketers to foresee and reframe their strategies, so that they can remain in the market and maintain and improve their standings.

Questions

1. What do you understand by consumer research? What are the main steps in conducting research?
2. What are the sources and importance of secondary data in consumer research?
3. What is sampling? What are the various methods of sampling?
4. What are scaling techniques. Describe a method of scaling to collect the primary data.

24

Changing Consumer Behaviour

IN THE INDIAN CONTEXT

"Think of the customer first, if you would have the customer think of you."

The consumption pattern and the behaviour of the consumer has been changing gradually. Since the last two decades we have seen many changes occurring in the attitude, perception, motivation, spending habits, purchase, and post purchase behaviour of the consumer,

The consumer of the 80's was austere and bought those things that were needed by him and the household. He was not very adventurous in spending habits. He had the restraint put on him by low income, the non availability of products and traditional methods of buying. Most of these were for all the classes of consumers the upper, or lower income groups. Even if they had the money and the willingness to buy, they could not purchase because of the limited choice of product, even after having booked the same a few years earlier (for example the waiting period for Bajaj scooters was almost four years and FIAT Padmin, over a year and a half). Many products were not available in the Indian market due to import restrictions, and the consumer had to depend on the product smuggled in, from foreign countries and paying heavy duty on them. Under these conditions the entire definition of consumer behaviour was put to limitations. "Consumer behaviour is a decision making process and physical activity engaged in while evaluating, acquiring using and disposing of goods and services."

Taking the case of Bajaj scooter, as it was the only dependable scooter available in 1900's. There was hardly any decision making as there was no choice for the consumer. The same could apply to cars. When the products available in the market were few there were hardly any physical activity to be performed. By physical activity we mean the effort made to analyse the products and do their comparative study, according to the desired attributes. This led to the evaluation of the product with every few and limited attributes that one could visualise. Even if the mindset for the purchase was positive, it was difficult to purchase as the products were in short supply and there was hardly any competitors. The process of evaluation purchase was reduced or had little to delve upon. Even after the purchase the factor of satisfaction and dissatisfaction had little meaning as you had to be satisfied with the best that was available, and the customer could not aspire for more than what was offered. One could dispose off the product after use with little difficulty.

In the new millennium however, the consumer behaviour has changed much. The consumer of the 80's had less discretionary income and with liberation in 1985 to globalization taking place since 1991 a whole lot of goods flooded the Indian market. Like refrigerators, washing machines, black & white TV, colour TV, VCR's Cars, Scooters, Moter Cycles, cosmetics, gas cylinders, cellular phones, microwave ovens, internet, ATM cards etc, Marketing through TV and internet became possible. Moreover, fast food centres with home delivery of snacks food and drinks gave the consumer options. A lot of avenues were opened for travel and communications, PCO, STD, FAX, photocopy machines were available almost at every crossing.

New innovative marketing techniques, branding the product, suited the Indian style. Branding Maharaja Burger instead of Big Mac, hot sams instead of Samasas and like Indianisation of fast food brands and lowering the price to suit the Indian consumer. The Indian consumer is very price conscious, and to suit the consumer changes in the product (several ranges, models, colours sizes) as mentioned above were made. There were changes in the price, range of prices, instalment offers; promotion offers (buy 2 take one free). In distribution extra pains are taken to reach the goods to the consumer (free delivery) have been some of the innovations in the marketing techniques. Changes have taken place in the Indian consumer due to innovation in the product, in liberalisation and the marketing mix.

The behaviour of today's customers is changed due to the economic liberalisation and economic crisis. He does not have to buy sub quality and shoddy products. He can dictate his terms, and as somebody has rightly stated. "The customer is not only the king but also the queen, the prince and the princess." He can choose from a plethora of brands, return the product if not approved. Can take a free trial, negotiate & bargain. He can reject and accommodate. He can use credit cards, buy houses cars, flats on easy instalments and can even get rebate from taxes, by taking a loan for a home etc.

He can access abundant information through the internet. The marketer is happy to provide service to him free of cost. It is the service that plays an important role in promoting products and brands. Marketers are all out to differentiates their products with plans of service, price, packaging, branding, promotion etc. Celebrities are being used to promote products Coco Cola, Pepsi "Yeh Dil Mange more", Maharaja of Air India and other brands have been globalised.

The marketers have adopted a new strategy. They have modified the old strategies, broadened their visions and are aware how they have to provide services. Adjust themselves to the customer and not the customer to them. The marketers are not satisfied with just satisfaction. They are going beyond the expectation of the customer and are delighting the customer and even to make them ecstatic with the product and services offered.

Many of the hotels greet you with the sign on the television as you enter the room. The sign—"Welcome Mr. & Mrs. Singh to our hotel, and have a pleasant stay." Besides this there are fruits in a tray, and the fridge is full of soft drinks, fresh fruits and eatables.

The millennium is witnessing dramatic changes in the market place, changes in the life style of the consumers and a radical revolution in information technology. The behaviour of the new generation of customers has seen drastic changes. He knows his rights. His expectations have increased, he has become more knowledgeable and is also aware of the multiple options satisfying his needs. He can switch over to new brands to get more value for his money. There are increasing number of competitors, both domestic and global, offering higher value for his money—added products and process through innovation. The customer has more purchasing power and can access information i.e. E-commerce and E-business.

The marketer must take the following points into consideration—

(i) The customer has become more demanding there is demanding.
(ii) There is greater liberalisation.
(iii) There is increasing competition.
(iv) The overall costs are rising.
(v) There are lower margins of profits.
(vi) The customer has more purchasing power.
(vii) The customer has more information about product, markets, companies, prices etc.

The marketer must act accordingly—

- The marketing effort is directed at the customer.
- The companies allows the customer to dictate their specification and standards.
- The marketers continuously tracks the needs of the customer.
- The marketers adopts the marketing concepts in its entirety.
- The strategy is aimed at delivering greater customer value than their rivals.

This is the age of modern marketing. The age of taking risks. The age to establish your identity through the use of marketing mix. Providing services, giving that little extra to the consumer that created the required differentiation between one product and the other. The age of positioning, the age of providing service. The age of relationship marketing and the age of studying the further expected changes in the behaviour of the consumer. Communicating with the customer is the core of good customer service.

"Coming together is the beginning, keeping together is progress and working together is success."

Questions

1. What is the reason for the change of the behaviour of consumers of the new generation?
2. Why do we term this decade as an age of Modern Marketing?

25

Case Studies

Case I Factors Affecting Consumer Behaviour

Martin Incorp. was a company carrying on business in cosmetics and perfumes. They were not following the marketing concept and were catering to a target market which was using their products. In other words, they only concentrated on what they would make, and did not bother about changes in preferences of their target market.

They were later joined by Mr. Ash, a marketing graduate who advised the company regarding the changing consumer preferences, and the changes that were necessary to be incorporated in the product. He emphasised upon the income factors, and social factors only. He modernised the products to a great extent, and invested about 30 lakhs on new packing, etc. Even after six months of these changes brought about by him, the company did not seem to have a proportionate increase in sales.

The assistant manager and the product manager were not very happy with the changes, and thought that although an effort has been made in the right direction, some important factors concerning consumer behaviour had been neglected.

Questions

1. Do you agree with the assistant and product managers, and why?
2. What other factors, if any, could have been considered? Elaborate in detail.

Case II Organisational Buying Behaviour

Miss Michael was working as a purchase manager in a small scale company, where raw materials and other products were purchased solely at her discretion. The company was doing very well and the credit was given to Miss Michael for all the progress of the company.

Later she got a job in a medium scale company with a turn-over of about five crore. She was appointed incharge of purchases, and as the procedures of the purchase made by this company were different from those of the previous company, it took her quite sometime to get familiar with the procedures of purchase, etc. under her jurisdiction.

On one occasion, she has to urgently place an order of raw material worth about two lakhs, which was essential for the supply of a timely order. Considering the situation an emergent one, she placed the order without informing, or calling a meeting. Although the order was supplied in time, during the audit it came in for severe criticism, and Miss Michael was given a show-cause notice, as to why she had taken the decision alone. Miss Michael was very perturbed about the situation, and wanted to explain her position to the manager.

Questions

1. Where did Miss Michael go wrong?
2. How can you help her to reply to the show-cause notice issued to her?

Case III Family Influences

A certain store was keeping a number of brands of washing machines. They had washing machines to cater to the needs of all the segments of the society. They were stocking IFB, Videocon, BPL, National, Godrej, and local made washing machines as well. They had both automatic, semi-automatic and manual machines. The automatic machines were bought by the higher income group. The middle income group were content with semi-automatic machines. Manual hand operated machines were for the lower class of clientele, and also those living in the rural areas, where electrification was not complete, or the electricity went off for days together.

It was observed that when customers came to buy an automatic machine, they usually came with their spouses and they looked mainly at the colour, style of functioning, electric consumption, care for handling, price factors, etc. Many customers would not buy on their first visit. They would come back after an interval of time, and bought the machine after careful considerations of the attributes that they were looking for. Many would lower their choice, and come back to buy semi-automatic, instead of automatic machines.

The sale was observed to be highest during marriage seasons and at festival times. There was a great influence of the house-wives in buying these, as they were the ultimate users.

With a lot of information imparted by the media, and the children being exposed to it for several hours, in a day. They seemed to have a good knowledge of the attributes, and had a great say in the purchases and their opinions were also given weightage by the parents.

Since a chain store is more interested in the sales to materialise, rather than pushing any particular brand, the salesmen are directed to satisfy the customers or the family. This should be their first consideration.

Questions

1. Do you feel that group interaction helps the buyer too, in his decision-making process? Elaborate.
2. What should be the role of the marketer in the above case regarding, advertisement, promotion, persuasion and closing the sales.

Case IV Health Conscious Consumer

Consumers are becoming health conscious and would like to consume foods which are balanced, and have all the required nutrients, in proper quantities. These ingredients are cholesterol, salt, sugar, fibre, calories and additives. The consumers are not only concerned about such goods for themselves, but also their families.

A survey was made by a company to find out the food attitudes of consumers. This was done to find out how products could be designed, advertised and positioned, to attract health conscious consumers. The survey of food attitude was carried out as food related items. These attitudes were food conscious, cooking attitudes, brand loyalty, instant foods, price sensitivity, value, etc. The analysis revealed that basically customers could be classified into three categories.

Category I: Older consumers

These were health conscious older people, who because of medical consideration, had little choice, and these people were concerned about sugar, salt, greasy foods, etc. They ate meals regularly, at regular timings, and took great precautions for their food. They used branded products, and played very safe in eating outside and not consuming food not prescribed for them.

Category II: Buyers of convenience food

These are younger consumers keeping busy mostly outside the house, who skip lunch or breakfast. They rely on convenience food and fast foods. They have a hectic lifestyle. They are upwardly mobile, use ready to eat and frozen foods. They work mostly outside the house and are pressed for time. They have an irregular schedule for meals. They also dislike cooking and want to utilise time for leisure and other activities rather than for cooking. They are not very concerned about a balanced diet, and would have greasy burgers or any other fast foods to suit their convenience. They can also be categorised under impulse buyers, rather than careful shoppers. If the product has appeal, it will be bought, and the price and brand name are not the main considerations.

Category III: Cooking own food

They like to cook their own food and get involved in the kitchen. They love to make an assortment of dishes. This is also done to cut costs. They like to buy their own groceries and cooking stuff, and do not want to waste money on fancy packings. They do not try new products, i.e. they are not innovators, but try to be a late majority, and buy a thing, when it has established itself in the market. They tend to have a big family, and have to economise, as well.

Questions

1. What inferences can be drawn by marketers from the above study? How does it help them to formulate strategies for advertisement, positioning, etc?
2. Do you require any other information and why?

Case V A.T.O. Model of Consumer Behaviour

A consumer wants to choose a three room flat by applying the A.T.O. model.

First Flat

It is available in the heart of town in the main market. The underground parking facility is provided. The cost of the flat is 20 lakh. The builder is not very reliable. Most flats are under construction, and the model flats on display do not seem to have a very good finish. The ventilation is O.K. but the galleries, etc. seem congested. Ample security is also provided.

Second Flat

These are already constructed, many people are living in them, and are appreciative of the facilities provided. The cost of the flat is 17 lakh, and it is situated about 4 km away from the main market. The construction, lift, power and water facilities are good, and there is good ventilation in the corridors as well, and these corridors are well lighted. Security and other factors are also good.

Third Flat

These are situated about 6 kilometres away from the main market. Have a beautiful view of the river and the university. They are across the river, i.e. one has to cross over from a bridge to come to this area. Although the traffic is free flowing, but on many occasions since it is near the university and political rally ground, many a times there is a traffic jam, and some inconvenience is caused to the owners to reach their destination. These are costing about 16 lakh, and have other facilities which are good to satisfactory. They are near another comparatively smaller market which is at a distance of 3 km from there.

Quality of construction is O.K.

Questions

1. Giving your preference on a one to five scale for the following and weightages as given. Show the process of choosing between the three flats.

Attributes	Weightages	*Your preference on 1 to 5 scale*			
		Flat One		*Flat Two*	*Flat Three*
Cost	40%	to	3	2	2
Location	20%	3	4	4	2
Facilities	20%				
Quality of construction	20%				
	Total				

2. What are the functions of attitudes and it affects on purchases?

Case VI Vending Machines (Motivation)

Thomson was a limited company manufacturing vending machines. These machines could be used for automatic vending of cigarette packs, match boxes, tea, coffee, cold drinks, chocolates and many other products. The vending machines had to be programmed for vending various items. One machine could handle a variety of products as well. These were to be installed at shopping centres, cinema halls, public places, hotels, etc. The manufacturer started with installing these machines in various parts of the city for selling coffee and tea. The machines became popular, as they served the customers with both tea/coffee at a standard price, and the customer had the choice of having strong or light, with or without sugar, more or less milk depending on his choice. As they became popular, more and more machines were set up at strategic places like bus stations, railway platforms, etc. so that the customer had an access to the beverage, whenever he needed it. In the beginning, an attendant was also required to stand with the machines, as they were not fully automatic. Later, fully automatic machines were developed, which could work without the help of an attendant. The attendant had to come only once, to replenish the stocks, and take out the cash from the machines. A difficulty that was faced, was that these machines did not accept torn notes, or some coins which got stuck in them. To overcome this difficulty, the company was contemplating to introduce a card system, which could be purchased with Rs. 100, or its multiples, and on using these cards, the amount would get debited automatically and the balance would be known by the consumer.

The survey showed the results, but a lot of effort would be required to motivate the consumers to buy these cards. The company also contemplated providing the consumers with other products as well. These could be cigarettes, soaps, oils, cold drinks, chocolates, biscuits, etc.

Questions

1. Do you think that the company will succeed in selling other products along with the tea/coffee they are already selling?
2. How can the company motivate the consumers to buy other products, as well as, to use the cards instead of cash?

Case VII Buyer's Behaviour

In the U.S. cereals are taken at breakfast time. Cereal manufacturing is an industry of great magnitude. Cereals are manufactured in various shapes, flavours and colours and the advertisement is directed at children. The leading manufacturers are Kellogg's, General Mills, General Foods, Quaker Oats, and Champion. Kellogg's share was constantly being eaten away by other manufacturers who were introducing new cereals. Kellogg's therefore thought of introducing a new cereal, which they had not done for a long time. The cereals were not only consumed by children, but a substantial portion formed the adult market as well.

Kellogg's developed a new plan to come out with a cereal which would be tasty, nutritious, free of sugar and made of gain. The cereal consisting of the above attributes was named "Nutrigrain". These were available in four types. Nutrigrain Corn, Wheat, Barley and Rye. These were introduced together, and no test marketing was done to avoid competition.

These products were advertised heavily and targeted at adults. To promote the product further, discount coupons were freely distributed, which gave a cut of about 30 per cent in the retail price of the product. Coupons were also inserted in the Nutrigrain boxes' so that customer would return to take advantage of these coupons, and make repeat purchases. A lot of information and advantages of consuming Nutrigrain was boldly printed on the packages for the information of the consumers. Proper display in the shelves of stores was also taken care of.

There efforts brought results, and the stores were loaded with orders and most adults started eating these cereals, because of promotion, curiosity, etc. After one year, the sales declined because there were very few repeat purchases. This started the extensive thinking as to where they had gone wrong. Consequently, they withdraw two of their brands—Barley and Rye. These were replaced by raisin and wheat varieties.

They also found out later, that there was a shortage of time for the adults, which prevented them from having cereals. If they could get out of bed 10 minutes early and devote these ten minutes to breakfast, they would probably enjoy the cereals. They also found out that though people were clamouring for sugarless cereals, yet they loved to satisfy their palates with sugar coated cereals.

Questions

1. Should Kellogg's have done test marketing and gradual product introduction?
2. What can you comment on the habits of the consumers and their preferences?
3. Suggest methods of increasing the market share of the adult market?

Case VIII Promoting Beauty Products (Marketing Strategy)

India is in the limelight with the success of several Indian beauties winning the Miss Universe and Miss World contests, one after the other, in a short span of a few years:

1. Sushmita Sen (Miss Universe)
2. Aishwarya Rai (Miss World)
3. Yukta Mookhey (Miss World)
4. Lara Dutta (Miss Universe)
5. Diya Mirza (Miss Asia Pacific)
6. Priyanka Chopra (Miss World).

This has put India in the centre stage, and many producers of beauty products and marketers, are trying to find out the reason for success of beauty pageants, and also how to promote their beauty products in the market. These products naturally are targeted at the beauty conscious, aspiring, upwardly mobile, outgoing ladies and girls, who want to make a mark in life, and believe that their face is their fortune.

India Times has through interviews come out with some information:

1. India's beauty product market is growing at the rate of 30 per cent.
2. The MNC's are also trying to penetrate the market deeper. Revlon for one, is feeling the pules of the Indian market, and is making suitable changes in their products.
3. The beauty products are being targeted in the developing countries, where women want to look their best and want to keep abreast of the international trends.
4. While targeting the products at the consumer, the price strategy is also considered along with the moods, the occasion, the shades, classic shades for longer use, colour stay for lipsticks.
5. The Indian climate is hot, and in manufacturing the product, care is to be taken for it not to melt. Cleansing, moisturising and applying sun screen to avoid blemishes and discolouration when outdoors, are required.
6. Further, the Indian women are educated to use the right colours. This is done by beauty advisors and continuous learning programmes imparted through various media.
7. There is a lot of response of beauty products from the cities of Delhi, Bangalore, Mumbai, Kolkata, Ahmedabad, Chandigarh, etc.
8. MNC's like Revlon, Lakme, L'Oreal are competing with each other to win customers. Continuous research is also going on, and the Indian market in beauty products is growing at a much faster pace.
9. Another product that is making inroads into the beauty product market, is herbal products. Many beauticians of east and west are recommending herbal beauty products, as they are natural and harmless. They are mild, and suit soft skin well.

10. Many consumers are switching over to herbal products, which is increasing the share of the herbal beauty market as well.

Questions

1. As a marketer do you see this as an opportunity, and how can you cash on it?
2. What strategy is to be adopted to enlarge the market and make consumers of lower and middle class more conscious about beauty products.

Case IX Organisation Buying

M.K.B. Products was an industrial company, undertaking the manufacture of chewing tobacco products. For the packing of these products, tin containers were required in huge quantities. The company was buying these containers from Shaz Metals, who were supplying the empty containers to M.K.B. Product @ Rs. 1.60 per tin container. This arrangement carried on for more than ten years.

M.K.B. Product was later joined by a young M.B.A., who advised the owner of M.K.B. Product, to go in for backward integration (To make the tin containers themselves, instead of buying them from Shaz Metal Works).

The matter was put under deliberation, and it was decided to join for partial backward integration, i.e. to start the manufacture of their own tin containers, as well as, keep buying from the supplier (Shaz Metal) in a lesser quantity, till such time that the company M.K.B. Product could become self sufficient.

In the pursuit of backward integration, another semi-automatic tin container manufacturing plant was set up by the company, and it started its production and initially faced a lot of teething troubles. They however, overcame them and started functioning smoothly.

A number of suppliers were interested in supplying tin sheets (out of which tin containers are made) for M.K.B. Product. After buying randomly from a number of suppliers, the company came to terms with one Mr. Wali, who undertook all the raw material supplies of tin sheets to the company at reasonable rates. He would make deliveries as and when necessary, and developed a good relationship with the owners of M.K.B. Product. The supplies were reliable, they were reasonably priced, were regular and timely.

This arrangement lasted for a decade. Later Mr. Wali, the tin supplier told the company that they would be charging an additional two per cent on the prices quoted by them, due to the rise in prices, and the delivery time would have to be re-scheduled, and the company would have to pick up, or order for the entire material consumed by the quarterly, instead of monthly arrangements.

This set the owners and managers of M.K.B. Product thinking whether to agree to Mr. Wali's terms, or look for another supplier. After a little research, they came across a supplier in scrap tin industries, who were happy to supply to M.K.B. Product at the rates and terms of conditions at which Mr. Wali was originally supplying. They agreed to monthly deliveries, and relaxed their terms of payments, as well.

When the deal was about to be finalised with the scrap tin industries, Mr. Wali sent a telegram to M.K.B. Product, that the increase in rates was cancelled, and they were willing to renew their contract, or continue with the supplies at the earlier rate for the next 12 months.

This again set the company thinking, because they had good relations with Mr. Wali for a considerable period of time, and also the fact that in industrial buying, market price plays a secondary role, but the quality, uniformity of products, timely and regular suppliers are the dominant factors.

Questions

1. What should the company do in this situation and why?
2. Should the company try scrap industries who are an unlisted supplier, and what precautions should the company take for the future?